NEW YAWK TAWK

A DICTIONARY OF
New York City
EXPRESSIONS

NEW YAWK TAWK

A DICTIONARY OF
New York City
EXPRESSIONS

Robert Hendrickson

Volume V:
Facts On File Dictionary of American Regional Expressions

Checkmark Books™
An imprint of Facts On File, Inc.

New Yawk Tawk: A Dictionary of New York City Expressions

Copyright © 1998 by Robert Hendrickson

Checkmark Books
An imprint of Facts On File, Inc.
11 Penn Plaza
New York NY 10001

Library of Congress Cataloging-in-Publication Data

Hendrickson, Robert, 1933–
New Yawk tawk : a dictionary of New York City expressions / Robert Hendrickson
    p. cm.—(Facts on File dictionary of American regional expressions ; v. 5)
    Includes bibliographical references and index.
    ISBN 0-8160-2114-7 (hardcover).—ISBN 0-8160-3869-4 (pbk.)
  1. English language—Dialects—New York (State)—New York—Dictionaries.
2. English language—New York (State)—New York—Terms and phrases—Dictionaries.
3. English language—Spoken English—New York (State)—New York—Dictionaries.
  4. English language—New York (State)—New York—Slang—Dictionaries.
      5. Americanisms—New York (State)—New York—Dictionaries.
  6. Figures of speech—Dictionaries. I. Title. II. Series: Hendrickson, Robert, 1933–
    Facts on File dictionary of American regional expressions ; v. 5.
                    PE3101.N7H46 1998
  427′.97471—dc21   97-51156

You can find Facts On File on the World Wide Web at http://www.factsonfile.com

Cover design and illustration by Cathy Rincon

Printed in the United States of America

10 9 8 7 6 5 4 3 2 1

(pbk) 10 9 8 7 6 5 4 3 2 1

This book is printed on acid-free paper.

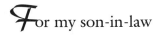For my son-in-law

Robert Walsh

"... million-footed Manhattan ...

The nest of languages,

the bequeather of poems ..."

—Walt Whitman,
"A Broadway Pageant," 1881

INTRODUCTION

*T*his wordbook or almanac of New York talk, a large selection of expressions and pronunciations that are commonly associated with the New York metropolitan area or that originated here, is meant to be a book of entertaining, often little-known stories about the *Big Apple,* or *Big Onion,* as well as a dictionary. The reader will find hundreds of references to the observations of writers ranging from the greats of a couple centuries past such as New Yorkers Washington Irving, Walt Whitman and Herman Melville, and New Jerseyan Stephen Crane, to authors of this century such as James Baldwin, Robert Benchley, Jimmy Breslin, Claude Brown, Richard Condon, Jack Conway, T. A. Dorgan, F. Scott Fitzgerald, Brendan Gill, Pete Hamill, Evan Hunter (writing under his own name and as Ed McBain), Ring Lardner, Norman Mailer, Henry Miller, Joseph Mitchell, O. Henry, Dorothy Parker, S. J. Perelman, Mario Puzo, Leo Rosten, Henry Roth, Damon Runyon, Sapphire, Walter Winchell, Thomas Wolfe, Tom Wolfe and many, many others. Included, too, are prominent figures from the sports and entertainment industries, the financial world and many other occupational groups in what Whitman called "million-footed Manhattan." I wish to thank them all and to thank the far more numerous people I've listened to in the streets of New York over a lifetime, for this book is as much a distillation of what I've heard through the years as it is a compilation of the experiences of others. I should also note that anyone writing an etymological work today has to be deeply indebted to the still unfinished *Dictionary of American Regional English,* edited by Frederic G. Cassidy and Joan H. Hall, and the also uncompleted *Random House Historical Dictionary of American Slang,* edited by Jonathan Lighter. Journals such as *Verbatim* and *Maledicta,* word scholars such as Peter Tamony and Professor Gerald Cohen, and syndicated columns such as William Safire's "On Language" have proven invaluable too. On a more personal note, many thanks are due to my wife, Marilyn, for her invaluable help.

I must confess at the outset that (contrary to most Americans) no dialect these days winds more gently through my ears than New York talk (often called New Yorkese and Brooklynese in these pages), the clipped 78-rpm patois to which I was to the manner born and raised and to which I reacted (the first few times I hoid my verse played back on a tape recorder) by cringing slightly if not by shuddering and clapping hands over ears.

Far sweeter American sounds have I heard (Southern talk, for example), but I've become comfortable (cumtabull) with my cacophonous birthright, so often slurred as "Slurvian" (so named because New Yorkers are said to commonly slur their pronounciations), and not because I delude myself into thinking I am not really speaking it, except when or because I wanna. Why, I've hoid the most kind, the most gifted, the most brilliant, the most beautiful of people speak in New Yorkese.

Of course, New Yorkers don't by any means all speak alike; there are in fact often great variations in the metropolitan area between those of different educational and cultural backgrounds. As the Federal Writers' Project *New York Panorama* (1938) eloquently put it, "A product of scores of nationalities, thousands of occupations and millions of people in necessary and constant contact, of whom some never leave the city while others come and go in a day, the New York language reflects every facet of a multifarious environment." No survey of this "ever-bubbling linguistic amalgam" can claim to be complete or definitive, not about a dialect (or subdialect) that has been touched by practically every other dialect in the country, or on earth for that matter. Not about a dialect in which the same speaker might ask "Where are you going?" in one instant and "Whe' y' goin'?" in the next, depending on the situation.

Damon Runyon's characters, for example, are often cited as typical New York speakers, but as critic Heywood Broun pointed out long ago: "Runyon has chosen a single segment out of New York. He has followed Broadway—not even all of Broadway. Every one of his stories can be located as having its principal routes somewhere between Times Square and Columbus Circle." It would make just as much sense to say that the characters in the works of Herman Melville and Walt Whitman, the two greatest American authors and both native New Yorkers, typify the speech of New York. Or, for that matter, Edgar Allan Poe. Poe, after all, spent much of his adult life in New York and some of the dialect must have rubbed off. Could it be possible that Poe and not Orter Anonamous really wrote what has been called "Da Brooklyn National Antem," dese woids about boids foreshadowing his raven:

> Da Spring is sprung,
> Da grass is riz,
> I wunneh weah da boidies is?

Da boid is on da wing?—dat's absoid!
From what I hoid da wing is on da boid!

To be even less serious, New Yorkese, or its exaggerated sibling Brooklyn-ese, has been defined as what you have a bad case of if you recite the sentence *There were thirty purple birds sitting on a curb, burping and chirping and eating dirty worms, brother,* as "*Dere were toity poiple boids sittin onna coib, boipin an choipin an eatin doity woims, brudda.*"

"Whadsa madda wid dat?" Well, maybe nuttin', brudda, but a better explanation of New Yorkese is surely called for. The dialect's most noticeable "peculiarity," as H. L. Mencken kindly put it (as kindly as the old aristocrat put anything), is the reversal of the *er* sound and *oi* diphthong sound. Thus, the *er* sound (which can also be spelled *ear, ir* or *ur*) changes in words like *nerve, pearl, girl* and *murder* to *noive, poil, goil* and *moider*. Conversely, the *oi* sound (which can be spelled *oy* as well) changes in words like *boil* and *oyster* so that we are left with *berl* and *erster*. There are many more examples, including *coil* (curl), *foist* (first), *adjern* (adjoin), *thoid* (third), *loin* (learn), *toin* (turn), *terlet* (toilet), *nerz* (noise), *hersted* (hoisted) and *Greenpernt* (Greenpoint). However, this switch-ing of sounds does not occur when the *er* sound is last in a word but isn't a suffix. In such cases, the *er* would be pronounced *uh* in New York talk: as in *were*, which is pronounced *wuh;* or as in *her*, which becomes a grunted *huh.*

The pronunciation of the voiced and unvoiced forms of *th* as *t* and *d* (try *wit* and *dat* for *with* and *that*) isn't as common in New York speech as it used to be, thanks to several generations of dedicated schoolmarms stressing funda-mentals on fundaments, or banging their rulers on desks and blackboards. The first writer to comment on the pronunciations, back in 1896, noted that it "does not take place in all words, nor in the speech of all persons, even of the lower classes; but the tendency exists beyond all doubt." This could still be said. And so we have *muddas, faddas, bruddas* and *uddas* as well as the *dems, deses* and *doses* that experts trace to the Dutch settlers of New Amsterdam or to later immigrants. But there are subtle differences in the use of all these forms, depending on both the speaker's audience and what he or she is talking about. In the case of *dis* and *dese,* for example, Professor William Labov, who taught at a local university, listened intently and found that some New Yorkers say *dis* for *this* and *dese* for *these* when talking about an emotion-charged event, such as a bad accident or a close call. However, when talking to teachers or reading aloud—that is, when watching themselves—New Yorkers tend to say *dis* and *dese* much less frequently.

Other important parts of the New York or Brooklyn dialect (Brooklynese may strictly be a subdialect of New Yorkese, but it's hard to see why it shouldn't be termed just an exaggeration of it) are the *aw* sound in words like *tawk* (talk), *fawk* (fork), *wawk* (walk) and *Noo Yawk;* the dropped *r*'s that transform *paper* into *papah, bar* into *bah, beer* into *beeah* and *super* into *soupa;* the omission of the letter *d* within contractions, making *didn't* into *dint;* and the *k* and *g* clicking sounds that can best be explained by the example of *Lunk Guylin* (Long Island), home now, it sometimes seems, to half of old Brooklyn.

By no means is that all of it. *Oncet* and *twicet* (*once* and *twice*) are bona fide Brooklynese, even though they were first recorded in Philadelphia and Baltimore by Noah Webster and are also heard in the Ozarks. And New Yorkers, like others, frequently add an *r* in words such as *idea* (*idear*) and *sofa* (*sofer*). Middle-class New Yorkers pronounce all their *r*s more than the poor or the rich do, however, out of concern for speaking "properly," and being grammatically "correct." Contractions, too, are plentiful in Brooklynese, telescoped words and phrases unconsciously tailored to meet the needs of the hurried, harried city dweller. Just a few samples that come to mind are *shudda* (should have), *dijuh* (did you), *ongana* (I'm going to), *alluh* (all the), *smatter* (what's the matter), *wuntcha* (wouldn't you), *juhhimee* (do you hear me) and of course the word *for* almost always blended into the following word, as in *finstins* (for instance). Then there are the many verbal shortcuts such as *Lex* for *Lexington Avenue*, the *Met* for the *Metropolitan Opera House*, and the *Garden* for *Madison Square Garden*.

Typical New York grammatical "errors," or differences, include the use of *should* for the infinitive *to* (*I want you should see it* instead of *I want you to see it*); using *leave* instead of *let* (*Leave me alone*); overuse of *like* (*Like, I like her*); and the use of *being* for *because* (*Being that I'm sick, I can't leave,* instead of *I can't leave because I'm sick*). Among a host of similar expressions, *that* is often substituted for *who* (*She's the one that went* instead of *She's the one who went*), and *if* is omitted in dependent clauses (*She asked him would he go* instead of *She asked him if he would go*).

Speakers of the dialect are not nearly so rude as they are portrayed. Instead of a simple *thank you,* New Yorkers will often say, "I really appreciate it." One of the most common terms heard in New York City is the apologetic *personally,* as in "Personally, I don't believe it," instead of the franker "I don't believe it." While this addition serves to show a certain humility, or worldliness—often one and the same thing—other typical interjections are completely superfluous, such as the *already* in "Let's go, already"; *here* in "This here book is mine"; and *there* in "That there coat is hers."

A feature of New York speech that now seems to be fading inspired a hundred years ago the popular designation *Joe Echoes*. People known as *Joe Echoes* (or *Johnny Echoes, Eddie Echoes,* etc.) in late 19th-century and early 20th-century New York weren't so called because they echoed *other* people's words. Those bearing this common nickname, usually the offspring of poor, recent immigrants, echoed *themselves* in sentences such as "I betcha ya can't do it, I betcha," or "I tell ya it's mine, I tell ya!" Today such repetition is still common with words like *says* (meaning *said*), as in an example I heard recently: "I says to him, I says, I'm goin' to be there, I says, no matter what you says, I says."

Youse—the so-called generous plural—is in a class by itself as a New Yorkism, though the expression is definitely heard in several parts of the country, including other Eastern cities and the Midwest. New York editor and author Barbara Burn, a New England transplant with a fine ear for regional speech, theorizes that *youse* is usually employed when a speaker is referring to the second person plural, helping the speaker differentiate between one person in the group he is speaking to and the group as a whole. It is the New York counterpart of the Southern *you-all* (a biblical precedent which can be found in Job 17:10), the "mountain tawk" *you-uns,* and the localized *mongst-ye* heard in Norfolk and on Albermarle Sound.

New Yorkers would not qualify as gentlemen under Palm Beach sportsman Charles Munn's definition of the "refined" species: "Someone whose family has pronounced tomato [as] *toe-mah-toe* for three generations." Many New York families have instead been pronouncing it *tamahter,* and calling pretty girls the same, for that long and longer. I have known only one native middle-class or poor New Yorker who pronounced the word *toe-mah-toe* and she, dear lady, suffered from delusions of grandeur worse than most of us do.

New Yorkers, too, have their special names for things. That long sandwich crammed with edibles on Italian or French bread and called a *poor boy* in the South and a *grinder* in New England (it has about a dozen names throughout the country) is a *hero* in most of the metropolitan New York speech area. A *stoop* (from the Dutch for *step*) is the front porch and steps of a New York house, while a sliding *pond* (possibly from the Dutch *baan,* track) is a metal slide in a New York playground but nowhere else. A *patsy* (one who is readily deceived or victimized) is another term that originated in New York. The word comes from the Italian *pazzo* (a crazy person or fool) and is first recorded in 1909. *Pazzo* may also be responsible for *potsy* (a New York City name for hopscotch), which may in turn take its name from the *potsy* (the object thrown into the hopscotch boxes)—like a victimized *patsy,* the *potsy,* too, is kicked around.

"I shuddah stood [stayed] in bed widda doctor!" is early Brooklynese rarely heard anymore in this life, though *stood* is still often heard for *stayed.* ("I should of stood at the Statler.") Native New York kids still *have a catch* (whereas other American youngsters *play catch*), their parents often omit the preposition *to* and *go over Harry's house* or *go down the store,* where (as they did in the schoolyard when the teacher kept them "in line," or orderly "on line") they stand *on line,* not *in line* as other Americans do, to pay for their groceries (though once they are *on line* they ideally *stay in line*). The New Yorker will usually ask for change *for* a dollar, not *of* a dollar, and he will *get a haircut,* never *have a haircut.* He will rarely today use *on* for *with* as in "Do you want zucchini or salad on your spaghetti?" (at least I don't hear the usage much anymore). While New Yorkers do say they *go to work,* they sometimes *go to business,* too, and they often *play piano* (without the *the*) as well as *play the piano.* They always *go to the beach,* never *go to the shore,* as neighboring Jerseyans in the same metropolitan area put it. They don't go to the supermarket but to Waldbaum's, Gristede's, D'Agostino's, King Kullen's, etc. Their frequent synonym for *You're welcome* is a modest *No problem.*

New Yorkers call New York City *the City* or *New York,* never *New York City.* If they come from any of the other four boroughs and are going into Manhattan, they say, "I'm going to the City." But when asked where they hail from, the answer is always "I come from the City," or "I come from New York," and this includes anyone who hails from any of the five boroughs, not just Manhattan. Practically no one says, "I'm going to Manhattan," either, and *au courant* expressions like the *Butcher Shop* are used jokingly or sparingly, if at all. As for the borough of the Bronx (Fred Allen used to call it South Yonkers), it is always called just that—*the Bronx*—not *Bronx.* "Let's go to Queens" (or Brooklyn, or Staten Island, or the City) is fine, but never "Let's go to Bronx." Staten Island, incidentally, is never called Richmond County or Richmond. And when people in the Bronx go *downtown* they're going to Manhattan; Queens and Brooklyn commuters go *uptown* to Manhattan.

Outlanders often call New York *the Big Apple,* but this foreign term is rarely used seriously by New Yorkers. A common nickname for New York City since the 1960s (though recorded by Walter Winchell in 1927), *the Big Apple* was first used in New Orleans. In about 1910, jazz musicians there used it as a loose translation of the Spanish *manzana principal* (the "main apple orchard"), the main city block downtown, the place where all the action is. *The Big Apple* was also the name of a popular dance in the 1930s. New York City has also been called *the Big Burg, the Big Onion, the Big Smear* (these last two by tramps), *the Big Stem* and *the Big Town.*

It isn't generally known that New York is ultimately named for a duke of York who ruled over York in England. It gets complicated. The name *York* itself comes from the Celtic *Eburacon* (the place of the yew trees, which are certainly not what New York is famous for). This became the Latin *Eburacus,* but to the Anglo-Saxons who ruled England after the Romans, *Eburacus* sounded like *Eoforwic* (their "boar town"), and to the Vikings, who invaded when the Romans left, *Eoforwic* sounded like *Iorvik.* Over the years *Iorvik* was shortened to *Iork,* which was finally transliterated into *York.* Then in 1664 James, duke of York and Albany, was granted the patent to all lands in America between the Delaware River and Connecticut by his older brother, King Charles II. The duke gave away the Jersey portion but held on to what was then the Dutch colony of New Netherlands. York became the patron of Colonel Richard Nicholls who that same year set sail for the New World, captured New Amsterdam from the Dutch, and named both the city of New Amsterdam (New York City) and the colony of New Netherlands (New York State) after the duke. New York State's capital, Albany, is also named for the same duke of York and Albany.

Since 1898 *Manhattan* has been the name of New York's central borough and has since about 1920 been a synonym elsewhere for New York City itself. It is named for the Algonquian Manhattan Indians who sold Manhattan Island to the Dutch in 1626. From the same Manhattan Indians, indirectly, the world also has the *Manhattan* cocktail, made with whiskey, sweet vermouth and bitters, first mixed about 1890; *Manhattan clam chowder,* made with tamaters, unlike the traditional milky New England clam chowder; and the *Manhattan Project,* the code name for the secret scientific group that developed the first atomic bomb. *Manhattanization* is a word that seems to have originated only recently. In the 1971 fall elections, San Francisco residents were urged to vote for an amendment halting the construction of tall buildings, to avoid the "Manhattanization of San Francisco."

Wall Street, which is both a street and a term symbolizing varying views of American capitalism in general, is of course located in downtown Manhattan, at the southern end of the island, and takes its name from the wall that extended along the street in Dutch times (a wall erected against the Indians and parts of which the same Indians used for firewood). The principal financial institutions of the city have been located there since the early 19th century. *Wall Streeter, Wall Street broker, Wall Street plunger* and *Wall Street shark* are among the American terms to which the street gave birth, *Wall Street broker* used as early as 1836, and Wall Street being called *the Street* by 1863. The New York Stock Exchange (NYSE) was first named the New York Stock and Exchange Board (1817), taking its present name in 1863. The American Stock Exchange (AMEX), which took its present name in 1953, was formed as the New York Curb Exchange in 1842 (because it was composed of *curbstone* brokers who worked on the sidewalk and were not members of the New York Stock and Exchange Board).

Flea markets across the country also owe their name to New York, as does every tough district called a *tenderloin. Flea market* as an American expression goes as far back as Dutch colonial days, when there was a very real Vallie (Valley) Market at the valley or foot of Maiden Lane in downtown Manhattan. The Vallie Market came to be abbreviated to *Vlie Market,* and this was soon being pronounced *Flea Market.* The original *tenderloin* was the area from Twenty-third Street to Forty-second Street west of Broadway in Manhattan. Gambling and prostitution flourished in this district, giving police officers "delicious opportunities" for graft. In fact, one notoriously corrupt police captain named Alexander "Clubber" Williams was so happy to be assigned to the old Twenty-ninth Precinct covering the area in 1876 that he said he'd been eating "chuck steak too long," but from now on he'd "be eating tenderloin." His remark led to the area's being dubbed *the tenderloin,* and that name was eventually transferred to similar places throughout the country. Many residents of New York's *tenderloin* were sent *up the river;* the river referred to is the Hudson, and *up it,* at Ossining, is Sing Sing Penitentiary, which was founded in 1830.

The *Bronx,* one of New York City's five boroughs, takes its name from Jonas Bronck, a Dane or Swede who first settled the area for the Dutch West India Company in 1641. The *Bronx cocktail* was named in honor of the borough, or invented there, in about 1919. Long associated with baseball, the razz, or raspberry, called the *Bronx cheer,* wasn't born at the borough's Yankee Stadium, home of baseball's New York Yankees, as is generally believed. It may derive from the Spanish word *branca* (rude shout) or have originated at the National

Theatre in the same borough of the Bronx, however; we only know certainly that the term is first recorded in 1927.

Since we've dwelled nostalgically upon New York and the Bronx, it's only fair that the origins of New York City's remaining three counties or boroughs be mentioned. *Kings County*, better known as Brooklyn, is named for King Charles II of England; *Queens County* honors Catherine of Braganza, Charles's queen; and *Richmond*, better known as Staten Island, is named for King Charles's son, the duke of Richmond. Since New York County, or Manhattan, was named for King Charles's brother James, duke of York, that leaves only the Bronx of New York City's five boroughs that isn't named for Charles II's royal family.

The *Coney* in Brooklyn's long-illustrious resort *Coney Island* should logically be pronounced (but never is) to rhyme with *honey* or *money*. The word derives from *cony* (or *cony* or *cuny*), the adult long-eared rabbit (*Lepus cunicula*) after which the place was named. However, *cony* (pronounced *cunny*) came to mean *cunt* in English slang. Proper Victorians stopped using the word, substituting rabbit, which previously meant just the young of the cony species. The only trouble remaining was that *cony* appeared throughout the King James Bible, which had to be read aloud during church services. The Victorians solved this problem by changing the pronunciation of *cony* from *cunny* to *coney* (rhymes with *Tony*), which it remains to this day in *Coney Island* as well as in pulpit readings from the Bible.

The fabled American *hot dog* also has a Coney Island connection. According to concessionaire Harry Stevens, who first served grilled franks on a split roll in about 1900, the franks were dubbed *hot dogs* by that prolific word inventor and sports cartoonist T. A. Dorgan after he sampled them at a ballgame. "Tad" possibly had in mind the fact that many people believed frankfurters were made from dog meat at the time and no doubt heard Stevens's vendors crying out, "Get your red hots!" on cold days. Dorgan even drew the *hot dog* as a dachshund on a roll, leading the indignant Coney Island Chamber of Commerce to ban the use of the term *hot dog* by concessionaires there (they could only be called *Coney Islands, red hots* and *frankfurters*).

Coney Islands and *Coney Island bloodhounds* are rarely used to mean a hot dog in New York anymore. Similarly, only one dictionary of slang I've consulted records the Americanism *Coney Island whitefish* for a disposed condom floating in the water, though I've heard it twice that I can remember and guess that it dates back to about the 1930s, despite lack of evidence. In typical New York humor it says much about the often dirty waters off the famous resort, just as its synonym *Manhattan eel* does about the waters around Manhattan.

Even more famous worldwide than Brooklyn's Coney Island are Brooklyn's incomparable Brooklyn Dodgers, who became comparable after a traitorous owner moved them to Los Angeles in 1958. The team was dubbed *the Dodgers* because Manhattanites contemptuously referred to all Brooklynites as "trolley dodgers" at the turn of the century, the bustling borough being famed for its numerous trolleys, especially in the central Borough Hall area. Attempts were made to change the name to the Superbas, the Kings and the Robins, all to no avail.

The legendary nickname "Bums" for the Brooklyn Dodgers beloved of memory was given to them by an irate fan seated behind home plate at a home game in Ebbets Field during the Great Depression. Particularly incensed by one error he shouted, "Ya bums, ya, yez bums, yez!" and his words, reported by a baseball writer, stuck as an endearing nickname for the team. *Dem Bums* are responsible for the national expression "Nice guys finish last." The cynical proverb has been attributed by *Bartlett's Familiar Quotations* to former Brooklyn Dodger manager Leo "the Lip" Durocher, who wrote a book using it as the title. Back in the 1940s Leo was sitting on the bench before a game with the New York Giants and saw opposing manager Mel Ott across the field. "Look at Ott," he said to a group of sportswriters. "He's such a damn nice guy and they'll finish last for him." One of the writers probably coined the phrase *Nice guys finish last* from this remark, but the credit still goes to the Lip. This is one of the few baseball expressions that have become proverbial outside the sport.

No one has been able to prove beyond a doubt the origin of New Yorkese. The dialect is native to Brooklyn, the Bronx, Manhattan, Queens, Staten Island and Nassau and Westchester counties, and extends across the river into New Jersey's Hudson, Bergen and Essex counties, among others, finding some of its most accomplished practitioners in Joisey City and Hoboken. It is the language of tens of millions, and you will in fact come upon it anywhere within a 100-mile radius with Manhattan as the center. The circle would include Suffolk County on eastern Long Island, southeastern Connecticut, Rockland County (to the west of Westchester) and northeastern New Jersey. Echoes of Brooklynese can even be heard in Chicago, Miami, the Gulf Coast area (where politicians commonly refer to "mah woythy opponent"), San Francisco, which New Yorkers were prominent in settling, and the Jewish district of west Los Angeles, which for half a century has been well known for its perpetuation of New York City dialect and idiom. Recognized immediately all over the world, traces of Brooklynese are heard in parts of Britain and Australia.

Stretching the point a bit, one could say that New Yorkese is also spoken (without any derogatory associations, by the way) in South Carolina, New Orleans and other Southern areas where the peculiar *er* to *oi* sound reversal in words like *thirty* (*toidy*) is heard almost as commonly as in New York—although most scholars would say the opposite: that *toidy boids*, etc., flew north from Dixie. People have persisted in calling the accent Brooklynese (often to the dismay of speech experts) because the borough has always been the butt of jokes and because the accent was once at its exaggerated best in northern Brooklyn, especially in Williamsboig and Greenpernt.

Denounced as "vulgar" by H. L. Mencken in his seminal *The American Language,* New York talk may have its roots in German or Yiddish. Certainly the characteristic melodic rhythm of the dialect, which rises and falls in the midst of a sentence and is so sung by almost all of us speakers (whether we know Yiddish or not), seems to be Yiddish-influenced. Yiddish has contributed hundreds of expressions to those who *schmooze* (stand around and gab) New Yorkese, but research doesn't bear out the theory that Brooklynese is simply an offshoot of Yiddish, as many people believe. Though Yiddish strongly influenced the dialect, New York talk has had influences too numerous to mention since the Dutch and Indians gave it words and ways of speaking, especially regarding vocabulary. Nevertheless, Yiddish terms do abound. Leo Rosten's *The Joys of Yiddish* (1968) alone collects over a thousand such terms. This does not include expressions such as *All right already!, Who needs it?* and *Get lost!,* which owe their presence in New York talk to Yiddish or Jewish influence. *Webster's Third* contains some 500 Yiddish words common in American English, especially in the New York area, and almost any expression can take on Yiddish coloring by what Rosten calls "unusual word order" (*Smart, he's not*), "blithe dismissal via repetition" (*Fatshmat, so long as she's happy*), "contempt via affirmation" (*My son-in-law he wants to be*), and other linguistic devices that convey "exquisite shadings of meaning" and have been adopted, often subconsciously, by almost all New Yorkers.

One of the better-known Yiddish New Yorkese expressions, *mazel tov,* is often believed to mean "good luck to you." However, Rosten says it has come to mean "Congratulations" or "Thank God!" rather than its literal meaning of "Good luck." Advising us that this "distinction is as important as it is subtle," he offers an example: "Say *mazel tov!* to an Israeli ship captain when he first takes command: this congratulates him on his promotion; don't say *mazel tov!* when the ship reaches port; this suggests you're surprised he got you there." Though Rosten and most others say *mazel tov* literally means "good luck" (from *mazel,* luck and *tov,* good), *mazel* is actually the Hebrew for "star," so the expression literally means "May a good star shine upon your days."

The common greeting *What's new?* has been traced back to 1880s New York and is thought to be a translation of the *Was ist los?* of German-Jewish immigrants, as is the general belief regarding the similar expression *What's with you?* Interestingly, one respected authority offers the surprising theory that *kike,* a vulgar, highly offensive term of hostility and contempt, often used by anti-Semites, offends not only persons of Jewish descent and religion but the Italians and Irish as well. The *Random House Dictionary of the English Language* suggests that it is "apparently modeled on *hike,* Italian, itself modeled on *mike,* Irishman, short for Michael." In other words, the deliberately disparaging term painfully illustrates the transfer of prejudice from one newly arrived immigrant group to the next. This view runs counter to the prevailing theory, however. Mencken and others, including *Webster's Third,* believe that the word "derived from the *ki* or *ky* endings of the surnames of many Slavic Jews." Neither theory seems susceptible to absolute proof.

The New Yorker's habit of "talking with his hands," a kind of frenetic ballet accompaniment to the music of his voice, is often associated with Yiddish, but it is a habit common to many language groups in the city, especially to Italian speakers. One wonders if American Indians could have communicated with New Yorkers unknown to them through ideographic signs, as late 19th-century experiments showed they were capable of doing with deaf-mutes. In any case, New Yorkers use a good number of the "700,000 distinctive movements of the hands, fingers, arms and face by which information can be transferred without speech"—perhaps more of them than any other Americans. Watch a New Yorker talking in a silent film and you might think he or she is speaking some form of Ameslan (*American Sign Language*).

H. L. Mencken considered Brooklynese a class dialect rather than a regional or geographical one. Originally it was "Bourgese," the Sage of Baltimore noted, a New York City speech pattern associated with "lower-class" colloquial speech. The word *Brooklynese* itself doesn't seem to have been coined until the late 1920s, though the subdialect that grew in Brooklyn was observed and joked about 50 years earlier.

Called "The English of the Lower Classes" by E. H. Babbitt, the Columbia professor who first gave it scholarly attention in 1896, Brooklynese may well be rooted in Gaelic. The theory here is that the dialect first appeared after a late 19th-century tsunami of immigration from Ireland flooded New York with future cops, firemen, cabbies, longshoremen, socialites, politicians and poets. Francis Griffith, a retired Hofstra University professor who has studied the Brooklyn dialect for nearly half a century, argues that the trademark Brooklyn diphthong *oi*, as in *moider* (murder), which exists in no British dialect, is found in many Gaelic words, such as *barbaroi* (barbarian) and *taoiseach* (leader). Griffith, who used to have a sign over his blackboard admonishing "There's no joy in Jersey" when he taught public school in Brooklyn, doesn't accept the traditional Dutch derivation for *dese* and *dem*. He points out that neither Gaelic nor Brooklynese has a *th* sound; *th* becomes a hard *t* or *d* in both languages, giving us rough Brooklynese like *da dame wid tin legs*. It should be noted, however, that in addition to the Irish, none of New York's polyglot immigrants (into the 1930s New York City subways had No Smoking signs printed in English, German, Italian, Yiddish, Chinese and Russian) pronounced *th* or *dh* sounds in their native languages and also substituted the nearest equivalents, *t* and *d*, for them.

A number of classic New York expressions do come directly from Gaelic. A *card*, or joker, as in "Wudda card he is," could be a corruption of the Gaelic *caird* (an itinerant tramp). The expression "Put da kibosh on it" (Put an end to it) may derive from *cie bais* (pronounced *bosh*), "the cap of death," a facecloth that was put on a corpse in southwest Ireland.

But it is hard to imagine mellifluous Gaelic or an Irish *brogue* (the word derived perhaps from the heavy *brogan* shoes that Irish peasants wore) becoming rapid-fire guttural Brooklynese, even in the midst of the most manic civilization in history. The Gaelic theory is just that: a theory—and one without sufficient proof. *Put the kibosh on it,* for example, may not derive from *cie bais* at all. One etymologist traces the words to a Yiddish term used in auctions and meaning an increase in a bid so that the bidder's opponents are quashed. Another word-detective suggests the Italian *capuce,* a tin lid used by street vendors of ice cream; to *put the kibosh on,* according to this last version, first meant to put the lid back on the container.

Facts can always be stretched to cover any theory. For instance, in his essay "A Form of Thanks," Cleanth Brooks shows how the King James Version of the Song of Songs would have been pronounced in 1860 Sussex, England:

1. De song of songs, dat is Solomon's.
2. Let him kiss me wud de kisses of his mouth; for yer love is better dan wine.

Brooks is writing about the roots of the folk language of Mississippi and how it sprang from a great lineage; yet these isolated words certainly could be used to make a case for a Brooklynese-Sussex connection as well.

Of the many theories about the origins of Brooklynese the most startling is the guess that long before Shoiman boined Atlanter, New York entrepreneurs, who for more than a century had a strong trading relationship with the South, picked up the famous Brooklyn accent from the Southern planters of Mobile, New Orleans and, to some degree, Charleston. These merchants, in turn, passed on the corrupted patrician Southernese sounds to the New York lower classes. The ironic suggestion that we bums who moider the language derived our speech habits from Southern aristocrats has been put forth as hypothesis, "not even a theory, really," by Dr. Marshall D. Berger, a speech professor at New York City College and a native New Yorker himself. Berger's best example of Brooklynese as corrupted Southern talk is the expression *The worm has turned.* Southern planters made that come out *The whum has tuhned,* which eventually arrived in New York as *The whuim has tuined* and finally became *Da woim has toined.* We shouldn't oughta have went South maybe.

While Brooklynese may derive from Southern speech, it is never called a charming dialect like its possible parent; even if it sometimes seems quite as lackadaisical, Brooklynese is clearly not a dialect of the upwardly mobile—not even in New York, as Professor William Labov shows in his book *The Social Stratification of English in New York City* (1966). One can hear the differences in speech among personnel in uptown and downtown stores and even within the same store, distinctions that correspond to price and service. The upper class, prep-schooled "honks" of Tom Wolfe speak a different language from that of the "wonks" of the "lower classes"; I've often heard the gentrified *rawther* uptown. Education, economic status, ethnic ties and age groups have always made a uniform New Yorkese impossible—to which most speech teachers would add, "Thank God!"

But by no means can we moan, "Dose were da days" or "Bon verge (bon voyage), Brooklynese." The thesis that Brooklynese is dead is a lot of *baloney* (Brooklynese that probably derives from the Irish *blarney*, not the German *bologna*). True, one finds nowadays few speakers around of the "a nerzy nerse annerz an erster," or "Doity Goity from Bizoity" variety, though the species is not extinct. True, Brooklyn itself is now more than half nonwhite and filled with the musical sounds of Spanish and the liquid tones of various species of Black English. But Brooklynese is not yet dead and a less exaggerated Brooklyn accent has spread out from Greenpernt more than 100 miles in every direction; the strains of it won't soon disappear from the land. Columnist Russell Baker, for example, has written a linguistic guide for Yurpeans (Europeans) visiting the United States in which he calls the language spoken here "American" but which strongly resembles Brooklynese, as this sample shows:

> Q. *Ahdaya gettu Rootwun?*
> A. *Dake a leffada nexlite, gwate bloxun daycoride tillya kumdooa big facdree, unyul see toorodes. Dake a rodetuuda lef unya cantmissit.*

If you hear someone hail a cab in New York, you might well hear him shout "KEE-ab," according to sociolinguist Labov, who has been studying changing Northeastern accents over the past four decades. Professor Labov has predicted the beginnings of a historic realignment in the pronunciation of American English, one that may be as far-reaching as that which occurred between Chaucer's and Shakespeare's time. At present this change is most prominent among New York's white lower-middle class. Just as few New Yorkers say *Toity-toid* today (incidentally, my own investigation reveals that many old-time New Yorkers insist this pronunciation was more often *Tedy-teyd*, Thirty-third Street and Third Avenue being *Teyd-teyd n Teyd*), other features of their dialect may wither away. Especially noticeable, says Labov, is the short *a* picking up a long *e* before it. Labov has found that a good number of New Yorkers (he doesn't give a percentage) have adopted this new speech habit, using it in some words (e.g., *cab* and *bad*) but not in others (e.g., *cat, back, pack, bang, bat*).

I'd like to second Professor Labov's findings, but I have never heard the distinct pronunciation KEE-ab (said quickly) for *cab*, or BEE-ag for *bag* in my extensive, almost daily travels and eavesdropping through the New York City metropolitan area on subway, bus and foot. Nor was I able to elicit such pronunciations on the 20 or so occasions that I tried to trick people into unself-consciously saying these words. I did hear *beer* pronounced BEE-ah, however, though that is nothing new. I agree with Labov that while *frog* is *frahg*, the New York *dog* is often (but not always) pronounced DOO-awg, and while *on* is *ahn* usually, *off* is often oo-AWF.

Neither could I find complete support for Labov's contention that while a *choral* group of singers is pronounced *coral, coral*, as in a coral reef, is pronounced CAH-rel. This is supposed to be some kind of New York shibboleth, but of the 10 New Yorkers I questioned, all pronounced both words as *coral,* though I admittedly have heard the *cahrel* pronunciation in the past (only among college-educated people, if I remember correctly). But then my methods are primitive; I mention the results only for the little they are worth. I have noticed the pronunciation of *OK* being shortened to a more hurried *K* in the New York City area and elsewhere; I noted this in *Human Words* (1972) and the pronunciation has become much more common since, though no dialectologist seems to have recorded it. Young people in particular often say "K" in place of *OK,* and recently I have heard the expression pronounced even more quickly—like the *k* in *kitty.*

Labov points out that the merger of vowel sounds has tended to cause confusion of meaning, telling of a New York family sharply criticized by neighborhood kids because they gave their son a girl's name—the name was Ian, which the kids all pronounced *Ann.* Again, I've been unable to confirm this (friends with a son named Ian said they had never heard the name pronounced *Ann*), but I am nowhere near the scientist that the professor is, his methods truly original and clever, as this admiring account of one of his field tests indicates:

> Labov's method for testing the fate of the final and preconsonantal *r* in speakers of different social levels consisted of choosing three New York City department stores, each oriented to a completely different social stratum. He approached a large number of salesladies, asking each of them about the location of a certain department that he knew to be on the fourth floor. Thus, their answers always contained two words with potential *r's* "fourth" and "floor." This shortcut enabled Labov to establish in a relatively short time that the salesladies in the store with richer customers clearly tended to use "*r*-full" forms, whereas those in the stores geared to the poorer social strata more commonly used "*r*-less" forms.

Scores of people rich and poor from all over the world have brought words and pronunciations to New York over the last four centuries, many of which have entered the national vocabulary. There is even a theory that the word *gizmo,* for a thingamajig, comes from the Arabic *shu ismo* (the same), which may have come to New York with Moroccans or been brought back by American soldiers who served in Morocco during World War II. New York has been a world city longer than any other American metropolis and is more so today than at any time in its history. The Magnificent Mongrel has a population of 7.3 million, of whom 2.1 million were born in another country. Walt Whitman's million-footed Manhattan has become 100-million-footed Manhattan. There are more Greeks here than in any place but Greece, more Russians than in any place but Russia, more Chinese than in any place but China and Taiwan. New York City has more Ethiopians (about 3,000) than several states have black people. Similar statistics could be cited for pages. At P.S. 89 in Elmhurst, Queens, 38 different languages are spoken by students, half of whom do not come from English-speaking homes (there are more than 113,000 such children in the New York City school system). People migrate to the city from every part of America and the world, most of them affectionately regarding it as home rather than "a nice place to visit," as the old saw goes. Travel about New York City and you will find little neighborhoods of people newly arrived from England, France, Germany, Greece, Iran, Israel, Italy, Poland, Portugal, Romania, Russia, Yugoslavia, Puerto Rico, Argentina, Colombia, Guatemala, Cuba, the Dominican Republic, Ecuador, Mexico, Panama, Peru, Barbados, Grenada, Guyana, Haiti, Jamaica, Trinidad, India, Japan, Korea and the Philippines, among other countries—this in addition to older enclaves like Chinatown and Little Italy. The new immigrants are of all kinds and classes. And all of them are slowly changing the nature of New York talk with new words and accents, just as the words and rhythms of Black English and Spanglish are doing.

New York City is truly "the nest of languages, the bequeather of poems," as Walt Whitman observed in "A Broadway Pageant." Every year hundreds of new words and expressions are coined in New York, which has long been the communications capital of America. Most of these are obsolete within a few years, but many last. An old one, surprisingly, is *outta sight*. Often regarded as college slang of the 1960s, *outta sight* (for something remarkable or wonderful) has been part of the language since the 1840s, in the form of the Bowery expression *out of sight*. Stephen Crane used it in its present form in his first novel *Maggie: A Girl of the Streets* (1896): "I'm stuck on yer shape. It's outa sight."

Class dialects in New York are generally similar to those in other parts of the country. As noted, middle-class people tend to pronounce their words more carefully, while the rich are supremely sure that whatever they say is right and the poor are too busy trying to eat to give a good damn. Black English probably has its capital in New York, if this class dialect can be said to have a capital; many new black expressions originate here at any rate. The class dialect Spanglish, in its Puerto Rican form, has also contributed local words and expressions to New Yorkese. No one seems to have established whether New York's Puerto Rican women favor the white New York dialect and Puerto Rican men lean to the black vernacular—which Professor Labov says is the case in Philadelphia. In any event, individuals of all classes and ethnic and social groups in the city frequently switch from New York talk to "network English," depending on the occasion. And in New York, as elsewhere, when members of these classes and groups have specialized occupations they often use words and expressions from the jargons or lingos of the workplace. Thus a New York City police officer calls his protector his *rabbi*, recognizing "his influence with the higher-ups" at headquarters, while a New York mugger talks of *doing time* (not of *serving a jail sentence*). New York stockbrokers, lawyers, legislators, garment workers, longshoremen, waiters, retail clerks, hotel workers, bartenders, truckers—these and hundreds more professionals have their own special expressions that often enter the mainstream of New York talk, as the police term *rabbi* and the lawyer's term *takeover* have.

New York printers contributed the national expression *lobster shift* to the language. *Lobster shift* for the newspaper shift commencing at four in the morning is said to have originated at the defunct *New York Journal-American* early in the century. The newspaper's plant was near the East Side docks, and workers on the shift came to work at about the same time lobstermen were putting out to sea in their boats.

Not long ago, a Bronx candidate for head of the Boston public school system was asked by his examiners if he couldn't "get rid of that New York accent"; he didn't get the job, though to what extent his accent played a role in his rejection isn't known. People across the United States often regard New Yorkese as negatively as the Dutch did the *click-clack* dialect of the South African Khoi-Khoin tribe to which they gave the derogatory name *Hottentot* from their *hateran en tatern* (to stutter and stammer). One Texan congressman had the noive to say New York City "isn't an English-speaking place" to which a Bronx borough president replied, "Texans speak a language no one understands!" But Americans generally do like Texan speech better if one can judge by a poll conducted by the Linguaphone Institute to ascertain where the best English in America is spoken, from the standpoint of diction. New York City came in dead last, with no votes. New York just *don't never get no breaks* (this triple negative, common in the area, is, however, not restricted to New York).

Protest groups have arisen like the Society Against Disparaging Remarks About Brooklyn, which had 40,000 members in the 1950s and replied to 3,000 slurs about Brooklyn speech in the media. But native New Yorkers do often shed whatever New York accents they possess while climbing the social ladder, either by emulating the local upper class or by hiring voice coaches to teach them General American. "There is nothing more tarnishing, more cheapening in life than a New York accent," advises one speech consultant. "It's so very *vulgar*. It robs even the most beautiful, intelligent person of any *dignity*." She is one of a good number of metropolitan area teachers who charge up to $100 an hour to make anyone speak as they think everybody should. Television and radio do their bit in homogenizing here, too—as they do everywhere, only more so. The theory is that New Yorkese turns off more people than any other accent, thus encouraging local media stars who want to become national media stars to lose their New York accents with the help of exercises done in front of mirrors. (Lesson One: To stop replacing *th* sounds with *d* sounds, as in *my udduh bruddah,* push the tip of the tongue against the cutting edge of the upper teeth and practice saying rapidly: *the, these, them, those, that.*)

But there are many who like the philological flavor of the polyglot city, who don't think of the New York accent as slurvian, sleazy, monotone, nasal and staccato (a charge that some Britishers level against all Americans). Happily there are those who, given the choice, stick to their subtler shades of *da, dis, dem, dose,* and *dat.* They may not believe New Yorkese is beautiful, but the real choice is whether one is willing to deny one's deepest origins by spurning one's native talk. With this, even outlanders agree. "In a country already suffering from terminal blandness, regional accents and dialects should be treasured, not trashed," Carl Grossman wrote in a letter to the editors of the *New York Times* on May 1, 1984.

> As a child growing up in Oklahoma, I relished the chance to hear a New Yorker talk. Every strangely shaped vowel brought pictures to my mind of towering buildings, hot, gritty sidewalks and Ebbets Field. And the fast-clipped speech made me imagine the speeding subways and hurrying pedestrians I had never actually seen. When at age thirteen I arrived in the city on vacation with my parents, my first wish was to hear the banter that was uniquely New York. Now, even after living here for eleven years, I find it is still accent that separates transplants like myself from "real" New Yorkers. And it is still accent that, for me, helps make New Yawk New York.

Along these same lines linguist Dr. Harold Bender says New Yorkese "is no upstart. It has a fine tradition going back to the early Dutch burghers. Despite its age, it is still virile and is spreading." Others who would agree include:

Jimmy Breslin, author, Pulitzer Prize winner, and sometime politician and broadcaster, who hails from Queens and who has been quoted as saying: "You are what you are."

Bella Abzug, the late congresswoman, who contended: "Nah, politically, my accent has never been a problem, and I've been all over the country. They loved me in Peoria, and they loved me in Nashville. I think people should be what they are."

Rocky Graziano, former fighter and television personality, who observes: "Da only reason dey use me on TV is cawsa my accent. I'm outta bizness widout it."

Leo Durocher, the "practically Peerless Leader," who when he managed the Brooklyn Dodgers, threatened Brooklyn's archrivals the New York Giants with: "It's gonna be Poil Hahbuh fuh de Gints."

Joan Rivers, New York comedian, who explains why she talks so fast: "We [New Yorkers] tawk fast becaws we don't know how long we're gonna *live* . . . I can do my whole act waiting for the subway doors to close."

Henry Winkler, "The Fonz," who could once be found black leather jacket and all hanging out on every Brooklyn street corner and still haunts the borough.

Geraldine A. Ferraro, whose New York accent may have helped her lose her bid for vice president in 1984. Do aliens detest the dialect so much? Should Ms. Ferraro go to accent-eradication school? Anyway, Ms. Ferraro, a trial lawyer, hails from Queens, the borough of homes, represented Archie Bunker's Ninth Congressional District in Elmhurst (*Ellimheyst,* locally), and should be saluted for her bravery—this stalwart New Yorker didn't try to change a word.

Honorable mention goes to Bugs Bunny, Betty Boop, the Dead End Kids (especially Leo Gorcey), early Tony Curtis, the late Nelson Rockefeller (who mixed a lot of *youses* wid his broad honk *ahs*), and finally, that well-remembered guy named Jerry with the white blowfish belly sticking out from under his shirt who did those outrageous furniture commercials on local New York TV ("That's the stor-ieeee . . .") As for the best all-around rendition of the Brooklyn accent I've seen in print, I'd have to vote against Damon Runyon and pick Thomas Wolfe's piece "Only the Dead Know Brooklyn" from his *Death to Morning* (1935), despite the fact that it is somewhat snobbish and the dialect is exaggerated.

But the champion of all New Yorkese speakers is John Occhiogrosso, formerly of Brooklyn, whose superb pronunciation of the Kings (County) English won him an expense-paid trip back to Brooklyn in a "Best New York Accent in Houston" contest some years ago. (A half-dozen contestants were eliminated because they didn't know or remember that you play stoop ball with a *Spaldeen,* not a Spalding, in New York.) Occhiogrosso's test of skill included the proper New York pronunciation of a room-service order from a certain floor of a certain New York hotel, which went: "Oim owan da toidy-toid flohwah, od da Noo Yowak Stadla. Can oi hab a cuppa kowafee an a glazza watta?" Though he had in the past even faced job discrimination on account of his accent, the winner said, in translation: "If people don't like me for what I am, the hell with them. That's the New York way."

NEW YAWK TAWK

A DICTIONARY OF
New York City
EXPRESSIONS

a Of or to, in telling time. "'What's the time?' he asked the doorman. 'Five a twelve.'" (Jimmy Breslin, *Table Money*, 1986)

absoid A pronunciation of *absurd* sometimes heard in New York.

ace boon coon Black English for one's best friend, first recorded in 1962. The word *coon* when said by a white person is a racial slur for a black person. It possibly has nothing to do with the animal called a raccoon or a coon. *Coon* here may come from the last syllable of the Portuguese *barracões*, which is pronounced like *coon* and meant buildings especially constructed to hold slaves for sale. The word *coon* is (obviously) also used by blacks, as is the word *nigger*, but is of course considered highly offensive when uttered by whites. "I knew K.B. about a year before we became ace boon coons." (Claude Brown, *Manchild in the Promised Land*, 1965) *Boon coon* alone dates back to 1958 and was originally a Harlem term too.

ackamarackus Pseudo-Latin slang for nonsense, bullshit. "Now of course this is strictly the old ackamarackus, as The Lemon Drop Kid cannot even spell arthritis, let alone have it . . ." (Damon Runyon "The Lemon Drop Kid," 1931) *The Random House Historical Dictionary of American Slang* (1994) cites the first recorded use of the term in a Runyon *Collier's* story in 1933, two years later, and cites Eugene O'Neill's use of it in a letter. *Ackamaracka* is among other variants of the word.

Adams' New York Gum No. 1—Snapping and Stretching The world's first modern chewing gum (previously there were gums made of spruce sap, paraffin and other substances), concocted by Thomas Adams Sr. on his Jersey City kitchen stove around 1869 and later manufactured in New York City. Adams' was the first commercial gum to be made with chicle and this milky liquid from the sapodilla tree was supplied to the inventor by General Antonio López de Santa Anna, Mexican conqueror of the Alamo, who was exiled in Staten Island at the time. Adams first tried to make a cheap rubber substitute from the chicle, as Santa Anna had urged him to

1

do; he failed but then came up with the great gum idea. Later his company merged with eight others into the American Chicle Company.

adjern   A New York pronunciation of *adjoin*.

ahn   Sometimes heard in New York as a pronunciation of *on*.

ailanthus   *See* TREE GROWS IN BROOKLYN, A.

ain't   A common contraction in New York speech, as it is elsewhere. *Ain't,* first recorded in 1706, began life in England as a contraction of *am not* (an't). Once widely used among all classes and quite proper, it became socially unacceptable in the early 19th century when people began to use it improperly as a contraction for *is not* and *are not,* as well as *am not.* But "proper" or not, *ain't* is still widely used wherever English is spoken.

ain't he (she) a caution   Isn't he or she remarkable, unusual or funny; an old term still heard infrequently. Probably a variation of the more common *Ain't he a corker,* once frequently heard among Irish Americans.

ain't no big thing   Describes something that isn't of much importance. *Big thing,* for something extraordinary, is first recorded in 1846.

airy way   Once a common term in Brooklyn and Queens for an areaway of apartment houses. In the *airy way*

garbage cans, rarely called trash cans, were kept for the garbagemen (sanitation workers today) to pick up, usually to the side of a building against a fence. Garbagemen in the 1930s, when the term probably originated, lifted not only garbage but cans of coal ashes so heavy that they required two men to dump them into the garbage truck (sanitation van today). Sometimes called the *air-ree.*

a.k.   1) A crotchety old man; an old fogy. *Variety* probably invented the story that these initials stood for *ant*edeluvian *k*night. It is actually an abbreviation of the Yiddish *alter kocker,* which loosely means "old fart," ultimately from the German *alter* (old) and *kock* (defecate). The initials are first recorded in 1942. 2) An abbreviation of *ass kisser;* a sycophant, an apple polisher. The term *a.k.* in this sense is first recorded in 1939 and has been common (far more common than the abbreviation meaning *alter kocker*) in New York City, especially among school kids, for almost 60 years. 3) To ass kiss. "He a.k.'s every teacher in the school."

a la famiglia   A mob toast; Italian for "to the family." *See also* FAMILY.

Albany beef   Sturgeon. The fish was once so plentiful in New York's Hudson River that it was humorously called *Albany beef.* The term is first recorded in 1791 and was in use through the 19th century; sturgeon caviar was so cheap in those days that it was part of the free lunch served in bars.

Alexander A cocktail made with cream, crème de cacao and other potent ingredients. It is said to have been invented by and hence named after New York wit Alexander Woollcott in the 1920s, although some say it was named after Alexander the Great, perhaps beause you have to be a hero to drink more than one. "The lethal mixture tasted like ice cream," Helen Hayes once said, recalling her experience with Alexanders at a party. "I drank one down and took another and drank it down, and I was blind." Searching for something to say, fearing everyone would think her drunk if she didn't, Miss Hayes remembered that she would soon be moving to a smaller apartment and wanted to get rid of her large piano. But her words came out, "Anyone who wants my piano is willing to it." After a long, terrible silence, playwright George S. Kaufman said, "That's very seldom of you, Helen." *See* BRONX COCKTAIL; MANHATTAN COCKTAIL.

Algonquin Round Table *See* MEN SELDOM MAKE PASSES / AT GIRLS WHO WEAR GLASSES.

all right already Stop it, that's enough!; stop talking! "The only appropriate reply that came to mind was Brooklynese; all right already. It took an act of will for him to limit himself to merely, 'Yes.'" (Henry Roth, *From Bondage*, 1996) *Enough already* is a variation. Both are common expressions influenced by Yiddish.

All the News That's Fit to Print *See* NEW YORK TIMES.

alluh A common contraction of *all the* among New York speakers: "Alluh king's horses and alluh king's men . . ."

almighty dollar New Yorker Washington Irving coined the phrase *the almighty dollar* in a sketch first published in 1836: "The almighty dollar, that great object of universal devotion throughout the land . . ." But Ben Jonson had used "almighty gold" in a similar sense more than 200 years before him: "that for which all virtue now is sold, / And almost every vice—almighty gold."

Alphabet City A nickname, for the past 15–20 years, for the part of Manhattan's East Village located between Avenue A and Avenue D.

already A very common superfluous interjection, as in "Do it already," "Where is she already?" etc.

alrighnik A Yinglish (*Yi*ddish & E*ng*lish) term for a recently successful person who boasts about his or her success; someone nouveau riche and crudely ostentatious.

alter kocker Yiddish for "an old fart"; a crotchety old man who can't do anything properly. Also called an *a.k.*

Amazin' Mets An affectionate nickname for the New York National League baseball team since the team was formed in 1962. Said to be coined by Casey Stengel, the team's first manager, when he watched them win their first exhibition game: "They're amazin'!!" Later, however, he would lament: "They're amazin'! Can't anybody here play this game!" Also called the *Amazin's*. *See* STENGELESE.

and how!   Indicating intensive emphasis of what someone else has just said, *and how!* is a popular catchphrase first recorded in 1924. The expression possibly derives from the German *und wie!* or the Italian *e come!*, both meaning "and how" and once very common in New York among Americans of German and Italian extraction, respectively.

annerz   A New York pronunciation of *annoys*. "She really annerz me."

appernt   An old Brooklynese pronunciation of *appoint* that still survives in New York. "I've got a dentist apperntment today."

Apple   The Apple is a nickname for New York City. *See* BIG APPLE.

appleknocker   An abusive term meaning a stupid person, especially a rustic stupid person, that is still used by city dwellers. The term is recorded in this sense in a 1939 *New Yorker* story: "I had a reform-school technique, whereas them other sailors was apple-knockers. They were so dumb they couldn't find their nose with both hands." *Appleknocker* first meant a fruit picker, deriving from the mistaken urban belief that fruit is harvested by being knocked from trees with long sticks.

Archie Bunker   *See* ELLIMHEYST.

arrow chase   An old children's game, seldom if ever played anymore. "The side that starts first is provided with chalk, with which the players mark arrows upon the pavement, pointing the direction of their course. The others follow when five minutes have passed, tracking the pursued by the arrow marks until all are caught." (*Journal of American Folklore*, 1891)

ash can   A loud firecracker resembling a miniature ash can or garbage can in shape.

asparagrass   A pronunciation of *asparagus*, probably influenced by the vegetable's resemblance to grass (hence the old folk etymology *sparrow grass* or simply *grass*, both of which are still heard in New York City among old-timers). *Asparagas* and *asparagus* are much more common pronunciations.

assawayigoze   That's the way it goes. A pronunciation recorded in the Federal Writers' Project *Almanac for New Yorkers* (1938).

ast   A common pronunciation of *ask*. "'I shoulda ast you first. But I really thought this was your money, Sal, I didn't know . . .'" (Evan Hunter, *Criminal Conversation*, 1994) *See also* AX.

astorperious   Stuck up, haughty, self-important. An eponymous word, probably obsolete, from New York City black slang that is a blend of *Astor*, the last name of one of America's oldest rich families, and *imperious,* haughty, dictatorial, overbearing.

Astor Place riots The eminent American actor Edwin Forrest (1806–72) was a great rival of the older English tragedian, William Macready, who at 78 played his last role, as Macbeth, and who died in 1873 at the age of 100. In 1849 both actors were appearing in New York, where each had ardent fans, the "common man" favoring Forrest and the elite supporting Macready. The rivalry degenerated into "a struggle between democracy and Anglomania," in one critic's words, and on May 10 a mob led by E. Z. C. Judson (writer Ned Buntline), possibly encouraged by Forrest, attacked the Astor Place Opera House, where Macready was playing Macbeth. In the Astor Place Riots 22 people were killed and 36 wounded, making this probably the worst such theater disaster of all time. Judson went to jail for a year for his part in the affair.

Atlanter A typical New York pronunciation of the city of *Atlanta.*

atomic wedgie To have an *atomic wedgie* is to have one's underwear gathered in an extremely uncomfortable position between the buttocks. Specifically it refers to having the waistband of one's underwear pulled up from the waist by abusive friends.

Heard on the New York–inspired television comedy *Seinfeld.*

Aunt Hagar's children A once commonly heard reference in New York City as well as in the South for African Americans in general. So called after Hagar, Abraham's wife and Ishmael's mother (Gen. 21.9).

avenoo Commonly heard as the pronunciation of *avenue* in all five boroughs of New York City. Recorded in the 1920s, it is indeed probably the prevalent pronunciation of the word, though the standard pronunciation *avenyuh* is also frequently heard.

away *See* BONAC.

awchit *See* BONAC.

awdah New Yorkese for *order.* "Are you ready to awdah now?"

awfice Office. "Come into my awfice, it's all right by me."

awluh A pronunciation of *all the,* as in "He's god awluh money."

awmobile Sometimes heard in New York as a pronunciation of *automobile.*

awways Always. *See quotation under* DIN.

ax A pronunciation of *ask. See quote under* COME OFF IT!

baaad Commonly heard in New York among blacks. This slowly pronounced form of *bad* has long been black slang for something or someone good, and recently this meaning has come into general usage to a limited extent. The variation is so old that it is found in the American Creole language Gullah of three centuries ago, when *baaad* was used by slaves as an expression of admiration for another slave who successfully flaunted "Ole Maussa's" rules.

ba-ba-deh-boom A humorous term imitative of the sound a gun fired and used to indicate someone was killed by a gun, generally up close. First recorded in the film version of Mario Puzo's *The Godfather* (1972) in which the word is used by James Caan, playing the godfather's oldest son, Sonny Corleone. *Ba-ba-deh-boom* was probably around long before it found its way to the printed page, however. Heard frequently since *The Godfather* film it is usually said while simulating a gun with the thumb and index finger. Can also be written as *babadehboom* to indicate how quickly it is said.

baby A common term of address used by one male to another in New York City, especially among blacks. "I can say 'baby' to another cat, and he can say 'baby' to me." (Brown, *Manchild in the Promised Land*) *Baby* as a form of address between men is recorded as far back as 1835, but the term didn't have much currency until the 1920s and wasn't really widespread in use until the 1960s in New York.

babushka One of the few Russian words widely used in English. *Babushka*, a woman's kerchief or scarf, derives from the Russian *baba*, "grandmother," because the scarves have long been worn hoodlike by old women in Russia, plus the diminutive Russian suffix *-ushka*. In New York City a triangular head scarf tied under the chin is generally called a *kerchief*. This same kerchief is usually called a *babushka* in New York when worn by old women, especially eastern European immigrants.

back in the woods Outdated, not with it. Usually black slang. ". . . I should have been their parents, because I had been out there on the streets, and

I wasn't as far back in the woods as they were." (Brown, *Manchild in the Promised Land*)

backyard tree A local name for the tree of heaven or ailanthus tree, the famous tree that grows in Brooklyn. So called because it grows in many backyards in all the boroughs with great resistance to any type of air pollution. *See TREE GROWS IN BROOKLYN, A.*

badmouth To speak badly of someone, put someone down. Originally African-American slang and possibly deriving from a Vai or Mandingo expression, to *badmouth* came north with Southern blacks and is now used widely among whites as well in New York City, among other areas. It is first recorded, however, in a 1941 *Saturday Evening Post* story by James Thurber: "He badmouthed everybody."

Bagdad on the Hudson O. Henry's favorite name for New York City. The "King of Story Tellers" chronicled the diverse lives of everyday New Yorkers, "the obscure and exploited masses of New York, the waitresses and hat-pressers, soda-jerkers and bums, the taxi drivers and policemen, O. Henry's 'Four Million'," as Upton Sinclair put it. The years from 1902 to 1910 have been called New York's *O. Henry age*. O. Henry drank an average of two quarts of whiskey daily, but this never prevented him from writing his 50–65 "wellmade" short stories a year (some 600 over his lifetime). The immensely prolific author wrote tales characterized by ironic, surprise endings—"twists," "stingers" or "snappers"—which while they aren't supposed to be fashionable anymore are still widely used by authors and known as *O. Henry endings*.

O. Henry was the pen name of American writer William Sydney Porter (1862–1910). While working as a bank teller in Austin, Texas, Porter was indicted for the embezzlement (really mismanagement) of a small amount of money and fled the country to South America. On returning to his dying wife, he was imprisoned for three years and adopted the pseudonym O. Henry to conceal his real identity when he began writing and selling the stories that would make him famous. Released from prison he pursued his literary career in New York, where he published at least 15 books of short stories, including such perennial favorites as "The Gift of the Magi," which he wrote in three hours to meet a deadline while his editor dozed on the couch in his furnished room. O. Henry suffered from hypoglycemia, the opposite of diabetes, his classic summary of the condition being "I was born eight drinks below par." He died with only 33¢ in his pockets; his famous last words, quoting a popular song, were "Turn up the lights, I don't want to go home in the dark." Then came an O. Henry twist he would have liked. His funeral, in Manhattan's Little Church Around the Corner, was somehow scheduled at the same time as a wedding.

bagel [It is my opinion that a good bagel can't be made with anything but

New York water as an ingredient, but I won't go into that here.] Bagels were possibly invented by a Jewish baker in Vienna in 1683. The anonymous baker, so the story goes, made the roll in the shape of a riding stirrup, in honor of Polish king John Sobieski, who had saved Vienna from Turkish invaders and whose favorite hobby was riding. The great invention was first called a *bugel,* the German for "stirrup." This information and much more about bagels can be found in Marilyn and Tom Bagel's (this is their real name) very entertaining *The Bagel Bible* (1992). The Bagels are not supported by Leo Rosten, however. Rosten claims in *The Joys of Yiddish* (1968) that the first mention of *bagels* came in 1610 when a community regulation in Kraków, Poland, decreed that bagels "be given as a gift to any woman in childbirth." He cites the German *Beugel,* a round loaf of bread, as the source of *bagel* and advises that a bagel was considered lucky by Jews because it is circular, "the perfect form." Other authorities derive *bagel* from the Middle High German *bouc,* "bracelet," which became the Yiddish *beggel*—the bagel, of course, resembling a bracelet in shape. "Bagels, begorrah!" Macy's bakery once advertised on St. Patrick's Day in word-rich New York City from which the bagel was introduced to the rest of the country. *See also* BIALY; SHMEER.

bag lady A destitute homeless woman, so called because many *bag ladies* carry all their belongings in shopping bags, which they keep close to them in their sleeping places in the subways, building lobbies, parks and other public places. The designation, at first limited to New York City, seems to have been first recorded in 1972, but I heard it several years before then. There is no equivalent expression for a homeless man living the same way; a *bagman* is a man who collects or distributes payoff money.

bah A pronunciation of *bar;* a tavern.

Baked Alaska This dessert of ice cream baked briefly in a hot oven to brown its meringue topping into a crust was invented in Manhattan by Charles Ranhofer, chef at the famed Delmonico's restaurant, in 1867 to commemorate the U.S. purchase of Alaska from Russia.

baleboss A Yiddish term deriving from the Hebrew for "master." *Baleboss* (pronounced BOL-eh-boss) can mean the head of the house, a store owner, a manager or anyone in authority. His female counterpart is a *baleboostch* (pronounced bol-eh-BOSS-teh).

baloney Al Smith, an East Sider who became governor of New York and an unsuccessful presidential candidate in 1928, helped popularize this expression with his remark "No matter how you slice it, it's still baloney." But *baloney* for "bunk" dates back to at least the early 20th century, bologna sausage having been pronounced *baloney* as early as the 1870s when there was a popular song entitled "I Ate the Boloney." There are those who say that *baloney* for "bunk" has nothing to do with bologna sausage, however, tracing it to a corruption of the Spanish *pelone*, "testicles," and claiming that this meant "nonsense" or "bunk" just as *balls, all balls,* and *nerts* did. The word is also spelled *boloney. See also* PALOOKA.

Bandits Roost   *See* TENEMENTS.

bar mitzvah   A solemn but joyous ceremony held in a synagogue, usually on the Saturday morning closest to a Jewish boy's 13th birthday, to recognize the boy as an adult member of the Jewish community. *Bar mitzvah* can also mean the boy himself, a *bar mitzvah boy.* The word comes from the Hebrew for "son of the commandment." The equivalent ceremony for girls is called the *bas mitzvah.*

barnyard epithet   Used to indicate that an expletive has been stated. Bullshit. New York City hasn't had any barnyards for years, but this euphemism was coined as recently as 1970 by a *New York Times* editor, in reporting the reply of David Dellinger, one of the Chicago Seven tried for conspiracy to disrupt the 1968 Democratic National Convention, to a police version of his actions. Dellinger's actual words were "Oh, bullshit!" The editor reported that Dillinger had used a "barnyard epithet."

barrio   A Spanish-speaking neighborhood or district. The first such neighborhood appeared in New York City above Canal Street shortly before World War I. It was composed mostly of people from Spain and South America. *El Barrio* is presently the name for a neighborhood in East Harlem whose inhabitants are Spanish-speaking. El Barrio lies between One Hundred Twentieth Street and Ninety-sixth Street and Third and Fifth Avenues.

batlan   Pronounced BOT-lin, this Yiddish term comes from the Hebrew for a "man who does nothing." It is applied to a jobless person, an idler or someone unsuitable for any employment.

Battle of the Aesthetes   Irish-born author Ernest Boyd (1887–1946) became an important literary figure after immigrating to New York in 1913. His essay "Aesthete: Model 1924," which appeared in the first issue of H. L. Mencken's *The American Mercury* that year, attacked the young idealists of Greenwich Village and launched what was called the Battle of the Aesthetes. Before it was over, a terrified Boyd suffered insulted would-be aesthetes picketing his apartment house, throwing stink bombs through his window, jamming his doorbell with pins and making obscene phone calls to him in the early hours of the morning.

bawss   A pronunciation of *boss.*

beanshooter   A term often used instead of *slingshot* in New York of the 1940s and 1950s.

beard   Police lingo for an undercover agent, after the beards grown by such operatives as disguises.

Beau James A nickname for James J. Walker, the effervescent, high-living, cocky mayor of New York from 1925 until he resigned in 1932 after being investigated by the Seabury Committee about the "high, wide and handsome government" he gave the city. *See* FUN CITY.

beautiful! There are many New York variations on the exclamation *beautiful!* It can mean everything from the very worst to the very best, depending on the situation and one's tone of voice. Someone might say, "This new virus can wipe out a whole city in a matter of days," and the reply might be an ironic, disgusted "Beautiful!" On the other hand, *beautiful!* is used to express one's extreme happiness with something.

bedbug A crazy person; someone who acts crazy. Often used in the old expression *crazy as a bedbug,* after the bedbug's frantic running around in all directions when exposed An example would be "I don't know who shot him—who knows who done it with all the bedbugs in this country?"

beeag A pronunciation of *bag.*

beep A term used for a New York City borough president. First recorded in 1980 and patterned on *veep* for the vice president of the United States.

beerbelly A big stomach or potbelly that is attributed to drinking too much beer over the years. Often called a *booze belly* in other regions.

beeuh A pronunciation of *beer.*

begorrah! This Irish exclamation, heard almost always in a comic sense, if heard at all, is actually a euphemism for *By God!* and dates back to the 19th century. *See quote under* BAGEL.

being Sometimes used for *because,* as in "Being that I'm sick, I can't leave," instead of "I can't leave because I'm sick."

Belgian block A square stone about a foot long, used extensively a century ago to pave streets but now, due largely to cost, used primarily for driveways or to make low borders in gardens, etc. Some of New York's streets built with *Belgian block* remain today. Also called *Belgian.*

believe me A very common interjection, as in "I'm going! Believe me!" or "Believe me, it's hot!"

belly laugh *See* PALOOKA.

bellywhopping Used in New York City and on Long Island, among other places, to describe a sledding technique: first one runs, holding the sled up, and then one throws the sled down and falls down belly first onto it.

Ben Slang for a $100 bill, named in honor of Ben Franklin, whose picture is on the bill. The term isn't common in New York except among gamblers but is frequently heard in Philadelphia and parts of New Jersey, especially Atlantic City. "'That's worth a Ben at least!'" (Frank Freudberg, *Gasp,* 1996)

Ben Day   A New York City printer named Benjamin Day (1831–1916) invented the Ben Day process of the quick mechanical production of stippling, shading or tints on line engravings. The process, which has been used since about 1879, eliminated the shading of a drawing by hand. *Ben Dayed* means produced by the *Ben Day* photoengraving method.

berl   A pronunciation of *boil* still commonly heard in New York City, especially Brooklyn. "Gimme those eggs hard berled."

Betty Boop   *See* POPEYE.

beyoodyful   Beautiful. "What beyoodyful skin," Mr. Kaplan said. (Arthur Kober, "You Mean Common," 1940)

b'hoy   An Irish pronunciation of *boy* common in the 19th century. His female counterpart was a *g'hal*. The *b'hoy* was usually a young worker, flashily dressed, who belonged to one of New York's many fiercely competitive and colorfully named fire companies, such as the Black Joke, the Dry Bones and the Bean Soup. Their speech was called *flash,* and it is said that it contributed many words and phrases to the language—though this last is doubtful. *See* FLASH.

bialy   A round bread roll topped with flakes of onion. A *bialy* (plural *bialys,* not *bialies,* and pronounced bee-OLL-ee) takes its name from Bialystok, Poland, where it was first made or perfected—long before its name was recorded in English. The bialy is not, as the bagel is, empty in the center; it does have a center depression, however, and has thus been called "a virgin bagel." The word is actually short for *Bialystoker begel,* that is, a bagel made in Bialystok. *See* BAGEL.

bidness   A common pronunciation of *business.* "'. . . Marowitz thinks that anybody in our bidness is glamorous, like a movie actor or something.'" (Richard Condon, *Prizzi's Honor,* 1982)

Big A   A shortened form of *Big Apple,* a name for New York City. Also a common designation for the Aqueduct racetrack in Queens, because there's bigtime racing there. *See* BIG APPLE.

Big Apple   A common nickname for New York City since the 1970s that is used only jocularly by residents, often in the shortened form of *the Apple,* mainly because it has been pushed by the local tourist bureau in advertisements and commercials. The term is first recorded by gossip columnist Walter Winchell in 1927, but no one is sure of the name's etymology. The *Big Apple,* according to one story, was invented in New Orleans in about 1910. There, New Orleans musicians used it as a translation of the Spanish *manzana principal,* the "main apple orchard," referring to the main city block downtown, or loosely the place where all the action is. Later, they brought the term to New York. New York City has also been called the *Big Burg,* the *Big City,* the *Big Onion,* the *Big Smear* (these last two of tramp language), the *Big Stem,* and the *Big Town. See also* DIRTY SIDE; FATHER KNICKERBOCKER; FROG AND TOE; GOTHAM.

Big Board   A nickname for the New York Stock Exchange; first recorded in the early 1930s.

Big Burg   A nickname for New York City; first recorded in 1933 but used before that for big cities in general.

big butter-and-egg man   New York City speakeasy owner Texas Guinan may have coined this expression for a wealthy big spender during the Roaring Twenties. According to the story, one of her patrons kept buying rounds for the house all evening and showering $50 bills on the chorus girls. Guinan asked him to give his name and take a bow, but he would only identify himself as being in the dairy business so Guinan put the spotlight on him, asking from the patrons and employees, "a hand for my big butter-and-egg man." In any case, George S. Kaufman used the phrase as the title of a Broadway play in 1925, giving it greater currency.

big casino   1) A very important person. 2) A major, often fatal illness, especially cancer. The term derives from the card game casino, in which the ten of diamonds is the most valuable card in the deck, worth two points, and is called the *Big Casino* or *Big Gus.*

Big City   A name for New York City common for nearly a century now and familiar throughout the U.S. *See* BIG TOWN.

Big City rhythm   See quote.

'The Big City rhythm' has been dealt with in the movies, radio, books and magazines, but the fact remains that everything which has been told is no more than a pale suggestion of the dominant moods of the town, the qualities that place it by itself in the world: the whirling, driving tempo of existence, the effots to relax within the battle to exist, the complicated individual adjustments to myriad personal relationships and to the whole process of the living city. (Federal Writer's Project, *New York Panorama,* 1938)

Big Gus   *See* BIG CASINO.

big house   Once common slang for a penitentiary, originating in about 1900, but now rarely used except humorously. Wrote F. Scott Fitzgerald in a 1940 letter: "I feel like a criminal who has been in a hideout, been caught, and has to go back to the Big House."

big (whole) megillah   Slang for a long, tedious explanation, as in "Don't give me a big [or whole] megillah, get to the point." From the Hebrew for "scroll," referring to the long, detailed *Book of Esther* read in synagogue during Purim.

big one   A $1,000 bill; any large denomination banknote. "He bet five big ones on the fight." Sometimes used also for a million dollars, as in a recent newspaper headline, "TRUMP WON TWENTY BIG ONES ON THE FIGHT."

Big Onion A nickname hoboes had for New York City a century before Big Apple became popular. Its origin is unknown, but the term could be a reflection of the fact that there are so many diverse layers to the city.

big shot This widespread term for a very important person has been traced back only to the 1920s in New York, where it is first recorded in Brooklyn-born humorist S. J. Perelman's *The Old Gang* (1927): "They are big shots but too well-known to shake loose an ankle with the gals." First applied to gangsters, the term is apparently patterned on the much older *big gun*, which is also still heard.

Big Smear A nickname for New York City used by hoboes long before *Big Apple* became popular.

Big Stem A name for the theater district in Manhattan, and sometimes for Manhattan itself. The *Big Stem* is first recorded in 1934, long after the *Great White Way* (1901) and *Big Apple* (probably the early 1920s).

Big Town A nickname, especially in the East, for New York City that is first recorded in 1902. In the West, the *Big Town* often means Chicago. *Big City* is a variation on the term.

Billy the Kid No one knows for sure if the famous western outlaw Billy the Kid came from New York or not—there were several young New York criminals who took that name. But there was a fabled gunman named Henry McCarty (1859–81) who took the sobriquet William H. Bonney; he was apparently dubbed "Billy the Kid" for his youth and small size after he killed at age 18 his first man (of 21) out West. He was perhaps the fastest draw in the West, and his shots often hit their mark before his gun was seen to leave his holster. He was killed by sheriff Pat Garrett, who caught him off guard. I recall, without supporting documentation, Billy being called "a homicidal maniac from Brooklyn."

bimbo Common term for a promiscuous woman, or a studied, empty-headed woman, since about 1930. Possibly originating among athletes, *bimbo* probably derives from the Italian *bambino*, "baby." (*The Bambino*, of course, was also a nickname for Babe Ruth). The word is almost always used disparagingly, humorously or not.

black frost A name sometimes heard in the metropolitan area for a frost that kills plants, sometimes turning them black or blackish; a killing frost. In the New York area the average date of the first black frost is about November 1.

Black Hand An old offshoot of the Mafia in New York at the turn of the century whose activities were usually limited to extorting money, often by violent methods, from storekeepers and others in Italian neighborhoods.

black Irish 1) An Irish person with black hair and dark complexion. 2) An Irish Protestant, used infrequently and usually in a derogatory way.

black money   Dirty cash made from illegal enterprises such as taking bribes and drug dealing. *Black money* has to be laundered, that is, made into *white money,* before it can be used. This is done by providing it with a legitimate history and source.

Black Rock   A nickname for the black-colored CBS building at Fifty-third Street and Sixth Avenue in Manhattan. The name, also applied to the television network itself, is said to have been suggested by the film *A Bad Day at Black Rock* (1953). In the trade NBC is called *30 Rock,* from its address at Rockefeller Center, and ABC is called *Hard Rock.*

Black Tom   A children's game of tag once commonly played in Brooklyn. *Black Tom* was the name of the player, usually called it in tag games.

bladder   Slang for a newspaper; from the German *Blatt,* "newspaper." ". . . the best thing to do is to put an ad in the Lost and Found columns of the morning bladders. . . ." (Damon Runyon, "Little Miss Marker," 1931)

blast from the past   The phrase was made popular by New York City disc jockey Murray the K in the 1960s as his way of introducing a great old song. Now used do describe someone or something that appears from one's past out of the blue, as in "Wow! Seeing him was a blast from the past!"

blickey   A Dutch word for a small tin pail. It used to be common in New York but is seldom heard anymore.

blintz   Ultimately *blintz* comes from the Ukrainian *blints,* "pancake," which became the Yiddish *blintzeh* and was then shortened to *blintz.* A blintz in Jewish cookery is a thin pancake folded or rolled around a filling of cheese, potatoes, fruit, etc., fried or baked, and often served with sour cream. The word is also spelled *blintze.*

Blizzard of '88   The great blizzard of 1888, which began on Sunday, March 11 and lasted until Tuesday morning, causing more death and destruction than any other storm in the city's recorded history.

block party   A party held outdoors by residents of a block or street; the food, music and other entertainment are provided by the residents, and the street closed to traffic.

blood   Used by blacks as a name for a fellow black; the word isn't widely used outside the black community.

Bloody Mary   A cocktail made of tomato juice, vodka and seasonings. Said to be named after Mary I, or Mary Tudor, queen of England (1553–58), who was called "Bloody Mary" because of her persecution of Protestants. But the name or drink is not recorded until about 1955. According to an article in *U.S.A. Today* (December 10, 1985), "The Bloody Mary made its debut in an ad that appeared in late December 1955. In it, [New York entertainer] George Jessel declared that he invented the drink at 5 one morning." Bloody Mary is also the name of a character in James Michener's *South Pacific* (1949).

bloody mouth Used to describe a member of the Mafia who enjoys killing people and making them suffer. "In their world this was an idiom for a man who went beyond savageness, an intimation of bestiality while doing a necessary piece of work." (Mario Puzo, *The Last Don*, 1996)

Bloomies A popular nickname for Bloomingdale's department store, founded in 1872 only a few blocks away from its present location on Third Avenue between Fifty-ninth and Sixtieth streets.

Bloomsday Every year *Bloomsday*, which was created by New York James Joyce-o-phile Enrico Adelman, celebrates the June 16, 1904, day of Leopold Bloom's odyssey through Dublin in Joyce's *Ulysses*. A marathon public reading by actors is always held (Bloomsday 1998 took place at Symphony Space at Ninety-fifth Street and Broadway) and lasts from 8:00 A.M. until Molly Bloom says "Yes I said yes I will Yes," some 40 hours later.

blue Slang for a uniformed police officer. The term dates back to the 19th century. "The two blues searching the alley were complaining." (Ed McBain, *Romance*, 1995)

blue-chip stocks The most valuable counters in poker are the blue chips. Since the early 1900s, Wall Street, borrowing the expression from another world of gambling, has called secure, relatively high-yielding stocks *blue-chip stocks*. Among the earliest terms for worthless or speculative stocks is *cats and dogs*, first recorded in 1879.

blueclaw The usual name in New York City among fishermen and crab lovers for the large crab *Callinectes sapidus*, which is blue in color, red when cooked. "We went scalloping (with nets) in Jamaica Bay for blueclaws. Caught some in traps, too." Rarely called the *blueclawed crab*.

bluecoat A New York City policeman. The term dates back to 1853 when the first completely uniformed full-time police force in New York City was formed, with the officers wearing a blue coat with brass buttons, gray trousers and a blue cap. Before this, policemen refused to wear uniforms because they felt that they were freeborn Americans and such "livery" would make them look like servants.

bluepoint oyster Originally the name of a delicious oyster harvested in the waters of Blue Point, Long Island; then applied to any oyster found off eastern Long Island. The term was first recorded in 1789 but is seldom heard today.

blue sailor An old name for the chicory plant, a blue wildflower very common along roadsides in New York City and vicinity. According to *American Wildflowers* (1949), the name comes from the

> legend of a beautiful girl who fell in love with a sailor. Her lover left her for the sea and so she sat day after day along the side of the highway looking

for his return. Eventually the gods took pity on her and turned her into a chicory plant which wears sailor blue in its blossoms and still haunts roadsides in the hope of meeting her returning lover.

The roots of chicory are often ground and roasted as a coffee substitute or flavoring.

blurb Humorist Gelett Burgess invented *blurb* in 1907 with the publication of his *Are You a Bromide?* Burgess's New York publisher, B. W. Huebish, later told the story:

> It is the custom of publishers to present copies of a conspicuous current book to booksellers attending the annual dinner of their trade association, and as this little book was in its heyday when the meeting took place I gave it to 500 guests. These copies were differentiated from the regular edition by the addition of a comic bookplate drawn by the author and by a special jacket which he devised. It was the common practice to print the picture of a damsel—languishing, heroic, coquettish . . . on the jacket of every novel, so Burgess lifted from a Lydia Pinkham or tooth-powder advertisement the portrait of a sickly sweet young woman, painted in some gleaming teeth, and otherwise enhanced her pulchritude, and placed her in the center of the jacket. His accompanying text was some nonsense about "Miss Belinda *Blurb*," and thus the term supplied a real need and became a fixture in our language.

boat race A fixed horserace. ". . . it is nothing but a boat race and everything in it is as stiff as a plank, except this certain horse." (Runyon, "The Lemon Drop Kid")

bobble A term dating back to the 1920s for a failure, as in "The dance was really a bobble." Rarely used today.

bobby *See* BONAC.

bo-bo A recent term for marijuana in New York and elsewhere; its derivation is unclear. Another term popular recently is *blunt* for a cigar with marijuana in it.

boccie An Italian variety of lawn bowling played on short narrow dirt courts in New York City Italian neighborhoods, often by elderly people. The name comes from *bocce,* the Italian name of the game. It is pronounced BOTCH-ee.

boddle A pronunciation of *bottle*. "Gimme a boddle of it."

bodega Originally a small Hispanic grocery store, often selling a large variety of items and including a wineshop; now often used to refer to any small grocery store. There are thousands of bodegas in the New York City area. *Bodega* derives from the Spanish for "storehouse"

boff To have sexual relations with. "'What I heard [about her], I wouldn't mind boffin her,' Sal said." (Hunter, *Criminal Conversation*)

boff-on-gool; bah-fong-goo Among the several pronunciations heard in New York for an Italian curse meaning "fuck you." The widespread curse is often accompanied by the common arm motion meaning the same. According to the *Random House Dictionary of American Slang,* the curse derives from the Italian *affanculo,* "I fuck you up the ass." *See also* FUN-GOO.

boin   A pronunciation of *burn.*

boip   A pronunciation of *burp* in the New York area.

boloney   *See* BALONEY.

Bonac   Roughly 100 miles from Times Square a community of Long Island fishermen called the *Bonackers* speak a dialect that retains the sound of Shakespeare's England and has rarely, if ever, been recorded in any language book. The Bonackers reside in East Hampton, a town they helped settle in the mid-17th century when it was founded as a whaling port by settlers from Connecticut across Long Island Sound. The Bonackers were not among the affluent settlers; they were, in fact, often the servants of other settlers, and at first they built shacks along the *Accabonac Creek,* which led the richer citizens to disparagingly dub them "Bonackers." Some 1,000 Bonackers live in the Hamptons today, many of them speaking the old English dialect called *Bonac* that retains much of the vocabulary and the same vowel sounds the original settlers employed. Many of the families are closely related. There are, for example, Posey Lesters and Devon Lesters and Roundswamp Lesters and Pantigo Lesters. The Posey Lesters take their name from a 19th-century ancestor who always walked the streets with a flower in his lapel, while the Roundswamp Lesters are named for the place where this branch of the family originated.

Bonackers call anyone born outside the eastern end of Long Island a *foreigner,* and the entire world outside the area is known as *away.* "Even my wife's a foreigner, she came from away," one old fisherman says. The salty dialect spoken by the Bonackers is often related to fishing, still the main livelihood of the people. "What you got *finnin'* over there?" a fisherman might shout to someone else pulling in a catch 100 yards away. "This spring I *caught* pretty *good,*" says a fisherman, "but I couldn't get a price for the *stock.*" A harbor is *hobboh* in Bonac, its *r*'s melting away as they often do in this dialect. The word *farmer,* for example, becomes *fammah.* One also hears words like *awchit* for *orchard, op'm* for *open, eebn* for *even, yit* for *yet, nawthin'* for *nothing* and *winnuhry* for *wintry.* In Bonacker homes, *durst* often takes the place of *dare not. Cattywumper* means "crooked" or "disorderly." No matter what your name is, Bonackers reply, "Yes, yes, *bobby,*" or "Yes, yes, *bub,*" when you ask a question. Bonac's nearest similarity to the voabulary of another area is in a few nautical phrases also heard in Massachusetts, these including *cutter,* a command to turn sharply, and *finestkind,* which means "A-OK."

Bonackers, who speak with something resembling an Irish brogue, try not to converse in Bonac when strangers are around, and it is seldom heard in the summer season when the population of this community made famous in the movie *Jaws* increases threefold from its 55,000 winter population. Yet these people cling to their dialect, which one of them calls "The King's English, only we come under an earlier king." They are "a stubborn bunch," in the words of another Bonacker fisherman, and resist all attempts by teachers to "get the Bonac out of their speech." They still live modestly, as their ancestors did, often on the same land, maintaining their dialect as a badge of pride. If Bonac dies, it will only be because the Bonackers have been forced from their land by rising prices and real estate development in this summer playground of the rich, which is fast becoming a year-round suburb of Manhattan.

bonebreaker An enforcer; a strong-arm man. "He had spotted Julia . . . with two men, one of whom was a Prizzi bonebreaker, Mort Violente." (Richard Condon, *Prizzi's Money,* 1994)

bonehead play The original *bonehead play* was made on September 9, 1908, by Fred Merkle, the New York Giant's first baseman, at the old Polo Grounds (torn down in 1964, in part with the same wrecking ball used to demolish Brooklyn's Ebbets Field). It was the bottom of the ninth, two outs, and the Giants had Moose McCormick on third and Merkle on first. The next man up singled to center and McCormick scored the winning run, but Merkle ran into the dugout instead of touching second base. Johnny Evers of the Cubs got the ball and stepped on second, forcing out Merkle. The winning run was nullified, and the game was not counted in the standings. Merkle's play became all the more significant later in the season when the Cubs and Giants finished tied for first place and the Cubs won the pennant in a play-off game. Though *boneheaded* had been used a little earlier, it was a New York reporter's use of *bonehead play* in reference to Merkle's blunder that popularized the phrase, along with the related *boner* and to *pull a boner. See* EBBETS FIELD.

bon verge A pronunciation of *bon voyage* heard in New York.

boo Marijuana. "Boo, cocaine and shit were for squares." (Condon, *Prizzi's Honor*)

boodle The Dutch in New Amsterdam (pre–New York City) called a bundle of paper money or a sack of gold a *boedal,* which served as the term for any property, goods or effects. The word's spelling gradually became *boodle,* and it was used as underworld slang for counterfeit money and graft or bribery money, later becoming slang for a large bundle of money or money in general, with no implication of dishonesty.

booting Bootlegging. "I think Judge Henry Blake figures to do a little booting on his own hook in and out of Canada." (Damon Runyon, "Madame La Gimp," 1929)

borax Several authorities say that the source for the term *borax,* for cheap furniture, or any cheap and inferior merchandise is a Yiddish expression used by Jewish immigrants on New York's Lower East Side in the late 19th century. It could have its origins, however, in the premiums of cheap furniture offered by early makers of borax soap.

borough   A designation for county in New York City. There are five boroughs comprising the city. The Bronx is the only New York City borough that is not named for King Charles II of England or a member of his family. *See* BRONX; KINGS COUNTY; NEW YORK COUNTY; QUEENS COUNTY; RICHMOND.

Borough of Churches   *See*   CITY OF CHURCHES.

borscht   A beet soup served hot or cold, often with sour cream, that is a great favorite in Jewish and Russian restaurants. The word derives from an East Slavic word meaning the same. Also spelled *borsht*.

borscht belt   A resort area in the Catskill Mountains of upstate New York. Famous for its abundant food and entertainment—many notable comedians and singers got their start there—the *borscht belt* caters largely though not exclusively to a Jewish clientele from New York City. It takes its name from the popular beet soup called *borscht* that was introduced to America by Russian Jews and is consumed in large quantities at the *borscht belt* or *borscht circuit* resorts.

boss   *Boss* was all the rage in the early 1960s to describe anything re-ally cool: *That's real boss* was the usual form. Today, the word seems to have largely passed out of use.

Bottle Alley   *See* TENEMENTS.

bow-and-arrow squad   A position assigned to a member of the New York City Police Department who has been relieved of his weapon, in other words, not any one real unit. "They relieve him of all armaments and assign him to units known, in police jargon, as Bow and Arrow Squads." (Jimmy Breslin, *World Without End*, 1973)

bowery   *Bowery* derives from the Dutch word for "farm," *bowerij*, and this was originally its meaning in New York. But the word came to be applied to an area in downtown Manhattan that was originally the site of a farm and became the city's most famous skid row, *the Bowery* long noted in song and story for its saloons and cheap hotels. It is also the name of a street, stretching from Chatham Square to Cooper Square, that was once an Indian path.

Bowery Boy   Huntz Hall, Leo Gorcey and the other Bowery Boys of movie fame with their extreme New York accents take their name from a number of real New York gangs dating back as far as the 1700s. Other gangs of the day, to name only a few, include the *Dead Rabbits,* the *Roach Guards,* the *Shirt Tails* and the *Plug Uglies.* Hell-Cat Maggie, a female member of the violent Dead Rabbits, "filed her front teeth to points and wore artificial brass fingernails," according to Luc Sante's *Low Life* (1991).

box ball A ball game, similar to tennis or Ping-Pong but played without racquets or a net, that has been popular among New York City children since at least the 1920s. It is played within two boxes of seamed sidewalk concrete with a rubber ball—usually a pink "Spaldeen" or a tennis ball. One player, facing his or her opponent, tries to serve the ball with his open hand over the seam into the second 4-foot square box, and the other player tries to slap it back into the server's box. This goes on until someone misses. If the server wins the volley he gets a point; if the receiver wins the volley, he becomes the server and tries to win points. Twenty-one points wins the game. *See* SPALDEEN.

boychik A term used in Yiddish for a boy or young man. It combines the English *boy* with the Slavic suffix-*chik* and is effective largely because both *boy* and *chik* (similar to *chick*) suggest someone young.

boyo *See* BOYOBOYOBOYO!

boyoboyoboyo! An exclamation used in many ways that may just be a variation on the common *boy oh boy*. On the other hand, it could be related to the Irish English *boyo* for a boy or lad. There may be a Yiddish influence, too, for the expression is often heard among elderly Jews as an expression of exasperation.

Boys of Summer A nickname for the Brooklyn Dodgers of the 1950s era that first appeared in Roger Kahn's book *The Boys of Summer* (1972), the title of which in turn comes from the Dylan Thomas poem "I See the Boys of Summer."

brain trust The group of experts forming the first *brain trust* were the advisers to Franklin Delano Roosevelt while he prepared presidential campaign speeches at Hyde Park, New York, in 1932. The *brain trust* consisted of Columbia University professors Adolf A. Berle Jr., Raymond Moley and Rexford G. Tugwell. The expression was coined by *New York Times* reporter James M. Kieran when he learned that they were in residence. Kieran originally called the group the *brains trust* in his *Times'* dispatches, but other reporters and headline writers soon eliminated the cumbersome *s*. By the time Roosevelt became president, *brain trust* was commonly being used for his larger group of supposedly nonpolitical experts. The phrase had been previously employed in sarcastic reference to the first American general staff, in 1901, not at all in the same sense.

braykidup Break it up. "A policeman's suggestion to any group of loiterers." A pronunciation recorded in The Federal Writers' Project, *Almanac for New Yorkers* (1938).

breadline In *The Dictionary of Americanisms, breadline* is said to be first recorded in 1900, but no specific account of its origin is offered. However, in his fascinating book *Here at the New Yorker* (1975), Brendan Gill attributes the expression to the Fleischmann family from whose yeast fortune rose the *New Yorker* magazine. The family ran the Vienna Model Bakery in New York City during the late 1870s:

> In order to call attention to the freshness of Fleischmann's bread and also, it appears, because of an innate generosity, Lewis [Fleischmann] made a practice of giving away at eleven every evening whatever amount of bread had not been sold during the day. The poor lined up to receive it at the bakery door; hence our word "breadline."

The term had its widest use during the Great Depression 50 years later.

breakers   *See* WAVES.

breeze   Black English for man or buddy, dating back to the 1960s. "Hey, breeze, what's happening?"

Breezy Point   The extreme western end of the Rockaway Peninsula in Queens, a part of Long Island, bordered on the south by the Atlantic Ocean and on the north by Jamaica Bay. "Far off [from Coney Island] he could see the sparse lights on the darkened smudge of Breezy Point . . . on a stretch of the most beautiful unspoiled beach left in New York [City] . . . Breezy Point was populated by lots of cops and firefighters and was still 90 percent Irish." (Denis Hamill, *House on Fire,* 1996)

bridge-and-tunnel   A term often used by Manhattanites to describe, usually negatively, suburban commuters to the city. "The place attracts a bridge-and-tunnel crowd."

bris   The Jewish rite of circumcising a male child eight days after his birth. Usually done by a *mohel* (MOY-el) trained in this surgery. Also called a *brith, berith* and *brit.*

broad   A woman. *See quote under* PANCAKE.

Broadway   Broadway is the oldest and of course the best-known street in New York City, though rivaled in fame by Wall Street, Park Avenue and Fifth Avenue. Famous for its theaters, restaurants and bright lights, it is also a synonym for professional theater itself. *Broadway* has in recent times become a nickname used to describe dapper dressers among baseball players and players in other sports. The first that comes to mind is Broadway Joe Namath, former quarterback of the New York Jets football team. According to the *Dictionary of Americanisms,* the first recorded use of the name Broadway for the street was 1673; before this it had been called High Street. Originally an Indian trail, it now runs 17 miles through Manhattan and four miles through the Bronx. It has been called the longest street in the world but doesn't come close, the record being held by Toronto's 1,178-mile-long Yonge Street.

broderick   His tactics wouldn't be officially approved today, but Johnny "The Boffer" Broderick is still remembered as a tough New York City cop who relied on his fists as much as his police revolver. Known as the world's toughest cop, Detective Broderick worked "the Broadway beat," dealing out punishment with his fists on the spot so often that *to broderick* became a synonym for "to clobber." Broderick once flattened the hoodlum Jack "Legs" Diamond, and he knocked out and captured Francis "Two-Gun" Crowley before Crowley could find the courage to shoot. Another time he battered two men molesting a woman, threw them through a plate-glass window and then arrested them for malicious destruction of property. In fact, Bellevue Hospital used him as an exhibit to show how much punishment the human hand could take. Broderick, an image of sartorial splendor, was used as a bodyguard by many celebrities, including Franklin Roosevelt and Jack Dempsey. Dempsey confessed that the detective was the only man he wouldn't care to fight outside the ring. This graduate of New York's gashouse district was immortalized by Damon Runyon as Johnny Brannigan and played by Edward G. Robinson in *Bullets or Ballots*. By the time he retired in 1947, after 25 years on the force, Broderick had won 8 medals for heroism. Broadway gamblers once gave 9–5 odds that he would be killed on any given day, but he died naturally in his bed in 1966, 72 years old.

broker Runyonese for one who has no money, is broke. "Feet Samuels is generally broke, and there is no percentage hanging around brokers . . . Feet Samuels is one of the worst brokers in this town." (Damon Runyon, "A Very Honorable Guy," 1929)

broker than the Ten Commandments A phrase common in the 1930s. "'Listen, bud, I'm flat broke. I'm broker'n the Ten Commandments.'" (Roth, *From Bondage*)

Bronx The *Bronx,* one of New York City's five boroughs, and the only one connected to the U.S. mainland, takes its name from Jonas Bronck, a Dane who first settled the area for the Dutch West India Company in 1641. Points of interest in the celebrated borough are the Bronx Zoo, the New York Botanical Garden, the Edgar Allan Poe Cottage and Yankee Stadium ("The House That Ruth Built"). *See* BOROUGH; KINGS COUNTY; NEW YORK COUNTY; QUEENS COUNTY; RICHMOND.

Bronx Bombers A nickname for the New York Yankees, more commonly called the *Yanks,* for at least the last 50 years. The name honors all the powerful sluggers who have played for the team and blasted, or bombed, the ball.

Bronx Bunnies An old humorous nickname for the New York Yankees; a play on *Bronx Bombers. See* BRONX BOMBERS.

Bronx cheer Long associated with baseball, the razz, or raspberry, called the *Bronx cheer,* wasn't born at Yankee Stadium in the Bronx, the home of baseball's New York Yankees, as many baseball fans believe. It may derive from the Spanish word *branca,* "a rude shout," and possibly originated at the old National Theatre in the Bronx. We only know for certain that the term was first recorded in 1929 and that many players have received Bronx cheers in Yankee Stadium.

Bronx cocktail A mixture of gin, sweet and dry vermouths, and orange juice created in Manhattan by Waldorf Astoria bartender Johnny Solon around 1900. Explained the bartender:

> The name? No, it wasn't really named directly after the borough or the river so-called. I had been at the Bronx Zoo a day or two before, and I saw, of course, a lot of beasts I had never known. Customers used to tell me of the strange animals they saw after a lot of mixed drinks. So when Treverson said to me, as he started to take the drink to the customer, "What'll I tell him is the name of the drink?" I thought of those animals and said: "Oh, you can tell him it is a 'Bronx.'"

See ALEXANDER; MANHATTAN COCKTAIL.

Bronx Indian *See* BROOKLYN INDIAN.

Bronx Zoo A derogatory nickname for the New York Yankees heard from 1979 until at least 1996 when the team won the World Series. The renowned Bronx Zoo is of course located in the same borough as Yankee Stadium, and the players seem to have reminded the fans of the animals in said zoo. The words were recorded for the first time in *The Bronx Zoo* (1979) by Sparky Lyle and Peter Golenbock, and may have been invented by the book's editor, Larry Freundlich, when he named the book.

Brooklyn The borough of Brooklyn is officially known as Kings County, but no one calls it that. In 1645 the area was named Breuckelen after an ancient village in the Netherlands; over the years this changed to Brockland, Brocklin, Brookline and finally Brooklyn. *Brooklynese* is a synonym for New York speech, or what some consider the worst of New York speech, coined in about 1945. It is, in any case, an extreme form of New York talk that had its golden age 60 years or so ago and has been heard less since. Someone long ago defined *Brooklynese* as what you have a bad case of if you recite the sentence *There were thirty purple birds sitting on a curb, burping and chirping and eating dirty worms, brother,* as "Dere were toity poiple boids sittin onna coib, boipin and choipin an eatin doity woims, brudda."

Brooklyn Bridge Called the "Eighth Wonder of the World" upon its opening, this bridge joining Brooklyn and Manhattan spans 1,595.5 feet between its towers and was at one time the longest bridge in the world. It was also the first suspension bridge to use steel for greater stability. John Augustus Roebling (1806–69), the inventor of wire cable, designed the bridge but died in a ferry accident during the early stages of construction. His son Washington Roebling (1837–1926) took charge after his father's death. In 1872 Roebling became paralyzed, suffering from the bends, a common affliction among the men working the massive bottomless caissons used to sink the bridge towers onto the solid bedrock beneath the East River. From then until the end of construction, Roebling's wife acted as his intermediary while he looked on through a telescope from the window of his Columbia Heights apartment. Twelve people were trampled to death in the crowd that rushed to cross the bridge when it first opened on May 24, 1883. Almost from that year on, *buying the Brooklyn Bridge* has become a phrase symbolizing gullibility—though it's doubtful that any con man ever really sold it to anyone.

Brooklyn Indian A disparaging, offensive term for a Jew, as is *Bronx Indian,* both terms first recorded in the 1940s and probably originating in the military during World War II.

Brooklyn National Anthem *See* DA BROOKLYN NATIONAL ANTEM.

Brooklyn side When a bowler hits into the wrong pocket of pins (the one opposite his bowling hand, for example, the 1-3 pocket if he's right-handed) the hit is called a *Brooklyn side* or a *Brooklyn,* as in "You've been hitting the Brooklyn side all night."

Brotherhood A synonym for the Mafia.

> "There are three laws of the Brotherhood which must become a part of you. The first—you must obey your superiors, to death if necessary . . . You must never betray any secret of our common cause . . . lastly, you must never violate the wife or children of another member . . ." (Condon, *Prizzi's Honor*)

Also called by the Italian name *Fratellanza.*

brudder A pronunciation of *brother,* as in "My uddah brudder's bedder."

Bruglione See quote.

> The other Mafia Families served chiefly as executive Barons, or *Brugliones,* who when in trouble went to the Clericuzio [family] hat in hand. In Italian the words "Bruglione" and "baron" rhyme, however in the Italian dialect "Bruglione" means someone who fumbles the smallest tasks. It was Don Dominico's wit, sparked by the Barons' constant pleas for help that changed the word "baron" to *Bruglione.* (Puzo, *The Last Don*)

bub *See* BONAC.

bubbe-mayse Yiddish for a grandma's story or old wives' tale. Said to derive from the title of a 16th-century book entitled *Buvo Mayse* (Buvo Story).

bubby John Bartlett's *Dictionary of Americanisms* (1877) states that *bubby,* a familiar name for a little boy, is a corruption of *brother,* claiming it as an Americanism first recorded in about 1848. More likely, it is from the German *bube,* "little boy." *Compare* BUBEE.

bubee *Bubee,* a Yiddish term of endearment that can be addressed to a child or any loved one, apparently derives from the Yiddish *bubeleh,* meaning the same, which probably comes from the Russian *baba,* "little grandmother," and the Hebrew *buba,* "little doll." *Bubee* is widely used in New York as an affectionate term for anyone. *Compare* BUBBY.

bubkes Usually pronounced BUB-kees, this Yiddish word from the Russian for "beans" means nothing or very little, a small amount, something trivial. "You know what I got for the job? Bubkes!"

bucket shop Any unethical brokerage firm; a boiler room operation. "It made the Rockefellers' little kerosene speculation look like a bucket shop." (O. Henry, "The Gentle Grafter," 1908) At the beginning of the 20th century many *bucket shops* were located on lower Broadway. At the time there were also saloons called *bucket shops* selling buckets of beer.

bug To annoy, irritate as might a mosquito or any small insect. The term has been common in New York since the late 1950s, probably popularized by jazz musicians some 10 years before that, and is widespread throughout the United States today. Some etymologists trace the *bug* in "don't bug me" to the West African *bugu*, "annoy." This may be so, but if the term did come to America with slavery, there should be earlier references to it than we have, *bug* only being recorded in this sense since the late 1940s. This meaning of *bug* may also have derived in some roundabout way from one of the many other slang uses of *bug*, including an obsessed person, a trick, or even *bugging* a person's phone calls surreptitiously, a term that arose from the underworld. It could also derive from *bugger* for sodomy.

Bugs Bunny Bugs's creator and voice, the late Mel Blanc, always insisted that the pesky wabbit had his (Blanc's) New York accent, combining Brooklyn and Bronx elements. *See* POPEYE.

bulldog edition In the 1890s several New York City newspapers brought out early morning editions that came to be called *bulldog editions*, possibly because the newspapers "fought like bulldogs" among themselves in their circulation wars. The first mention yet found of the expression is a reference to a "bulldog edition" of the morning *World* delivered to Brooklyn.

Bull Durham! A euphemism for *bullshit!* using the name of the long popular trademarked brand of tobacco. "'Bull Durham!' cried Zeddy, 'What was I going to let on about anything for?'" (Claude McKay, *Home to Harlem,* 1928)

bunk into Bump into. This pronunciation probably dates back at least to the turn of the century and is still heard, especially among older speakers, though not as frequently as in the past. There is little doubt that it originated in Brooklyn. "I bunked inta him on the subway last week, and we had a long talk."

buns Old slang for the buttocks; common in the New York City area. "Up your buns!" (Norman Mailer, *Why We Are in Vietnam,* 1967)

bunt The *bunt* in baseball, used mostly by a batter as a sacrifice play to advance another runner into better scoring position, is probably a corruption of the word *butt,* which does sound like *bunt* when spoken nasally. Hitters "butt" at the ball with the bat when they bunt. *Bunt* dates back to at least 1872, when the first recorded use of this strategy was made by a player named Pearce on the Brooklyn Atlantics.

burial society An organization that pays or helps pay for the burial of its members. One of the oldest is the Hebrew Free Burial Society, which pays for the burial in a Jewish cemetery of indigent Jews who otherwise would be buried in Potter's Field.

burn one with a feather A colorful example of old New York diner and luncheonette talk, meaning a chocolate malted milk with an egg mixed in it. Another example is *burn the British,* which means a toasted English muffin. Of these orders related to the chef by the waiter or waitress, a few have stood the test of time. Nobody, for example, has improved on *one to go* for a take-out order or on *nervous pudding* for Jell-O.

bustin' my onions A euphemism for *bustin' my balls;* punishing, disciplining, pushing or annyoing someone. "The boss was really bustin' my onions today." Also *bustin' my chops.*

busy as a one-armed paperhanger This phrase is often attributed to New York cartoonist and prolific word coiner T(homas) A(loysius) Dorgan (1877–1929) but may have originated with O. Henry, who wrote in a 1908 story: "Busy as a one-armed man with a nettle rash pasting on wall-paper."

buttinsky A meddler; someone who always butts into other people's affairs. Some authorities believe the *sky* ending is a play on Russian and Polish names ending in "sky," and *buttinsky,* a punning word formed around the turn of the last century when there were plenty of "greenhorn" immigrants among these ethnic groups who had to ask a lot of questions in order to survive. At any rate, the term was soon used in New York to describe all buttinskies and still is. *Kibitzer* is a similar word.

button man A soldier or low-ranking Mafia member. The name, first recorded in the 1960s, may come from the fact that such low-ranking members are paid very little, the equivalent of buttons. "'There are three thousand fucking button men out there who are millionaires. Just soldiers, button men, the dirty-work people, not even workers.'" (Condon, *Prizzi's Honor*)

buying the Brooklyn Bridge *See* BROOKLYN BRIDGE.

B'way This spelling of *Broadway* may have been invented by gossip columnist Walter Winchell. *See* BROADWAY.

by With. "She lives by her parents."

cabbie   *See* HACKIE.

cablegram   First used in 1868, the word *cablegram* initially met with some resistance, scholars condemning it as a hybrid derived from Latin (*cable*) and Greek (*gram*). Use the all-Greek *calogram* instead of the New York City–born monster, they suggested, but few agreed and the coinage proved durable. Such improperly formed words are of course common in English, and there is a liberal supply of like hybrids, including such common words as *because, dentist, grateful, starvation, talkative* and *parliament*.

café society   Said to be coined one night in 1919 by newspaper society columnist Cholly Knickerbocker (Maury Paul) when he saw a number of prominent socialites dining out at the Ritz-Carlton in midtown Manhattan. Up to that time, supposedly, most of this breed dined at home. Paramount Pictures later paid Lucius Beebe, another city newspaper columnist, $50,000 for using the term *café society* as the title of a movie starring Madeleine Carroll—thinking he had invented the expression. But it is fairly certain that Champagne Cholly (as Paul was also known) deserves the honor. He is also said to have invented *glamour girl,* an old standby, but is mostly responsible for such thankfully extinct cutesy coinages as *sweetie sweets* (nice people) and *doughty dowagers* (rich people).

calzone   A favorite Italian food in New York, consisting of a crisp Italian pastry made from pizza dough and filled with mozzarella and ricotta cheese, among other ingredients. So named from the Italian *calzone* for "trousers" because of its resemblance in shape to one leg of a pair of pants.

can   An old term for jail or prison. "He was thrown in the can last night."

Canary That Couldn't Fly   The nickname gangsters gave to Kid Twist Reles, who informed on Murder, Inc. in the 1930s and was consequently pushed to his death from the window of a Coney Island hotel while he was being guarded by lawmen. *See* MURDER, INC.

candy   *See* SHOULDER CANDY.

candy store   *See*   MOM-AND-POP STORE.

cannoli   A popular crispy Italian pastry, rolled and filled with a mixture of ricotta cheese, cream, candied fruits and other ingredients, that has become one of New York's many popular "international foods" in relatively recent times. ". . . Corrado picked up a cannoli and wolfed it down like a sword-swallower." (Condon, *Prizzi's Money*) The pastry is named from the Italian *cannolo* for "tube," being tubular in shape. But a *cannoli* is never called by the singular form, at least not in New York, although one such pastry should technically be a *cannolo*.

cannon   A name for a pickpocket, deriving from the Yiddish *gonif*. *See* DIP; FINGER.

can't anyone here play this game?
The famous question New York Mets manager Casey Stengel asked his team midway through their first season in the National League. The Mets of 1962 have been nominated as the worst team in any one season, losing a record 120 games that year. Wrote columnist Jimmy Breslin: "This is a team for the cab driver who gets held up in traffic and the guy who loses out on a promotion . . . losers, just like nearly everybody else in life."

capeesh   Pronunciation of *capisce*, Italian for "understand." "'Then he wants her to tell those banks to wire the money to the number accounts on the list of banks I'm gonna hand to you. Capeesh?'" (Condon, *Prizzi's Money*)

capo di tutti capi   Italian for "boss of all the bosses." "He was the sole United States 'friend' who had enjoyed a personal relationship with the late Don Calo Vizzini, who was so close as to be actually within the family of the present Capo de tutti Capi of Sicily. . . ." (Condon, *Prizzi's Honor*)

caporegime   A Mafia leader serving under the don or godfather who heads a Mafia family. The *caporegime* has an organization of his own and is in charge of a large area but must report to the godfather. Also called *skipper* and *captain*.

captain   *See* SKIPPER.

Carvel   Frozen custard or soft ice cream of any kind is often called Carvel in the New York area, so popular has the Carvel brand name become. In fact, I rarely hear anyone say *frozen custard* anymore; it's "I feel like a Carvel," or "Let's get Carvel." Thomas Andreas Carvelas, a Yonkers resident, invented his machine for making frozen custard in 1934, selling it from a truck he drove through city streets, where he competed with ice cream trucks like *Good Humor* and *Bungalow Bar*. Carvelas later changed his name to Tom Carvel and sold franchises that made the Carvel name a household word by the 1960s. Before then soft ice cream was usually called frozen custard.

Castle Garden   *See* ELLIS ISLAND.

Catch *The Catch* is a historical expression referring to a specific catch known to all New York City sports fans: the over-the-shoulder catch made by New York Giants centerfielder Willie Mays in the first game of the 1954 World Series of a long drive by Cleveland Indians first baseman Vic Wertz.

Cathedral of Commerce *See* WOOLWORTH BUILDING.

Catlick A pronunciation of *Catholic*. "You think your mother would tell you to lie? She's a Catlick, too." (Pete Hamill, *Snow in August,* 1997)

cattle call A large casting call for actors and actresses at Broadway theaters. The theatrical term is first recorded in the 1950s and is applied to any mass audition today. It apparently first referred to an audition held at a television studio.

cattywumper *See* BONAC.

caught *See* BONAC.

caught with the store An expression gin rummy players use when an opponent goes out or knocks with a large number of points in his hand. "You caught me with the store."

Cedarhurst Alley *See* HOWARD BEACH WAIT.

cellar *Cellar,* for the lowest position in league rank for a baseball team, is first recorded in a *New York Times* headline of July 9, 1922: "Red Sox Are Up Again. Leave Cellar to Athletics by Taking Final of Series, 4 to 1."

Central Park Work began on the great Manhattan park in 1857 based on designs by Frederick Law Olmstead and Calvert Vaux. The park was partially inspired by public grounds in great European cities and was meant to improve New York's reputation and provide a recreational area for its citizens. The original grounds covered 700 acres running from Fifty-ninth Street to One Hundred Sixth Street between Fifth Avenue and Eighth Avenue. Olmstead and Vaux's design called for a combination of pastoral settings and recreational facilities and included features such as Belvedere Castle, the Sheep Meadow and carriage drives. The park opened in 1859, and in 1863 its northern edge moved to One Hundred Tenth Street, increasing the grounds to 843 acres. In the 1930s Progressive reformers and Parks Commissioner Robert Moses built numerous playgrounds at the park's edges, constructed ballfields, renovated the zoo and increased recreational activities. Since its opening, the park has been an important part of New York life, particularly in summertime. Among the park's best-known features are the Children's Zoo, the Delacorte Theater, the Friedman Memorial Carousel, the Great Lawn, the Metropolitan Museum of Art and Tavern on the Green restaurant.

cerveza Spanish for beer; a word used mainly by Hispanics.

chalk player A horseplayer who only bets on favorites. Also called a *chalk eater,* which shows that such players are objects of ridicule.

challa *See* HOLLY.

Chanukah *See* HANUKKAH.

change for; change of Both expressions are used in New York, but I've heard "You got change for a dollar?" more frequently.

Chapin stigmata In his *City Editor* (1934), Stanley Walker wrote of another city editor, Charles E. Chapin, who was widely respected for his professionalism but generally hated for his cold-hearted efficient methods. Chapin fired 108 men when city editor of the *New York Evening World.* When *World* reporter Irvin S. Cobb heard he was ill one day, he remarked "I trust it's nothing trivial." Walker writes that "Today, men who develop traits and methods similar to his are said to be marked with the 'Chapin stigmata.'" Chapin died in 1930, in Sing Sing prison, where he was sent after killing his wife.

Charges Gina / Was Obscena / On La Screena *See* NEW YORK DAILY NEWS.

Charlie *See* MR. CHARLIE.

Chasidim *See* HASIDIM.

cheesecake; beefcake The old story is that in 1912 *New York Journal* photographer James Kane was developing a picture of an actress that included "more of herself than either he or she expected." As he looked at it, he searched for the greatest superlative he knew of to express his delight and exclaimed, "That's real cheesecake!" The word soon became synonymous for photographs of delectable models; however, not until 1934 is *cheesecake* first recorded. In the 1970s, *beefcake* became the male equivalent.

cheese it, da cops! This street cry didn't originate in Brooklyn, though it has often been heard there in fact, fiction and film. It dates back to early 19th-century England, the *cheese* in it probably a corruption of *cease it,* that is cease any criminal activity, the cops are coming.

chestnut stabber An old derogatory name for an Italian because hot chestnut carts in the city were often operated by Italian immigrants.

chewing gum *See* ADAMS' NEW YORK GUM NO. 1—SNAPPING AND STRETCHING.

Chicken à la King *Chicken à la King,* diced pieces of chicken in a sherry sauce, is now available canned or frozen and even found in army mess halls, which is a long way from the éclat tables where it was served in the late 19th century. The dish was not invented for a king, as is popularly believed, yet it's hard to pinpoint just who *chicken à la king* does honor. Some say that New Yorker Foxhall Keene, self-proclaimed "world's greatest amateur athlete," suggested the concoction to a chef at Delmonico's restaurant. The peerless Foxhall always claimed this was so.

chicken feed 1) Very common for many years in New York as an expression for a small amount of money. 2) Another name for the kernels of yellow, gold and white candy usually called *candy corn*.

chicken lobster; chick A small lobster up to one and a quarter pounds. The terms also once meant a lobster under the legal size limit. Sometimes advertised as *chix*.

chicken out To lose one's nerve and back out of a situation. "He chickened out at the first sign of trouble."

chicklets Slang for teeth; after the trademark candy-coated gum called *chiclets*.

chief cook and bottle washer A humorous name for someone doing a lot of menial work.

Chinese apple Common in New York for the seed-filled fruit generally known as a pomegranate.

Chinese handball A variation on handball in which the ball must bounce on the ground before it hits the wall.

Chinks' Once very common for any Chinese restaurant or its food, as in "Let's eat Chinks' today" or "Let's go to the Chinks'." The derogatory expression is fading from use.

chintz A pronunciation of *gents*, as in "*chintz room.*" Also used to describe cheap baubles and knickknacks or gaudy, tacky decorations.

choose-up A baseball (or softball, basketball or football) game without regular teams in which players are chosen in turn from the available talent by two captains who are frequently the best players. The worst players are usually chosen last, and those not chosen at all often umpire. Also called a *choose-up game*.

chopped liver Said of something or someone trivial. First recorded in a famous line of comedian Jimmy Durante: "Now that ain't chopped liver!" (*See* SCHNOZZOLA.) Often heard today in the half humorous complaint "What am I, chopped liver?"

chop suey *Chop suey* isn't native to China; in fact, most accounts of its origin say that the dish was invented in America. The widely accepted theory, advanced by Herbert Asbury in his *Gangs of New York* (1928), makes the tasty mélange the brainchild of a San Francisco dishwasher, though the Chinese dishwasher is sometimes promoted to a "cook in a California gold mining camp." I've traced the term's invention, however, to 1896 when it was concocted in New York by Chinese ambassador Li Hung-Chang's chef, who tried to devise a dish appealing to both American and Chinese tastes. Since the ambassador had three chefs, it's hard to say which one invented *chop suey*. The name has nothing to do with the English word "chop," deriving instead from the Cantonese dialect *shap* *sui,* which means "bits and pieces of mixed bits." The chef who invented it took leftover pieces of pork and chicken and cooked them together with bean sprouts, green peppers, mushrooms and seasonings in a gravy, serving it with rice and soy sauce.

Chunky   *See* TOOTSIE ROLL.

Church of the Holy Rifles   Preacher and author Henry Ward Beecher (1813–87), brother of Harriet Beecher Stowe, was a complex man whose interests ranged from involvement in antislavery movements to involvement with female members of his congregation. Beecher's Bibles, for example, were Sharp repeater rifles that the reverend, one of America's most famous and controversial preachers, raised money for at his Brooklyn Heights church in New York and shipped to Bloody Kansas in crates labeled "Bibles." Beecher encouraged his parishioners to join the "underground railroad" and even held mock slave auctions at Plymouth Congregational Church to illustrate the evils of slavery. The church, still in use, was called the "Church of the Holy Rifles" and is now a national historic shrine. Beecher once wrote that "the Sharp rifle was a truly moral agency . . . [had] more moral power . . . than a hundred Bibles."

Christmas Christian   Used in the New York area and elsewhere for someone who only goes to church on Christmas Eve or Christmas Day or who rarely goes to church.

Chrysler Building   A skyscraper on Lexington Avenue that was briefly the tallest building in the world. The story is told in *The New York City Guide* (1939):

William Van Alen, architect of the Chrysler Building, and his former partner, H. Craig Severance, became rivals when each was commissioned to design the world's tallest building. When the Chrysler tower seemed likely to terminate at 925 feet, the builders of the Bank of the Manhattan Company structure (or Manhattan Company Building) at 40 Wall Street (designed by Severance and Yasuo Matsui) decided to halt their operations at 927 feet. Meanwhile, steel workers were secretly assembling the rustless steel sections of the Chrysler spire which, when lifted through the dome and bolted into place, brought the building to its triumphant height of 1,048 feet. Subsequently the Empire State Building stole the laurels.

See EMPIRE STATE BUILDING; WOOLWORTH BUILDING.

chutzpah   *Chutzpah* derives from a Hebrew word meaning "insolence, audacity." Signifying impudence, gall, brazen nerve, incredible cheek and unmitigated audacity in Yiddish and in New York slang, it more often today indicates an admirable quality in a person: guts bordering on the heroic. Leo Rosten gives the classic definition of *chutzpah* in *The Joys of Yiddish:* "That quality enshrined in a man who, having killed his mother and father, throws himself on the mercy of the court because he is an orphan." (No one knows if this ever happened, but a 19th-century anecdote does mention such a man.) A study by the Lexis-Nexis information-retrieval system found that *chutzpah* is becoming very respectable nationally. From 1980 until 1993 the Yiddish word was used in fully 112 court decisions by judges across the United States, a large number of them in New York.

ciao   Italian for "goodbye" or "so long" that has been widely adopted into New York talk. Pronounced CHOW.

cinema   *See* PICTURE SHOW.

citizen   In black slang a *citizen* is something of a square, but in Runyonese the word simply means any person. "Among these citizens is The Seldom Seen Kid, who is called the Seldom Seen because he is seldom seen after anything comes off that anybody may wish to see him about. . . ." (Damon Runyon, "Money from Home," 1931)

city   Manhattan, one of the five boroughs of New York City, is *the city* to anyone living in any of the other four boroughs, and that person would usually say "I'm going to the city" if he or she was going to Manhattan, although "I'm going to Manhattan" might also be used. Out in the suburbs of Long Island, Connecticut and New Jersey, however, one might say "I"m going to the city" and mean he or she is going to the boroughs of Brooklyn, Queens, Staten Island or the Bronx as well.

City College   *City College* is the usual name for C.C.N.Y., the City College of New York. It is also a humorous name for the Tombs prison, on Centre Street, which was once the site of the Collect Pond where inventor John Fitch experimented with his steamboat in 1796.

City Hall   The gracious structure was completed by French engineer Joseph Mangin in 1812. When Mangin designed the building it was decided that City Hall stood so far north that few people would ever see the rear of it—surely there would be no growth northward. Therefore, the rear facade of the building was finished with red sandstone rather than the expensive marble used for the rest of the structure.

City of Churches   A nickname for Brooklyn, after its many churches of many faiths. Also *Borough of Churches*.

City of Towers   A century-old nickname for New York inspired by the city's numerous skyscrapers.

clam digger   A humorous nickname for residents of various bayfront towns near or in New York City; often because in years past they had a large population of people who clammed for a living. Residents of Inwood, New York, on the Queens border (next to Far Rockaway), for example, were often called clam diggers up until the 1960s, though the designation isn't much heard today except among oldtimers. The same could be said of Canarsie in Brooklyn and Broad Channel in Queens.

clean up hitter   Another term that comes to us from the sports pages of a New York newspaper: the *New York Evening Journal,* April 15, 1907. It means the player hitting fourth in a team's lineup, who is supposed to clear the bases of any of the three men preceding him and by extension has come to mean the most reliable person in any group.

Cleopatra's Needles   *Cleopatra's* Needles is a misnomer. The two originally pink obelisks—one 68 feet tall standing on the Thames embankment, and the other 69 feet tall standing in New York's Central Park—really have nothing at all to do with the queen of the Nile. Hieroglyphics on the needles show that Pharaoh Thutmose III erected them centuries before Cleopatra lived. Originally raised at Heliopolis in 1475 B.C., the obelisks were moved to Alexandria, under Augustus in about 14 B.C., where they adorned the Caesareum. In 1878 and 1880, Ismail Pasha made gifts of them to England and the United States, respectively, and it is said that they have suffered more from erosion in their present locations over the last century than they did over thousands of years in Egypt. The formerly rose-red syenite granite obelisks were probably named for Cleopatra because they stood outside the Caesareum, honoring her dictator lover.

click   *See* PALOOKA.

cliff-dweller   An old term used in New York to describe New Yorkers who live in tall apartment houses. The original cliff-dwellers were prehistoric peoples who lived on the rock ledges and in the natural recesses of cliffs.

clip   1) To steal, swindle. The term apparently originated in New York City in the 1920s. Wrote Walter Winchell in *Vanity Fair* (1929): "When a patron in a nightclub is 'clipped,' he isn't punched, he's 'taken,' or 'gypped' out of some currency, or he is overcharged." 2) To kill, assassinate, shoot. "'Irene will clip the bodyguard.'" (Condon, *Prizzi's Honor*)

clocker   See quote. "At the moment, they were both clockers, who were low-level people who sold cocaine on street corners." (Ed McBain, *Mischief,* 1993) For much more on *clockers* see Richard Price's 1985 novel of that name. *Clocker* probably derives from the older slang *Clock,* to watch for a prospective victim of a crime or to watch for a customer.

close the door, were you born in a barn?   *Born in a barn* has widespread U.S. use in describing someone with bad manners ("He acts like he was born in a barn."), but the above variation has been used in the New York City area since at least the 1930s, though it isn't frequently heard today.

clueless   *See* DON'T HAVE A CLUE.

cockamamie   *Cockamamie* means something worthless or trifling, even absurd or strange; a *cockamamie* excuse or story is an implausible, ridiculous one. The word may be a corruption of *decalcomania* (a cheap picture or design on specially prepared paper that is transferred to china, wood, etc.), a word youngsters on New York's Lower East Side early in the century found tiring to pronounce and impossible to spell.

coconut One dollar. ". . . he is a smart guy at his own dodge, and everything else, and has plenty of coconuts. . . ." (Damon Runyon, "Gentlemen, the King!" 1929)

coffee milk This term seems to be recorded only in Louisiana as the words for coffee and hot milk mixed together, a translation of the French *café au lait*. But I distinctly remember it being used in the 1940s and 1950s in the New York metropolitan area, where it means a little coffee (usually from an adult's cup) poured into a child's glass of cold milk as a treat, to coax the child to drink the milk by making him feel like a grown-up. It is also used in New York City to describe a coffee-flavored milk sold in stores.

coffeepot A common term in the 1940s for an old noisy junkheap of a car. Often used affectionately.

coffin nail Commonly used in the New York City area for a cigarette from the 1930s on.

coib A pronunciation of *curb*. "A little boid sat on the coib and choiped and choiped and choiped."

coil A pronunciation heard in New York for *curl*. "Her hair had lotsa coil to it."

coinel A pronunciation of *colonel*.

cold-ass Mary Slang for a cold woman, unresponsive sexually, perhaps frigid. "'Why would anyone wanna talk to Julia? She's the original Cold-Ass Mary.'" (Condon, *Prizzi's Money*)

colder than a blonde's heart I can only find this used by Damon Runyon in his short story "Broadway Financier," 1931: "Silk asks the copper why these people are raising such a rumpus in the street, instead of being home keeping warm, for it is colder than a blonde's heart. . . ."

cold one A very common term for a bottle of beer, as in "How about a cold one?" In the New York City area the term isn't used as a euphemism, as it sometimes is elsewhere.

cold slaw A frequent pronunciation of *coleslaw*.

cold-water flat The term was originally applied to apartment houses with common toilets in the backyard or hall and only cold running water in the sinks; it then came to mean any apartment with poor plumbing. "A walk-up cold-water Brooklyn tenement." (William Faulkner, *A Fable*, 1954)

College of the City of New York Popularly called C.C.N.Y. or *City College,* the public institution was founded in 1848. It moved to its present Washington Heights campus in 1920. *See* CITY COLLEGE.

Columbia University A lottery accounted for the financial support of King's College when its charter was granted on October 31, 1754. Thirty years later the name of the college was changed to Columbia College, which became Columbia University in 1891. The school moved to its present location in Morningside Heights in 1897. Of its many famous graduates, among the first are John Jay and Alexander Hamilton.

come aboard In 1945 Joanna Colcord wrote in *Sea Language Comes Ashore* that *come aboard* commonly meant "come in" to a person knocking at the door of a house located on eastern Long Island. If the term still exists, no one I've questioned in the area has heard it.

come off it! This is traditional New York talk for cut it out, stop it, don't be preposterous, etc. The phrase dates back at least to the late 19th century in the form of *come off!* In 1892 the *New York Mercury* recorded the following conversation: "How much does yez ax fer this book?' 'Six dollars,' replied the smiling clerk. 'Oh, come off!'"

communion A killing by a Mafia hammer or enforcer in which the body is made to disappear by burying it in the concrete of a building foundation, dumping it weighted down far at sea, etc. "'Remember, it will have to be a Communion. Their bodies must not be found.'" (Puzo, *The Last Don*) The term perhaps derives in some way from the bread and wine that is taken at Holy Communion by communicants.

con artist A professional confidence man; any deceitful person. "He was a natural born con artist." (Damon Runyon, *More Guys and Dolls,* 1937)

Coney Island 1) The *Coney* in *Coney Island* should really be pronounced to rhyme with *honey* or *money.* The word derives from *cony* (or *coney* or *cuny*), meaning the adult long-eared rabbit (*Lepus cunicula*) after which the Brooklyn, New York, community was named. However, *cony,* pronounced CUH-nee, became a term for the female genitals in British slang, and proper Victorians stopped using the word, substituting it with *rabbit,* which previously had meant only the young of the cony species. The only trouble remaining was that *cony* appeared throughout the King James Bible, which had to be read aloud during church services. The Victorians solved this problem by changing the pronunciation of cony: It became COH-nee (written *coney*), which it remains to this day in *Coney Island* as well as the Bible. 2) Now widely known as a synonym for a hot dog, *Coney Island* first meant an order of fried clams in the 1870s. Today it means different things in different areas of the country. In Texas a *Coney Island* can be a "weenie and chili," while in Oklahoma, Missouri and Ohio it can be a hamburger.

Cosa Nostra ■ 39

Coney Island butter A humorous term for mustard, the spread of choice on the millions of hot dogs (*Coney Islands*) sold at the Brooklyn sea resort each year.

Coney Island head The disparaging term describes a glass of beer that is all foam. It is heard in Los Angeles but not in New York.

Coney Island whitefish *See* MAN-HATTAN EEL.

confession magazine Both *confession magazines* and soap operas got their start in New York. Confessions, which have been with us now for about 75 years, are an American invention and an outgrowth of the long soul-searching letters sent to physical culture crusader Bernard MacFadden's *Physical Culture* magazine in 1919. MacFadden's first confession book was the New York–based *True Story*, the great-grandmother of the genre. The first stories dealt with sweet young things who were so wicked that they dared to elope against their parents' wishes, etc., while contemporary tales have virtually no taboo themes, ranging from well-written confessions about incest to stories such as "My Bride Is a Man" (where Julie was Jules before her sex-change operation). The yarns, which earn 5–10 cents a word, aren't all written by readers. Professional writers turn out a large number, perhaps the majority of them, though some magazines do require an author to sign a release saying his or her story is based on a true experience. The best

biography of MacFadden is Robert Ernst's *Weakness Is a Crime* (1991).

consigliori The chief adviser to the head of a Mafia family; hence in popular speech any person in an important advisory position. "The Consigliori was also what his name implied. He was counselor to the Don, his right-hand man, his auxillary brain. He was also his closest companion and his closest friend." (Mario Puzo, *The Godfather*, 1969)

contract hitter A professional killer who gets a contract, often from the mob, to kill someone. "'A person ain't a contract hitter, he don't throw away no weapon.'" (McBain, *Romance*)

Coogan's Bluff An old name for the Polo Grounds, the long gone Harlem home of baseball's New York Giants. It was so named for the hill behind the stadium.

cookie *See* PANCAKE.

corker Someone exceptional or extraordinary. The origin of the word is unknown, but it is often associated with New York speakers of Irish origin. It may have originally referred to someone or some group of people from Ireland's County Cork, although there is no proof of this. *See* AIN'T HE (SHE) A CAUTION.

Cosa Nostra Italian for "our thing" and another name for the Mafia. "'. . . Sonna cosa nostra,' Don Corleone said, 'these are our own affairs. We will manage our world for ourselves be-

cause it is our world, *cosa nostra!*"
(Puzo, *The Godfather*)

coulda A pronunciation of *could have. See quote under* WOULDA.

counteh A pronunciation of *counter.*

counterfeit lox *See* LOX.

couple Couple of. "Give me a couple them candies."

cowboy This word was first applied to members of Tory bands in New York State who rustled cows, but by the mid-19th century it came to mean a man who herds and tends cattle on a ranch in the West. Because of shoot-em-up Hollywood Westerns, *cowboy* had also taken on the meaning, in New York City and elsewhere, of any reckless person, such as a speeding automobile driver.

crackers A derogatory term for white people in general, sometimes used by blacks. "And the peoples, well some of them was peoples and some of them was vampire peoples. But the real peoples . . . You know crackers eating roast turkey and champagne and shit." (Sapphire, *Push*, 1996)

creamers Small potatoes, even smaller than new potatoes, that are often used whole in a cream sauce dish made with onions. The term, not recorded in *The Dictionary of American Regional English*, is used in Long Island's Suffolk County on the North Fork.

croaker Underworld slang for a doctor. ". . . I have Lily moved into a private room, and got her all the nurses the law allows, and the best croakers . . ." (Damon Runyon, "The Lily of St. Pierre," 1929)

Crossroads of the World A nickname for *Times Square*, for at least 60 years; the name had earlier referred to London's Picadilly Circus.

Croton cocktail A humorous old term rarely heard anymore for a glass of water. After the Croton reservoir system upstate, a major source of New York City's drinking water.

cruiser *See* HEAVY CRUISER.

cuccidata See quote. "[She brought] . . . homemade *cuccidata*, Charley's favorite, which were rolls of sweet pastry filled with cream made with raisins, dried figs, nuts, candied pumpkin, and pieces of chocolate." (Condon, *Prizzi's Money*) Those pastries, also called *cuccis*, are generally considered a Christmas holiday treat.

cumtabull A New York pronunciation of *comfortable.*

cupcake *See* MUFFIN.

cuppa A pronunciation of *cup of.*

curveball The word *curveball* has been traced to William Arthur "Candy" Cummings (1848–1924), a Brooklyn Hall of Famer, who is credited with inventing baseball's curveball over 120 years ago. Cummings's curve was inspired by the half clam shells that he skimmed across a Brooklyn beach as a youngster, but he perfected it by experimenting with a baseball that he bought for a nickel.

cutter *See* BONAC.

da A pronunciation of *the*.

DA Since the 1950s, *DA* has been short for a *duck's ass* haircut, the back of which is cut like a duck's tail.

Da Bronx Bar A new candy bar named after the Bronx. It is called "the chocolate bar with an attitude." *See* BRONX.

Da Brooklyn National Antem Written years ago by Orter Anonamus when Brooklynites all spoke Brooklynese:

> Da Spring is sprung
> Da grass is riz
> I wunnah weah da boidies is?
> Da boid is on da wing?—dat's
>   absoid!
> From what I hoid da wing is on
>   da boid.

dance To fight. "You wanna dance wid me?"

Danish The common term for a Danish pastry in the New York area. "A Danish and coffee, please."

Dapper Dan A nickname for a very well-groomed man; sometimes used ironically. In fact, the local poolroom where I passed too much of my misspent youth was called Dapper Dan's, after the always unironed old Dapper Dan who ran it.

Dapper Don *See* TEFLON DON.

dead men A crab's gills, the inedible part of a crab that is disposed when cleaning it. The crabs are always blueclaws, often from Jamaica Bay.

dead rabbit A historical term for a gang member; after the Dead Rabbits, a violent gang of New York toughs in the mid-19th century whose standard was a dead rabbit representing its enemies. One old story claims that the symbol and name derive from a dead rabbit one of the gang members threw at an opponent during a gang war.

dead soldier A widely used term for an empty beer can or bottle.

dead wagon Once fairly common for a hearse in the New York area, but not used much anymore.

Death Valley *This* Death Valley was in the Bronx, in Yankee Stadium: deep center field went by this name before the stadium was renovated recently and the fences were moved in. In Death Valley a ball hit 400 feet or more could be nothing but a long out.

dem; dose; dat Some experts claim that *dem, dose* and *dat* for *them, those* and *that* long ago ceased to be used by New Yorkers. But the pronunciations still persist, often used by older residents and sometimes, if not frequently, heard in the speech of younger people. The pronunciations were still common, especially in Brooklyn, in the 1940s and '50s.

dem Bums According to one story, a legendary Brooklyn Dodger fan named Sid Mercer dubbed Brooklyn *the Bums,* an affectionate nickname for the team from the 1930s until they left New York for Los Angeles. Mercer, who attended every game—always sitting behind home plate—and was known as "the Spirit of Brooklyn," got so disgusted with the team's play one day that he cried out in his stentorian voice, "Youse bums, youse!" A baseball writer reported his words and it wasn't long before *Bums* and *dem Bums* became part of the language. As for Mercer, he never set foot in Ebbets Field again. *Bum* for an unskilled boxer made its debut in New York long before this.

den A pronunciation of *then.*

de nada A Spanish phrase meaning "it's nothing," "don't mention it" that is frequently heard today. "'Thank you, sir, I appreciate your time,' Kling said. 'Da nada,' Presson said." (McBain, *Mischief*)

department store The term *department store* isn't recorded until 1887 when a New York establishment advertised itself as H. H. Heyn's Department Store; however, the idea of separate departments in stores can be found in print at least 40 years earlier.

dere A pronunciation of *there,* as in "over dere."

dey A pronunciation of *they.*

Diamond Jim Brady *See* DINNER ON HORSEBACK.

diddy-wah-diddy The name for an imaginary fabulous place. Used mostly by blacks; origin unknown.

did you ever! A common interjection, as in "Did you ever! Look who's here!"

dig To understand, as in "You dig." Popularized by jazz musicians and possibly of black origin, perhaps from the African Wolof language *dega,* "to understand."

dijuh A verbal shortcut for *did you* in New York speech: "Dijuh read Hawking's new book?"

dime A $10 bill, $10. "I had six dimes on that bum, but he took a dive."

din Didn't. "Din I awways smile at you?" (Kober, "You Mean Common") *See also* DITINT.

Dinner on Horseback A famous dinner given by millionaire C. K. Billings at Louis Sherry's restaurant in 1903. The guests, all men, lounged in the saddle astride horses that had been brought to the ballroom by elevator and ate pheasant from feed bags and drank champagne from large rubber casks. It was said that Billings spent $50,000 for the feast, including the planting of sod on the ballroom floor. A couple of years later, in 1905, millionaire Diamond Jim Brady topped Billings with a dinner he gave for his racehorse Gold Heels; it cost over $100,000, including the $60,000 he spent for diamond jewelry for each guest.

dint The letter *d* is often omitted within contractions in New York speech, turning *didn't,* for example, into *dint.*

dip A pickpocket. In a recent pickpocketing operation the *dip* works with an accomplice called a *steerer* who selects the *score,* or victim. The steerer then signals a *stall,* or *stick,* who blocks the score by slowing down or falling in front of him. A *shield,* or *shade,* walks on one side of the score, shielding him from witnesses while the dip, the actual pickpocket, moves in from behind and picks the score's pocket. Another accomplice called the *dish* takes the wallet or money from the dip and passes it to another gang member in a nearby car. Sometimes there is even a sixth accomplice called a *tailpipe* who watches well back of all the other players for police surveillance. This is the latest very common pickpocketing scheme in New York City, where a pickpocket is also called a *mechanic,* an *ocho* (a master pickpocket), a *cannon* (a white pickpocket), a *shot* (a black or Hispanic pickpocket), a *hook,* a *finger,* a *wire,* a *rouster* and a *spitter* (who "accidentally" hawks phlegm on his victims to distract them.). *See also* DONNEGAN WORKER.

dirt nap Criminal slang for death. "Cross me and you'll go down for the dirt nap."

Dirty Side A name in CB radio language for the New York City area. Also *Dirtytown,* both terms originating in the 1970s.

Dirty Spoon *See* TENEMENTS.

dis To disrespect, disrupt, disparage. Originally Black slang, dating back to the 1980s; now widely heard. "'I shouldn't have dissed him that way." (McBain, *Romance*) 2) A pronunciation of *this* that dates back at least a century and a half. "'Drink dis,' said the man, holding the glass to Raggle's lips." (O. Henry, "The Making of a New Yorker," 1904)

dish *See* DIP.

ditint A common New York pronunciation of *didn't. See also* DIN.

ditzy Scatterbrained, silly, irresponsible, dizzy, as in "That was a really ditzy thing to do." Used in the New York area since at least the 1960s, perhaps deriving from *dizzy*. A *ditzy* person is called a *ditz*.

Dixie Daniel D. Emmett, according to a biographer, composed his famous song "Away Down South in Dixie" (1859), the favorite marching song of the Confederacy, on his violin "while looking out on the cold dreary streets of New York City and wishing he were home in Dixie." Ironically, his song was sung by troops aboard the *Star of the West* on their futile mission to relieve Fort Sumter early in 1861; thus, it could be said that *Northern* not Southern troops first sang the song in the Civil War.

Dixieland One good though unlikely story claims that the first *Dixieland,* or *Dixie,* was in New York City. According to the *Charleston Courier* of June 11, 1885:

> When slavery existed in New York, one Dixie owned a large tract of land on Manhattan Island, and a large number of slaves. The increase of the slaves and of the abolition sentiment caused an emigration of the slaves to more thorough and secure slave sections, and the Negroes who were thus sent off (many being born there) naturally looked back to their old houses, where they had lived in clover, with feelings of regret, as they could not imagine any place like Dixie's. Hence it became synonymous with an ideal location combining ease, comfort, and material happiness of every description.

Although no slave "lived in clover," the explanation seems as good as several other theories about *Dixie,* whose origin remains unknown.

do a Brodie Intrepid amateur athlete Steve Brodie once angered fighter Jim Corbett's father by publically predicting that John L. Sullivan would knock out his son. "So you're the fellow who jumped over the Brooklyn Bridge," the elder Corbett said when the two met for the first time shortly thereafter. "No, I jumped *off* of it," Brodie corrected him. "Oh," replied Corbett, "I thought you jumped *over* it. Any damn fool could jump off it."

But Brodie's name became proverbial as the result of his famous leap in the form of to *do* (or *pull*) *a Brodie,* to take a great chance, even to take a suicidal leap. Brodie made his famous jump from the Manhattan side of the Brooklyn Bridge on July 23, 1886, to win a $200 barroom bet. Eluding guards on the bridge, the 23-year-old daredevil climbed to the lowest chord and plummeted 135 feet into the water below, where friends were waiting in a rowboat to retrieve him. He was arrested for endangering his life and reprimanded by a judge, but that didn't stop him from leaping off a 212-foot railroad bridge in Poughkeepsie, New York, two years later to win a $500 bet.

Brodie, who later became a successful saloonkeeper, always laughed at charges that he had really pushed a dummy off the Brooklyn Bridge. His leap was not an impossible one; in the mid-1960s a man leaped off New York City's George Washington Bridge from 250 feet up, hit the water at over

70 miles an hour and then swam 200 yards to shore.

do a dance   To be hanged. Said to be New York City police slang dating back over 60 years ago. Since convicted killers weren't hanged in New York State at the time, it's hard to imagine it originating here, unless hardboiled detectives coined it in reference to killers extradited to a state where they would be hanged for their crimes.

do an Arthur Duffy   Arthur F. Duffy held the world record for the 100-yard dash in the early 1900s. At the time, New Yorkers used to *do an Arthur Duffy* as a synonym for to escape, run away. "He did an Arthur Duffy out of the city." Also *take an Arthur Duffy*.

Doctor's Mob   "In a spirit of medical humor," one chronicler of the period wrote, a medical student, John D. Hicks, picked up the arm of a corpse he had just dissected and waved it at several young boys peering in through the window. "This is your mother's arm!" he shouted. "I just dug it up. Get out of here or I'll smack you with it." The children scattered into the dark, but one frightened boy took Hicks at his word. By a strange coincidence his mother *had* died recently. The boy repeated Hicks's threat to his father, who gathered some friends and hurried to the local cemetery. There by another strange coincidence he found his wife's grave empty. Whoever had robbed it hadn't even bothered to refill the hole, the coffin exposed and broken apart. The enraged man vowed to make someone pay for this desecration, leading his friends through the streets of lower Manhattan. Others joined them, and a mob of hundreds soon stormed toward the New York Hospital and its unsuspecting staff. The mob had heard too many stories about young interns stealing bodies from private cemeteries, and now they had "proof." The "Doctor's Mob" of April 13–15, 1788, one of America's first riots, had begun. Before it was put down at least eight people were killed and scores more were injured. *See also* ASTOR PLACE RIOT.

Dodgers   Those incomparable Brooklyn Dodgers (who became comparable after their desertion to Los Angeles in 1958) were called the *Dodgers* because Manhattanites contemptuously referred to all Brooklynites as "trolly dodgers" toward the end of the 19th century. The bustling borough was famous for its numerous trolleys, especially in the Borough Hall area. Attempts were made to change the team's name to the Superbas, the Kings and the Robins, all to no avail.

does Macy's tell Gimbels?   Although Gimbels department store has long gone out of business, this expression is still heard. The by-now proverbial words arose from a friendly, well-publicized and well-advertised retailing war between the two giant New York department stores. The expression possibly originated as a publicity gag, perhaps as a line in an Eddie Cantor comedy skit when a stooge asked Cantor to reveal some dark secret and the comedian replied, "Does Macy tell Gimbels?" Actually, Macy's often told

Gimbels and vice versa. One time Gimbels ran an ad calling attention to Macy's fabulous annual flower show, heading it: "Does Gimbels tell Macy's? No, Gimbels tells the world!" On another occasion, in 1955, both stores posted signs on their buildings directing shoppers to the other's store. The Gimbels-Macy's rivalry was further publicized in the film *Miracle on 34th Street* in which Macy's directs customers to Gimbels when it doesn't have a particular item in stock and flustered Gimbels executives, realizing their store has been made to look like "a profiteering money-grubber," have to adopt the same P.R. policy. *See also* NOBODY BUT NOBODY UNDERSELLS GIMBELS.

doesn't know his ass from his elbow A common term describing a person completely ignorant of something.

dog 1) A hot dog. 2) A worthless horse too slow to win. 3) A homely woman or man. 4) Among stock market players, a stock that doesn't perform well.

dog park The strip of grass between the sidewalk and the road where dogs are often walked by their owners.

doity A pronunciation of *dirty*.

dollar Used in mob talk, a *dollar* means a thousand dollars, when secrecy is required.

It looked like a sixty-dollar score. People in the environment liked to think of a thousand dollars as one dollar to confuse the tourists at Vegas, but the measurement became universal because so much money was lying around in heaps, pleading to be taken. Sixty dollars was sixty thousand dollars. (Condon, *Prizzi's Honor*)

D.O.M. Since the 1960s short for a dirty old man; any lecherous male, usually but not always elderly.

domblokadoor Don't block the door. A pronunciation recorded in the Federal Writers' Project *Almanac for New Yorkers* (1938).

do me a favor, drop dead *See* DROP DEAD.

domebeeztoopid Don't be stupid. A pronunciation recorded in the Federal Writers' Project *Almanac for New Yorkers* (1938).

do me a solid Do me a favor. Used by the character Kramer on the New York-inspired television comedy *Seinfeld*.

donker-goyndon An elevator operator's "Down car [is] going down!" A pronunciation recorded in the Federal Writers' Project *Almanac for New Yorkers* (1938).

donnegan worker A pickpocket who works the *donnegans*, or toilets, in public restrooms. He often drops change on the floor in a washroom and steals a victim's wallet from his coat where it hangs in the toilet compartment while the victim helps pick up the coins. *See* FINGER.

don't do me any big (small) favors A sarcastic remark made to someone who is viewed as doing you no favor at all.

don't even think it A stern warning to someone who might be about to do something. "He gave them a look that said *Don't even think it,* and they went on by." (McBain, *Romance*) Also *don't even think about it.*

don't get your bowels in an uproar Don't get excited, calm down, cool it. The expression may be a euphemism for *don't get your balls in an uproar.* In any case it has been around at least 70 years.

don't gimme that Short or euphemistic for "Don't give me that shit (crap, garbage, nonsense, etc.)."

don't have a clue Don't have any idea, don't know the first thing about how something is done, etc. "I like how Rita is, she shows the world, how to act and stuff. Sometimes I don't have a clue." (Sapphire, *Push*) Also *clueless,* as in "I'm clueless."

don't jerk my chain Don't harass or bother me, don't victimize me. Suggested by someone harassing a chained animal or man. Also *don't yank my chain.*

don't never get no breaks A common triple negative that, to be fair, is heard in other speech areas as well.

"The Mets don't never get no breaks."

dooawg A pronunciation of *dog.*

doofus Originally New York slang dating back to the late 1950s or early 1960s meaning a fool, jerk, dope or any combination of the three. Some writers claim the word is an alteration of *goofus* for the same, while others say it is of Yiddish or German origin. It can also mean the penis.

doper A dope addict. "'I think I'll watch the clockers and the dealers and the dopers doing their dance of death on the block in hell where I live, and I'll hope to stay alive.'" (Hunter, *Criminal Conversation*)

doppess A useless bystander who is of little or no help when help is needed. Said to have been coined in the New York garment center from the Yiddish *tipesh,* a "fool."

do-re-mi Money, dough. "It must have cost him plenty of the do-re-mi." (Damon Runyon, *Guys and Dolls,* 1929)

Dorothy Perkins rose Ranking with Peace and Crimson Glory as the best known of American roses, the *Dorothy Perkins* is a pink rambler introduced by the famous Jackson & Perkins Nursery of Newark, New York, in 1901. It is a small, cluster-flowering type, and although ramblers have bowed in popularity to larger-flowered varieties, this variety remains a sentimental favorite much mentioned in literature. The rose was named for the granddaughter of co-owner Charles Perkins.

do the number on To kill, assassinate. "'So first you put the fear on her. Then you find out where the money is. Then you do the number on her.'" (Condon, *Prizzi's Money*) *See* PUT THE FEAR ON.

double In Jamaica Bay and other New York waters, a *double* (not a *doubler*) is the name given to a pair of mating crabs (that is, a hardshell crab and a more vulnerable softshell crab) caught (scalloped) with a crab net. *Scalloping* for crabs is also called *walking*. The more colorful Chesapeake Bay terms "channeler and his wife," "cradle carrier" (for the male), and "buck and rider" are not often heard, if heard at all.

double-dipping The impolite act of placing a chip in a dip, taking a bite, and then dipping again for more with the same chip. Heard on the New York-inspired television comedy *Seinfeld,* but dates back to the 1970s.

double Dutch A jump rope game, with many variations, in which two jump ropes are used.

double-talk Fifty years ago there were many more practitioners of New York double-talk than there are today. For an example, here is an excerpt from the Federal Writer's Project *New York Panorama* (1938):

> Observe in this sample of Mr. Hymie Caplin's double talk the creation of gibberish having a distinctly "sensible sound," and the ingenuity with which it is woven into the entire melody line: "Well, take now you're in a restaurant. So you say to the waiter, 'Gimme the chicken and vegetables but portostat with the chicken with the fustatis on it.' So he says 'What?' and you say 'You know, the portostat, and moonsign the savina on the top, with the vegetables.'"

The same source explains that this "humorously conceived system of language corruption" is meant to seduce or *rib* the unknowing listener into believing that he is "either deaf, ignorant, or ready for a lifetime run in the part of Napoleon." Also called *talking on the double*.

douse the glim Joanna Colcord's *Sea Language Comes Ashore* (1945) defines to *douse the glim* as to put out the lights in a house and says the expression is used on eastern Long Island. If it is so used there today, I have been unable to confirm it.

D.P. The initials *D.P.* have been used in New York at least since the 1980s for a bottle of *Dom Perignon* champagne.

D.Ph. Humorous slang, based on transposing *Ph.D.,* for a damned fool. The Yiddish *phudnik* is a similar construction.

Dracula Old, perhaps obsolete, but colorful slang from the world of jazz musicians that describes a key-pounding piano player who brings his hands all the way up to his face.

dreads Short for the *dreadlocks* style of hair worn by some blacks, or for a person wearing the ropelike strands.

Dream Street   See quote.

> Now this Dream Street Rose is an old doll of maybe fifty-odd, and is a very well-known character around and about, as she is wandering through the Forties for many a year, and especially through West Forty-seventh Street between Sixth and Seventh Avenues, and this block is called Dream Street. And the reason it is called Dream Street is because in this block are many characters of one kind and another who always seem to be dreaming of different matters . . . Many actors . . . handbookies, horseplayers . . . fight managers . . . burlesque dolls, hoofers and guys who write songs, and saxophone players, and newsboys, and newspaper scribes, and taxi drivers, and blind guys and midgets . . . and I do not know what all else. (Damon Runyon, "Dream Street Rose," 1931)

dreck   *Dreck* is most heard recently in its meaning of cheap, worthless trash, anything of poor quality. It originally meant excrement, from the German *Dreck* meaning the same, and came into the language through Yiddish.

drip   Slang for a dull, boring, foolish person, obnoxious but not quite as foolish as a jerk. The word is first recorded in the early 1930s.

drop a dime   To make a phone call to the police informing on someone. A *dime-dropper* is a *rat*, a *snitch*, a *stool pigeon*. The term dates back to the 1960s, when a phone call cost a dime.

drop dead   1) This expression of rejection and contempt can be shouted forcefully in the heat of an argument or said almost casually when one is slightly annoyed; in any case, it has been commonly used since it was first recorded in 1925. Its classic local use came in a *New York Daily News* headline (October 30, 1975) when New York City was verging on bankruptcy and President Gerald Ford refused its request for aid: FORD TO CITY—DROP DEAD. "Bill Brink wrote it with Mike O'Neill," recalls author Jimmy Breslin, who was present at the creation. "It came out of the Garson Kanin line in *Born Yesterday*, 'Do me a favor, Harry. Drop dead.' They did it in fun first until they looked at it. Like, 'Here's one—"Ford to City: Drop Dead!"' And then someone said, 'Holy Christ, yes! Put it in the paper!'" 2) More recently an adjective form, *drop-dead,* dating back to about 1970, has appeared and means strikingly beautiful, sensational, as in "That's some drop-dead dress she wore."

duh   A word used to make fun of someone after that person has spoken, indicating that he or she is dumb or has said or done something stupid. The expression dates back to the early 1940s, and I wouldn't be surprised if it was introduced by ventriloquist Edgar Bergen's dummy Mortimer Snerd, a rustic moron who constantly had the word put in his mouth.

duhshuh-ul   The shuttle. An underground railway connecting Times Square and Grand Central Terminal. A pronunciation recorded in the Federal

Writers' Project's *Almanac for New Yorkers* (1938).

dummkopf German for a stupid person, blockhead. The term has been used in New York City since the 1700s.

dump; dumping To abandon an old person, usually one suffering from Altzheimer's disease, by leaving him or her in some public place, such as a hospital emergency room, without any identification. "'We'd really like to locate his people, whoever they are, whoever dumped him here.' Hospital personnel had picked up the media expression. Hardly anyone in a hospital called it abandonment. It was dumping, plain and simple. Like dumping your garbage. Only these were human beings." (McBain, *Mischief*)

Duncan Phyfe Duncan Phyfe's furniture workshop stood on the site of the present Hudson Terminal Building in New York City. The Scottish-born master craftsman had ar-rived in New York in 1783 at the age of 15 and later opened his own shop, changing his name from Fife to Phyfe. Duncan Phyfe and Sons employed more than 100 artisans at its height of popularity, but the master craftsman's best work was done in the early period up until 1820, when he evolved his own style, using the creations of Sheraton, Hepplewhite and the Adam brothers as models. This work has become known as the *Duncan Phyfe style*, characterized by excellent proportions, graceful, curving lines and beautifully carved ornamentation.

durst *See* BONAC.

Dutch courage An old term still used for the courage liquor inspires; courage that comes in a bottle.

dybbuk In Jewish folklore a demon or soul of a dead person that enters a living person's soul and takes possession of him or her. Pronounced DIB-book.

earl A still common pronunciation of *oil*. "Pass the earl and vinegar for dis salad."

East Side The East Side of Manhattan in New York City lies east of Fifth Avenue and is bordered by the East River. *East Sider* is a term used since about 1900 for a resident or native of the East Side. *See* WEST SIDE.

eat'm and beat'm A humorous name New Yorkers had for cafeterias where the food (generally sandwiches and drinks) were left out on tables for customers to choose from, each customer trusted to add up his or her bill honestly from the prices listed. Owners of these places generally agreed that people were quite honest about doing so, despite the cynical name given to such establishments. Nevertheless, few such places were left by the 1980s.

Ebbets Field Demolished for a housing development in 1960, this was the home field of the late lamented Brooklyn Dodgers from 1914 to 1957 when the Dodgers left New York for Los Angeles. It was named for its builder, Charlie Ebbets.

ecdysiast New York stripteaser Georgia Southern, or her press agent, wrote H. L. Mencken in 1940 asking him to coin a "more palatable word" to describe her profession. The Sage of Baltimore, who had hatched other neologisms (e.g., "bootician" for a bootlegger), gallantly responded, suggesting that "stripteasing be related in some way or other to the zoological phenomenon of molting." Among his specific recommendations was *ecdysiast*, which comes from *ecdysis*, the scientific term for "molting." Miss Southern adopted the last, and it was publicized universally; born to the world was a new word and a new union called the Society of Ecdysiasts, Parade, and Specialty Dancers. But not every artfully unclad body was happy with Mencken's invention. Said the queen of New York strippers, Gypsy Rose Lee: "'Ecdysiast,' he calls me! Why the man is an intellectual slob. He has been reading *books. Dictionaries.* We don't wear feathers and molt them off . . . What does he know about stripping?" Most would agree that *stripteaser* is far more revealing.

Edgar Allan Poe Cottage   Often called "New York's chief literary shrine," this little cottage at Fordham in the Bronx is the place where Poe's wife, Virginia, died of tuberculosis during the terrible winter of 1846–47 when they were desperately poor and close to starving. Poe wrote "The Raven" and "The Pit and the Pendulum," among other great works, in New York. He was paid $10 for "The Raven," immediately recognized as a work of genius when it appeared, and it was a year and a half before he pried loose his money from the *New York Mirror.*

eebn   *See* BONAC.

effing   *Effing* or *effen* has been a euphemism for *fucking* in America since at least the early 1960s, though it is first recorded in a *New York Times Magazine* article by Anthony Burgess in 1972: "I have already had several abusive phone calls, telling me to eff-off back to effing Russia, you effing, corksacking limey effer."

egg ball   One-half of a spaldeen ball, the result of the ball having been batted too much. It is used in a variation of stickball called *egg ball. See* SPALDEEN.

egg cream   No one has identified the genius who first concocted the *egg cream,* but this New York favorite was invented in the 1920s at a New York soda fountain. There are no eggs and no cream in an egg cream, so it is something of a misnomer. While no exact recipe for one can be given and egg cream lovers all seem to have their own methods and proportions for making one, it is generally agreed that its ingredients must be milk, seltzer from a seltzer bottle, and Fox's U-Bet Chocolate Flavor Syrup.

eggplant   A derogatory slang term for a black person, especially among Mafia members, who also use the term *melanzana,* the Italian for "eggplant." "'. . . a week ago, this eggplant shows up on my biggest construction job.'" (Puzo, *The Last Don*)

Eighth Wonder of the World   *See* BROOKLYN BRIDGE.

eighty-seven and a half   Restaurant slang used by waiters and countermen to indicate that a pretty woman is approaching; origin unknown.

eighty-six   To murder someone or to put an end to something. "Eighty-six his ass, I don't want to see him again." The expression derives from the restaurant waiter slang *eighty-six,* which, among other things, means to "deny an unwelcome customer service" or to cancel an order ("Eighty-six the eggs"), or which directs the cashier's attention to a customer trying to leave a lunchroom without paying his check. The code word has been used in New York restaurants and bars since the 1920s, but the extended uses of *eighty-six* have only been around for half as long. Its origin is unknown, although one theory suggests it may come from slang used during Prohibition to describe the back exit of a Village speakeasy, now known as Chumley's, on Bedford Street.

eighty-two pounder See quote. "'And you're an eighty-two pounder, right?' He's picked up on fighter talk, dropping the hundred off the weight." (Pete Hamill, *Flesh and Blood*, 1977)

el A metal or concrete subway or train structure elevated above the street on which trains run and where stations are located. "He had a candy store down by the el." A shortening of *elevated*, which it is rarely called.

elevated *See* EL.

elevator apartment An apartment in an apartment building with an elevator in it, rather than just stairs. The term has been in use for almost a century.

Elgin Gardens Few New Yorkers know that New York's Rockefeller Center was once the site of the famous Elgin Gardens, one of the first botanic gardens in America. The Elgin Gardens were established by Dr. David Hosack (1769–1835), who subsequently deeded them to Columbia University. Hosack, a professor at Columbia, is remembered for his many medical and botanical books, as well as for being a founder of Bellevue Hospital and the physician who attended Alexander Hamilton after his fatal duel with Aaron Burr. The *Hosackia* genus of herbs is named after him.

Ellimheyst The local pronunciation of *Elmhurst,* a neighborhood in Queens. It is the home district of Geraldine A. Ferraro, who ran for vice president in 1984 on the Democratic ticket and has a New York accent as good as Archie Bunker's (he also lives in the area).

Ellis Island The chief immigration station of the United States from 1892 until 1943. Previously *Castle Garden*, an old fort that had been converted into an opera house and amusement hall, had processed immigrants from 1855 to 1892 in Battery Park at the southern tip of Manhattan. Located in upper New York Bay, Ellis Island originally occupied three acres but was built up with landfill to 27.5 acres to accommodate the millions of people arriving there. During its use as an immigration center, the Ellis Island facilities processed 16 million immigrants, roughly 70 percent of all immigrants to the United States in that time period. People arriving there were screened for various undesirable qualities such as contagious illnesses or mental deficiency before being granted entry to the United States. When the government began screening prospective immigrants in their native countries, Ellis Island fell into disuse. The government offered it for sale in the 1950s but could not find an adequate buyer, and the island eventually became a national monument under the care of the National Park Service. In 1998, Ellis Island officially became part of New Jersey after many years of legal debate over whether it actually belonged to that state or New York. Ellis Island was also once called *Oyster Island* because of the abundant oysters in its waters.

emmis Confidential information known by insiders. ". . . whereas nobody had even been able to prove anything, it was very much on the *emmis* that the parrot business was a front for cocaine importing from South America." (Condon, *Prizzi's Money*)

Empire State Building In discussing the 13 original states President George Washington referred to New York State as "the seat of Empire," and it thereafter became known as the "Empire State." In 1931 the completed Empire State Building was named after the state nickname. Until 1972 it was the tallest building in the world at 1,250 feet. In New York today only the World Trade Center (1,350 feet) is higher, with the Sears Tower (1,450 feet) in Chicago being the tallest building in the United States. The tallest building in the world, the Petronas Tower, is presently found in Kuala Lumpur, Malaysia. *See* WORLD TRADE CENTER.

English basement An old term, not often heard anymore, for a basement at street level, often found in brownstones in Manhattan.

English sparrow People have compared the destructive *English sparrow* to the rat because of the damage it does in eating tree buds and grain. The bird is so named because eight pairs of them were brought from England to Brooklyn in 1850 and freed in an attempt to rid the area of a caterpillar pest called the inchworm. The birds thrived, ultimately proved more of a liability than an asset and are now ubiquitous pests throughout the country.

enjoy! A common expression meaning have a good time, enjoy yourself, be happy. Often heard as *enjoy, enjoy!*, the term was influenced by Yiddish syntax.

enough is enough already Said when someone has gone too far or something has been carried on too long, etc. Either Yiddish in origin or influenced by Yiddish speech patterns.

environment The world of crime and gangs. "Well, Jesus, he thought, no wonder Irene understands the environment. . . . Her own father was a worker for a Chicago mob." (Condon, *Prizzi's Honor*)

erl boiner A pronunciation of *oil burner*.

erster A pronunciation heard in New York for *oyster*. "The poil was in the erster."

Eskimo Pie Invented in 1919 and originally called an I Scream Bar, this still popular chocolate-covered ice-cream bar was manufactured in 1921 by Russell Stover (for whom the well-known chocolate-covered candies are named) and given the trade name *Eskimo Pie*.

ever   Frequently used before an adverb as an intensifier, as in "Am I ever mad!"

everything worthwhile doing is either immoral, illegal or fattening
A by-now proverbial saying attributed to New York wit Alexander Woollcott, a member of the Algonquin Round Table. *See* MAN WHO CAME TO DINNER, THE; MEN SELDOM MAKE PASSES / AT GIRLS WHO WEAR GLASSES.

excuse the expression   Pardon my language. A common saying influenced by Yiddish.

extremely dead   A good example of Runyonese, as in "Big False Face is extremely dead when they find him." (Damon Runyon, "The Brakeman's Daughter," 1931)

ey   Hey. Common words upon greeting a caller on the telephone or meeting someone on the street: "Ey, Louie, how're y' doin'?" Pronounced *ey* as in *hey,* which it is a shortening of.

eyeball   To stare at; frequently heard among black speakers. "Stop eyeballin' me, man."

Eye-tie   A mildly derogatory term for an Italian.

face   According to Douglas Le Vien, a former New York City Police detective, as stated in the *New York Times* (March 15, 1992), a *face* is "a guy who looks like a mobster's supposed to look. . . . They [the mob] send him to scare the hell out of someone, like 'Go send a face.'"

faddah   Father. *See* MUDDAH.

fahcrissake   A common pronunciation of *for Christ's sake*. "Fahcrissake, will you stop doing that?"

family   An original Mafia unit, headed by a don or godfather, operating in a clearly defined area, the members of which are not necessarily blood relatives; sometimes called a *crime family* by the media. The term *family* has been used to describe groups of professional criminals since the 18th century but was not applied to the Mafia much before 1963. Every Mafia family is responsible to a council composed of representatives of all the Mafia families.

family hammer   A hit man or assassin for a Mafia family. *See* HAMMER.

fammah   *See* BONAC.

fancy-shmancy   Something so fancy that it is pretentious. A Yinglish word, a blending of Yiddish and English, the Yiddish in this case being the *shm* sound that is often prefixed to a word to mock that word. Other examples are *Santa Shmanta* and *Oedipus-schmedipus*.

'fare   A black slang term for welfare, the welfare department in New York City, officially called Social Services. "They ain't no mutherfucking therapists on our side they just flunkies for the 'fare." (Sapphire, *Push*)

Fashion Avenue   *See* RAG TRADE.

fast lane   *See* SPEED LANE.

father-and-son business   A joking name for a shady enterprise that advertises "Going Out of Business" sales in the window for years and years in order to lure people looking for a bargain.

Father Knickerbocker   A synonym for New York City. The prominent Dutch Knickerbocker family settled near Albany, New York, in about 1674.

Among its prosperous descendants was the wealthy Harman Knickerbocker (b.1779), the great-great-grandson and namesake of the family founder, who became known as "the prince of Schaghticoke" for his great manor along the Schaghticoke River. So when Washington Irving burlesqued a pompous guidebook of the day with his *A History of New York from the Beginning of the World to the End of the Dutch Dynasty* (1809), he decided to capitalize on the old familiar name, choosing the pseudonym Diedrich Knickerbocker. Irving could not have concocted a better pen name in satirizing the stodgy Dutch burghers than this thinly veiled alias for the well-known Dutch "prince," although the first great book of comic literature written by an American was also a satire on Jeffersonian democracy, pedantry and literacy classics. Soon his humorous work became known as *Knickerbocker's History of New York*, but it wasn't until English caricaturist George Cruikshank illustrated a later edition in the 1850s that the Knickerbocker family name was bestowed on the loose-fitting, blousy knee breeches known today as *knickers*. In that English edition Cruikshank depicted the alleged author and his fellow Dutch burghers wearing voluminous breeches buckled just below the knee. His drawings of the style that the early Dutch had worn were widely copied for boys' knee pants, baggy golf trousers (called plus fours) four inches longer, and even silk underwear for women—all of which were dubbed *knickerbockers* after the family Irving had immortal-ized. Eventually, the name *knickerbockers* was shortened to *knickers*, and *knicks* in England. The trouser style is no longer worn by schoolboys but was revived relatively recently as a short-lived fashion for women. The British still call women's underwear *knickers*.

As a result of Irving's work *Father Knickerbocker* became an early synonym for New York City, *Knickerbocker* was adopted by a school of local writers called the *Knickerbocker Group* and an early New York City literary journal was called *The Knickerbocker Magazine* (1833–65). Much later it became the name of New York's professional basketball team, the New York Knicks. *See also* BIG APPLE; GOTHAM; KNICKERBOCKER RULES; NEW YORK.

fawk A pronunciation of *fork*.

faygeleh I have only heard the Yiddish *faygeleh* used as a term of endearment for a child, but several authorities give it as a derogatory term for a homosexual as well. It derives from the German *vogele*, "little bird," and is pronounced FAY-geh-leh.

fayuh A pronunciation of *fare*, as in "cab fayuh."

faz-ols Dollars. "He owes me two hundred faz-ols."

Feast of Dedication *See* HANUKKAH.

Feast of Lights *See* HANUKKAH.

Featherbed Lane According to the *Random House Historical Dictionary of*

American Slang, this humorous expression meaning any bad road dates back to at least 1698. The dictionary quotes a "doubtful" story about the term's origin told by a New York City dentist: "I was told as a child that Featherbed Lane got its name in the Revolution. The story was that Washington was afraid his troops would make too much noise marching through town at night, so to fool the redcoats he got all the housewives to pave the roads with their featherbeds so the army could move silently. . . ." Most likely the term refers to vehicles sinking in a muddy road as if in a bed of feathers.

Federal Hall The original building was New York's city hall and later served as the site of George Washington's inauguration as first president of the United States on April 6, 1789. In 1842 a new building was constructed at the site in downtown Manhattan. Today it is a museum.

feeuh A pronunciation of *fear*.

feh! A common Yiddish exclamation of disgust similar to *pew!, ugh!* or *yuck!* It is usually associated with a terrible smell, but can be used to express any distasteful experience. "Feh! This monkey business I don't like." (Arthur Kober, "You Mean Common," 1940)

fer A very common pronunciation of *for* heard among poor and rich alike for several centuries. "Get it fer me, will ya?"

fergit A pronunciation of *forget*.

figger A pronunciation heard in New York of *figure*, as in "Go figger."

filladuppigin Fill it up again (usually with beer or whiskey). A pronunciation recorded in the Federal Writers' Project *Almanac for New Yorkers* (1938). *See* YOUVADANUFFBUD.

films *See* PICTURE SHOW.

fin A synonym for a $5 bill that isn't heard as widely as it was even 20 years ago. It derives from the Yiddish *finif*, "five," and has been around since at least the 1920s. *See* FINNIF.

finestkind *See* BONAC.

finger Another name for the *mechanics, dips, cannons, goniffs, donnegan workers, moll buzzers* or *pickpockets* who work the city streets, one reputedly so skilled that she can steal the cheese from a mousetrap set deep in a man's pocket. Their accomplices are called *stalls* and *sticks* and *shades*. See CANNON; DIP.

finger-wringer An old theatrical term for an overemotional actress, "an actress given to emoting," as a *New York Times* article (March 11, 1928) put it.

finnif A $5 bill. "I am not giving finnifs to guys like Feet Samuels, and he finally offers to compromise with me for a deuce. . . ." (Runyon, "A Very Honorable Guy") *See* FIN.

finnin' *See* BONAC.

finstins   A telescoping of *for instance* often heard in New York speech.

Fithavnya   Fifth Avenue in Manhattan.

Five-O   The police, a policeman; after the popular television police series *Hawaii Five-O,* introduced in 1968. Often used by street criminals as a warning that cops are approaching.

Five Towns   A prosperous Long Island suburban area of New York City. It consists of the Nassau County towns of Inwood, Lawrence, Cedarhurst, Woodmere and Hewlett. *See* KEEPING UP WITH THE JONESES.

flahwah   A pronunciation of *floor.*

flash   Loud attire or lifestyle; sometimes called *flashfront.*

> "A jacket like this would stand out in New York. You don't want clothes for that. My father used to tell me that twice a week. . . . He means all flashfront stuff but what he is saying to me is it's better to stand out because of what you are than to let clothes or cars or diamond rings do it for you. For me, that is," he added quickly. (Condon, *Prizzi's Honor*)

See B'HOY.

flatfoot   A widely used term for a policeman in New York up until the last 20 or so years, when it has been heard less frequently. Before policemen were called *flatfoots* here, they were called *flatties,* a term common in the 19th century.

flat-foot floozy with the floy-floy   An expression well known in the early 1940s, when a popular song had the same title. A *floozy* was commonly used for a cheap or loose woman or a prostitute. The *floy-floy,* which isn't included in slang dictionaries I consulted, apparently means a sexual disease such as gonorrhea.

Flatiron Building   *See* TWENTY-THREE SKIDOO.

flea market   These bargain markets have nothing to do with fleas. *Flea market* has been an American expression as far back as Dutch colonial days when there was the Vallie (Valley) Market at the valley, or foot, of Maiden Lane in downtown Manhattan. The Vallie Market came to be abbreviated to *Vlie Market* and this was soon being pronounced *Flea Market.*

flip one's wig   To greatly enjoy, appreciate, be crazy about. "You flipped your wig over her just two weeks ago and now you won't give her the time of day?"

flip someone   Mob talk for to make someone a turncoat. "The cops paid a lot to flip him."

floor broker   *Brokers* today are associated with stocks or real estate, but all brokers were originally *brokières,* or men who opened up wine casks (usually to bottle and sell the wine inside). This old French word came to be transferred to wine salesmen, or brokers, and finally to one who sold anything at all. Wall Street brokers who work on the floor (or in the pit) of the exchange are called *floor brokers;* they were once called *$2 brokers* because they received a fee of $2 per transaction.

floor-through A word encountered only in New York City for an apartment in a small apartment building, such as a brownstone, that takes up an entire floor. "They rented a nice floor-through."

Flushing A neighborhood in Queens whose name is a corruption of the Dutch name *Vlissingen* for "the place."

FOB's A historical term heard in baseball during the heyday of the Brooklyn Dodgers, when it meant the bases were *full of bums* or *Brooklyns.* *See* DEM BUMS.

foist A New York pronunciation of first that is also heard in the South. "I'm always foist on linc for the movies."

foot Speed of foot. "'. . . the guy is too speedy for Shamus, who never has much foot anyway.'" (Damon Runyon, "Bred For Battle," 1931)

Fordham University This Catholic institution's name was St. John's College when founded in 1841 in the Bronx. In 1907 it took its present name.

foreigner *See* BONAC.

Fort Apache A widely known name, originally police slang, for the

41st Police Precinct in the South Bronx, among the most crime ridden areas in New York City. The name is said to have originated in the early 1950s, when it was suggested by the cowboy and Indian movie *Fort Apache* (1948).

Fort Pricks Punning slang for the army base Fort Dix in New Jersey.

for-two-cents-plain One serving of soda water, from the days when it cost two cents a glass at soda fountains. "'It was time to enjoy a "for two cents plain,"' only now it is for five cents plain." (Harry Golden, *For 2¢ Plain,* 1958)

Forty-Deuce Slang for West Forty-second Street, the Times Square area, since the 1970s. "I went down to Forty-Deuce."

Forty Thieves A common name in the mid-19th century for the Common Council of aldermen that governed New York City. The name was suggested by a dangerous gang of the time with the same name. Boss Tweed came from the ranks of the Forty Thieves council.

four-box baseball A variation on the children's game of box ball in New York City.

Four Hundred Society columnist Ward McAllister coined the *Four Hundred* in 1889, when he claimed that only 400 people formed New York City's high society. According to the traditional tale, 400 was chosen as the quantity because old Mrs. Astor's ballroom held only that number, but the truth is that she often invited twice that many people to parties held there.

Four Million   *See* BAGDAD ON THE HUDSON.

fox-trot   One story has it that actor Harry Fox's original trotting type of dance was a showstopper in a 1913 Broadway hit musical. The show's producers realized the dance had promotional value and hired the noted social dancing teacher Oscar Duryea to modify it and introduce it as the *Fox-Trot* to the public. This he did, and the *fox-trot* has been America's most popular slow dance ever since. The story does jibe with the fact that the term is first recorded as *Fox* (with a capital *F*) *trot* in an RCA Victor catalog in 1915.

Fratellanza   *See* BROTHERHOOD.

freaking   A commonly heard euphemism for *fucking*, as in "You're outta your freakin' mind."

free and easy   A common term in New York before the Civil War for a house of prostitution.

French ice-cream soda   Heard in Brooklyn for an ice-cream soda topped with whipped cream.

fress   To eat, often in large quantities or ravenously, from Yiddish. Frequently used mixed with English, as in "I never saw anybody fress like that."

friend of mine   In mob talk, someone you'd vouch for.

friend of ours   Someone who is a *made man* in the mob, who is a member of the "family." *See* FAMILY.

Frog and Toe   In the mid-19th century this was a name in underworld slang for New York City. The origin of the name is uncertain. *See* BIG APPLE.

from away   A term used on Long Island's North Fork, and apparently nowhere else in the metropolitan area, for someone not born there. "He's from away."

fuck   According to a recent *New York Times* story by Carey Goldberg, "Welcome to New York, Capital of Profanities," New York "appears to be the most foul-mouthed city in the nation, rivaling only prison and the armed forces in its penchant for profanity." This is especially true as regards the word *fuck,* the so-called *F-word,* which is used so often that it has lost its shock value among the underclass and overclass alike. The reason usually given is the stress of New York City life, but then what kind of release does a word that has become so namby-pamby or shock-valueless provide? In any case, according to Professor Lewis Allen, author of *The City in Slang* (1990), *fuck* "has become just an intensifier . . . like *shucks* and *golly* and *darn* that people used to say . . . and its -ing form (*fucking*) has become for many simply a substitute for 'very.'" The *Times* article points out that in *Do the Right Thing,* a Spike Lee movie set in Brooklyn, *fuck* and *fucking* are used fully 182 times.

fuck off!   Get out of here, go away, don't bother me. Very common slang in New York for the last 30 years or so, largely replacing similar terms such as *buzz off!* The phrase dates back, however, to the late 1800s.

fuhgeddaboutit   Forget about it. Usually the equivalent of "don't mention it," "it's no trouble at all," "no problem," etc. But it can also mean "no way," "I won't even consider it," etc.

Fun City   A nickname for New York City said to have originated with Mayor John V. Lindsay in 1966 on his first day in office when a reporter asked if he was happy he'd been elected. "I still think it's a fun city," Lindsay replied. Author Dick Schaap first capitalized the name in his *Herald Tribune* column "What's New in Fun City." Other New York mayors with a way with words include James J. Walker, who wrote the sentimental favorite "Will You Love Me in December as You Did in May?" before he was elected, and Mayor Fiorello LaGuardia, who in 1934 invented the phrase "No more free lunch!" (No more graft), which is a translation of the Italian "È finita la cuccagna," said to have been shouted by the Little Flower while he angrily shook his fist at City Hall.

fungoo   Very common since the 1940s for fuck you; from the Italian *affanculo,* meaning "I fuck you up the ass." Also pronounced *fongoo.* Usually accompanied by the appropriate arm or finger sign. *See also* BOFF-ON-GOOL; BAH-FONG-GOO.

funny as a crutch   The crutch here is short for someone on crutches, someone disabled permanently, which is of course not a funny matter nor something to laugh at. Thus something said that is decidedly unfunny or tasteless is often called *funny as a crutch.* The expression was more frequently heard in New York 50 years ago than it is today.

furgassi   Pronounced foo-GAZE-ee; mob talk for a fake, especially fake jewelry.

futz around   To fool around, play; often used as a euphemism for *fuck around. Futz,* possibly deriving from the Yiddish *arumfartzen,* is first recorded in 1929. *We futzed around all day* means we accomplished nothing, wasted the day. *Don't futz around with it* means don't touch it, don't mess around with it, leave it alone.

G Slang for a thousand dollars, short for a *grand*. "I am going to stake them to a few G's." (Runyon, *Guys and Dolls*) Also *G-note*.

gangbuster H. L. Mencken said, "*Gang-buster* was launched in 1935 to describe Thomas E. Dewey (a prominent New York District Attorney who prosecuted organized crime and later became Governor)." The radio program *Gangbusters*, introduced in 1936, popularized the term and it has since been applied to any law enforcement officer engaged in breaking up gangs. To *do gangbusters* is to be very successful as in "The show did gangbusters," while *come on like gangbusters* means to approach something very aggressively and energetically, like the opening of a *Gangbusters* radio program with its machine guns, sirens, etc.

gangland slaying A name in the past attached to almost every killing involving professional criminals. "And the next day in the *Daily News* there was a story about the body that was found in the Prospect Park lake and the cops . . . thought it was what they always called a gangland slaying. I was a kid and wanted to know where Gangland was. This new strange country that wasn't in the geography books." (Hamill, *Flesh and Blood*)

Gansevoort Street pier The pier where New York City–born Herman Melville spent the last 20 years of his life as a "most inglorious" inspector of customs, in complete obscurity. Ironically, the name Gansevoort honored his affluent maternal ancestors. A neglected *Moby-Dick* behind him, the writer lived for the evenings during which he could work on *Billy Budd* in his bleak Gramercy Park room. So little known was America's greatest novelist at his death that the *New York Times* at first failed to print his obituary. Belatedly the *Times* printed a brief item reporting the death of "Hiram" Melville.

garbageman *See* AIRY WAY.

garbage mouth Mob talk for someone who consistently "talks dirty."

Garden The *Garden* is the usual name for Madison Square Garden in New York City.

gate In the world of jazz a name that musicians have for each other, especially for someone who really swings. The word, very popular in the 1940s, had some general use in the expression, "Greetings, gate." *Gate* was popularized by Louis Armstrong, whose nickname as a boy was "Gate-mouth."

gavoones See quote. "The Boston area had too many murders, too many petty wars for power . . . If the Chicago Mafia were savages, then the Boston people were *gavoones,* or uncouth louts, ruffians." (Puzo, *The Godfather*)

Gaynor, William A reform mayor of New York, who was elected in 1909 and is the only New York City mayor ever to be assassinated. Gaynor was shot by a disgruntled city worker in 1910. The bullet was irremovably lodged below his right ear, and he died of his wound three years later.

Gay White Way Another name for Broadway in the early 1900s. *See* GREAT WHITE WAY.

geddin gout A pronunciation of *getting out.*

gee whiz *See* JEEZ!

gelati Italian *gelati* has become more popular in America, especially in New York, over the past 10 years. *Gelato* is the Italian for ice cream, and the delicacy, which is folded rather than churned when made, has a much higher butter fat content than any other kind of ice cream.

George Washington Bridge Completed in 1931, this magnificent bridge joining New York City and New Jersey was once the world's longest (with a central suspension span of 3,500 feet), but it has since been surpassed by the Golden Gate Bridge in San Francisco and the Japanese Akashi-Kaekyo Bridge—the current record-holder at 6,532 feet. New York also has a *Washington Bridge* (not *George* Washington) that crosses the Harlem River; it was built in 1889.

get a bun on To get very drunk. The expression has been common in New York for almost a century, but its etymology is unknown.

get a haircut A New Yorker *gets a haircut;* he or she doesn't *take a haircut* as many other Americans do. Few, if any, New Yorkers say "I'm going to take a haircut."

get lost 1) Get out of here, get out of sight, stop bothering me; as in "A dollar? Get lost. I haven't got a dollar myself." 2) Often said during an argument when one person expresses an idea unacceptable to the other. "Get lost, ya creep!" (Rocky Graziano, *Somebody Up There Likes Me,* 1955)

get makkes To get nothing, as in "You'll get makkes from me." A Yiddish term from the Hebrew *makot,* "plagues," "blows," etc.; pronounced MOCK-iss

get off the dime   To get started, take some action, as in "You'd better get off the dime while you still have time." Originally a term used by floor managers in dance halls, telling dancers to move from an almost stationary position. Ten cents was the cost of a dance.

get one's ears lowered   Though this saying for getting a fresh haircut isn't generally associated with New York City, I've heard it here a number of times over the years.

get one's pots on   To get drunk.

> . . . every time King O'Hara gets his pots on, which is practically every night, rain or shine, he is always bragging that he has the royal blood of Ireland in his veins, so somebody starts calling him King, and this is his monicker as long as I can remember, although probably what King O'Hara really has in his veins is about ninety-eight percent alcohol.   (Damon Runyon, "Princess O'Hara," 1931)

get out of here!   Usually not to be taken literally, these commonly heard words most often mean: that's preposterous, you've told me an unbelievable story, that could never happen, etc. The perfect New York pronunciation is *Ged ouda here!*

getty   Pronounced JET-ee. An old term for a street-corner organ grinder, usually one with a monkey trained to collect coins thrown by the audience. Sometimes the getty's monkey would climb up the apartment windows to get the coins. Today the term is mainly remembered in the old song "The Sidewalks of New York": "And the getty plays the organ on the sidewalks of New York."

gevalt!   *See* OY!

g'hal   *See* B'HOY.

gimme   A common pronunciation of *give me.* "Gimme a pack of Camels."

gimme a break   Don't be ridiculous, spare me the lies or exaggerations. Often heard as "Gimme a break, willya."

gin mill   A humorous name for any bar, but especially a low-class one; once widely used but now heard mainly from older speakers.

giobba   See quote.

> . . . the alien immigrant . . . Italian of a decade's residence began to astound more recently arrived compatriots with such expressions as *giobba* (job), *sanguiccio* (sandwich), and *sonomagogna* (son of a gun). With the acquisition of American words came the acquisition of something of the American's sweeping largeness of idea. (Federal Writers Project, *New York Panorama*)

give 'em the hook   This saying, as well as the practice of hooking a failing act from the stage, is said to have originated at Manhattan's Miner's Theater during an amateur night sometime in the early 1900s. The first *hook* was apparently a shepherd's crook (a prop from a play) tied to a long pole. The practice and saying spread from Miner's to theaters all over the world.

gizza A pronunciation of *give us.* "'Gizza kiss, Al.' He leaned over and kissed her cheek softly." (Condon, *Prizzi's Money*)

gladda Glad to. "'Lay on the romance and she'll be gladda marry you.'" (Condon, *Prizzi's Money*)

glamour girl A glamorous young woman, often a film star or model. *See* CAFÉ SOCIETY.

glass tea Tea served in a glass, not a cup. "Maybe you'd like a glass tea?" asked Mrs. Grass "Maybe a piece fruit you'd like?" (Kober, "You Mean Common")

glazza A pronunciation of *glass of.*

glitch This scientific word, meaning a sudden change in the rotation period of a neutron star, has its roots in the Yiddish *glitch*, "a slip," which, in turn, comes from the German *glitschen*, "slip." Possibly a scientist in the U.S. space program (c.1960) familiar with Yiddish is responsible for the coining, but he remains nameless. Today the term is most used in computerese for a mechanical malfunction or for any problem or emergency due to a defective or broken machine. On the other hand, some authorities say the word dates back to early radio days, when it meant an announcer's slip or mistake.

go Sometimes used to mean "say." "My mother she go go to the store for milk. I go I don't want to go, I'm busy."

godda Got to, have to, as in "We godda gedda bedder one."

godfather The head of a Mafia family. "Don Vito Corleone was a man to whom everybody came for help, and never were they disappointed . . . His reward? Friendship, the respectful title of 'Don,' and sometimes the more affectionate salutation of 'Godfather.' . . ." (Puzo, *The Godfather*)

God finally caught his eye New York playwright and wit George S. Kaufman's mock epitaph for a dead waiter. New York waiters were Kaufman's pet hate; he believed they were actually trained to exasperate him and other customers.

go down *See* TO.

God should be allowed to just watch the game Yogi Berra is supposed to have made this remark from behind the plate after watching Chicago White Sox batter Minnie Minoso appeal for divine intervention by drawing a cross in the dust on home plate. The story has become sports legend, but syndicated columnist William Safire recently contacted the former Yankee catcher and Yogi denied that he had ever said it. *Yogiisms* that Yogi hasn't denied include "I've been playing eighteen years and you can observe a lot by watching" (on his managerial abilities), "He can run anytime he wants—I'm giving him the red light" (on giving a player permission to steal a base) and the much quoted "It ain't over till it's over." *See also* STENGELESE.

go in the water To take a dive, intentionally lose or throw a fight. "They say he's a tank artist, a tomato can, a guy that goes in the water for a few bucks. . . ." (Hamill, *Flesh and Blood*)

go fight City Hall A saying of resignation, an admission of the futility of a situation, comparable to *it's like hitting your head against the wall*, which is often in New Yorkese *go hit your head against the wall*.

go figure An expression of frustration meaning something that defies logical thought, it beats me, I can't explain it, you try. "There they are, the best team in baseball—the best pitching, the best hitters—and they lose three in a row to these stumble bums. Go figure."

goil *Girl,* and a better rendering of the word, according to some experts, than the *gel* or *gairl* of Britain.

going, going . . . gone Any New York Yankee fan of the 1950s will remember this phrase, which became the trademark of Yankee radio announcer Mel Allen (1913–96) in describing a home run or a hit in the process of becoming a home run. Just as well known were the native Alabamians's words *How 'bout that?*, a comment about how pleasing or depressing or dramatic something was.

Goldberg Derogatory black slang for a Jew; first recorded in Claude Brown's *Manchild in the Promised Land* (1965) but older. "Calling you Goldberg in the bargain, [they'll] send you on your way." (Philip Roth, *Portnoy's Complaint,* 1968) *See* MR. CHARLIE.

Gold Dust twins I heard this expression several times in 1951 from two boys from the Bronx who were describing two girls from the Bronx. The girls were always together, as inseparable as the Gold Dust twins pictured in ads for Gold Dust Washing Powder.

gole joolry A pronunciation of *gold jewelry.*

goombah Italian for friend. From the Italian *compare*. "He's my goombah." Said to have been popularized by boxer Rocky Graziano in his appearances on the *Martha Raye Show* (NBC-TV) in 1955.

goniff *Goniff,* first recorded in 1839, is slang for a thief or a shady, dishonest person, the word deriving from the Hebrew *ganef* for "thief." It was given wider currency when used in George Roy Hill's film *The Sting* (1973).

good field, no hit This baseball catchphrase is sometimes applied jokingly to anyone who does one thing better than another thing, to someone who is good in one field and not another. The expression dates back to 1924, when coach Miguel "Mike" Gonzales scouted Dodger player Moe Berg for the St. Louis Cardinals. Observing Berg at Brooklyn's training camp that spring, Gonzales wired his boss the four-word evaluation "Good field, no hit" and the Cardinals didn't offer him a contract. The scholarly Berg, who spoke seven languages, became an American secret agent during World War II, spying on German atomic scientists.

good for another one thousand miles Heard recently in New York City from a barber on finishing someone's haircut: "Now you're good for another thousand miles"; and as the answer to a greeting on the street: "How y'doin'?" "Guess I'm good for another thousand miles." Probably originally used in reference to a car.

go over *See* TO.

go peddle your papers Far more common 50 years ago than it is today, the expression has a variety of meanings depending on the situation it is used in, including go away; get lost; be a good guy and leave; go away before you get hurt; mind your own business; leave us alone, etc.

gorill A stupid strong-arm man; also a hired killer. ". . . I never care to be around gorills when they are drinking. . . ." (Damon Runyon, "Dark Dolores," 1929)

Gotham Washington Irving first called New York City *Gotham* in his *Salmaguni Papers* (1807), because its residents reminded him of the legendary inhabitants of the English town of Gotham. An old tale has it that these villagers had discouraged King John from building a castle in their town, and taxing them for it, by feigning madness—trying to drown fish,

sweep the moon's reflection off the waters, etc. This legend had been the inspiration for more stories about the villagers, collected in a book called *Merrie Tales of the Mad Men of Gotham*, and Irving, reading of these alternately wise and foolish people, thought that they resembled New Yorkers. The name is still used: "'One worries for Scott that the fickle gods of Gotham will finally notice him wiggling on a mountain top,' says Baitz." (Peter Marks, "An Eye for the Id," *New York Times Magazine*, November 10, 1996) *See also* BIG APPLE.

go to business A term still used, mostly by older New Yorkers, for *go to work*. "It was often said of her that she went to business, which meant she had a job in an office. . . ." (Hamill, *Snow in August*)

go to the beach When New Yorkers take the subway to Coney Island or the Rockaways or drive out to Jones Beach or Orchard Beach, they *go to the beach*, never the *shore*, as neighboring Jerseyans put it.

go to the mattresses See quote.

Whenever a war between the [Mafia] Families became bitterly intense, the opponents would set up headquarters in secret apartments where the "soldiers" could sleep on mattresses scattered through the rooms. This was not so much to keep their families out of danger . . . since any attack on noncombatants was undreamed of . . . But it was always smarter to live in some secret place where your everyday movements could not be charted either by your opponents or by some police who might arbitrarily decide to meddle. (Puzo, *The Godfather*)

got to see a man about a dog   A humorous euphemism when excusing oneself to use the bathroom.

go west, young man, go west   In the United States, with the expansion of the frontier, the words *go west* came to stand for new life and hope. There is some controversy however, about who said *go west, young man* first. Horace Greeley used the expression in an editorial in his *New York Tribune:* "Go west, young man, and grow with the country." Later, as the phrase grew in popularity, Greeley said that his inspiration was John Babsone Lane Soule, who wrote "Go West, young man" in an 1851 article in the *Terre Haute Express.* Greeley even reprinted Soule's article from the Indiana newspaper to give credit where it was due, but several writers insisted that Greeley had given them identical advice before Soule had written the piece. William S. Verity said that the great editor had coined the expression a full year before Soule.

goy   *Goy* is a Yiddish word for a gentile and can be completely innocent or disparaging in meaning, depending on who is using it and how it is used. Leo Rosten notes that the word itself is not derogatory and discusses it at length in his excellent book *The Joys of Yiddish.* The word derives from the Hebrew *goy,* "nation," and dates back to at least the 19th century.

grade A   An old term for a glass of milk, especially at a soda fountain.

Grant's Tomb   A memorial along Riverside Drive to Ulysses S. Grant (1822–85), Union general in the Civil War and 18th president of the United States. It is said that after leaving a party on Riverside early one morning, humorist Robert Benchley wandered over to Grant's Tomb, not realizing that several friends were following him. After a while his friends saw him pick something up, write a few words on a slip of paper and then place the object back on the ground again. When he left, his friends came closer. There, outside the huge tomb, stood an empty milk bottle with a note in it, ordering: "One milk, no cream—U.S. Grant." *See* WHO'S BURIED IN GRANT'S TOMB?

grapevine   Some 15 years after Samuel Morse transmitted his famous What Hath God Wrought message, a long telegraph line was strung from Virginia City, Nevada, to Placerville, California. The line was so crudely strung, it's said, that people jokingly compared the line with a sagging grapevine. I can find no record of this, but, in any case, grapevines were indeed associated with telegraph lines, for by the time of the Civil War a report *by grapevine telegraph* was common slang for a rumor. The idea behind the expression is probably not rumors sent over real telegraph lines, but the telegraphic speed with which rumormongers can transmit canards with their own rude mouth-to-mouth telegraph system. It is said that New York City's Old Grapevine tavern, "a hangout and gossip center" in the 19th century, may have reinforced the coinage.

graveyard stew   A common humorous term during the Great Depression years for a meal of bread (or toast) and milk with sugar added. A steady diet of it, and you might wind up in the graveyard.

greaseball   An offensive term for people of Mediterranean or Latin American background heard since at least the 1920s.

Great Black Way   The part of Seventh Avenue that cuts through Harlem. So named because the area, populated mostly by blacks, rivaled Broadway (the *Great White Way*) for its nightlife, and its clubs and performers were renowned the world over.

Great Fire of 1835   A fire of unknown origin that leveled downtown New York to the ground.

Great Tight Way   A humorous name for Broadway at the turn of the century, in reference to all the drinking that took place there. Other humorous or once humorous names for Broadway over the years include *The Hardened Artery, The Grandest Canyon, Baloney Boulevard, The Big Gulch, Buzzard Boulevard, Phosphorescent Path, The Diamond Ditch, Gin Gulch, Beer Gulch, Aspirin Alley, The Flamboyant Floodway, Coffee Pot Canyon, Hooch Highway, The Milky Way, Artful Alley, Big Street, The Big Drag, Little Old Broadway, The Stem,* *Rue de Revelry, The Galaxy, Fraudway, Noisy Lane, Levity Lane,* and *The Dirty White Way.* Most were invented by newspaper columnists like Walter Winchell, O. O. McIntyre and Mark Hellinger. *See* GREAT WHITE WAY.

Great White Way   This nickname for Broadway and the Manhattan theatrical or entertainment district, a reference to all the lights there, was coined by Albert Bigelow Paine, best known today as Mark Twain's biographer. The words were first used as the title of Paine's novel *The Great White Way* (1901).

green hornet   A name for New York City patrol cars, which in the 1940s were green, black and white. Probably suggested by *The Green Hornet* radio series (1936–52).

Greenpernt   The usual pronunciation of the area officially known as Greenpoint in Brooklyn.

Greenwich Village   A lower Manhattan district of New York famous as a literary and artistic community since the early 20th century—earlier than that if one considers that Thomas Paine wrote *The Crisis* there and that Edgar Allan Poe lived in the Village for a time. It's called the *Village* because it was a separate village through the colonial period and into the early 19th century.

> In a little district west of Washington Square the streets have run crazy and broken themselves into small strips called "places." These "places" make strange angles and curves. One street crosses itself a time or two. An artist once discovered a valuable possibility

in this street. Suppose a collector with a bill for paints, paper and canvas should, in traversing this route, suddenly meet himself coming back, without a cent having been paid on account! So, to quaint old Greenwich Village the art people soon came prowling, hunting for north windows and eighteenth-century gables and Dutch attics and low rents. (O. Henry, "The Last Leaf," 1906)

gridlock A term describing the halting of vehicular movement in part or parts of the city because key intersections are blocked by traffic. I have it on good authority that the word was coined by Sam Schwartz, head of the New York City Department of Transportation, in 1975.

guido An insulting stereotype for a young Italian male since the late 1980s; from the Italian name Guido. An article in *New York Newsday* (March 22, 1991) defined *Guidos* as "guys who usually have [hair]brushes in their pockets, drive expensive American muscle cars, wear Bugle Boy jeans, like dancing . . . and are mostly Italians." Italian young women with similar interests are sometimes called *guidettes*. ["Guido Nazzo is nazzo guido," drama critic George S. Kaufman wrote in a 1930s review of a young operatic tenor of that name. The wisecrack was so widely repeated that it nearly ruined the singer's career. Kaufman was so truly sorry that he apologized to Nazzo and offered him a part in one of his plays.] *See* GUIDO.

Guinea Another offensive name for an Italian, this one dating back to the late 19th century. Before then it was the name for a black from Guinea in West Africa, which is probably the origin of the word. *Guinea* has also been applied to any southern and central Europeans and to Hispanics in general. *Guinzo, wop, greaseball* and *dago* are also derogatory names for Italians, as is *Eye-tie. See* GUIDO.

Guinea red A derogatory name for any cheap (though often good) red Italian wine often made at home.

Guinea stinker A slang term for a strong cheap, foul-smelling cigar, called *el stinko* elsewhere; it is usually long and twisted, often smoked down to a stub. Also *Guinea rope.*

gumnt A pronunciation of *government,* believe it or not.

gun moll Female accomplices of criminals did not carry their guns for them. The *gun* in the term *gun moll* does not refer to a firearm but derives from the Yiddish *goniff,* a "thief," and *moll* is 18th-century slang for a woman. A *gun moll* in the 1920s was a female pickpocket, before newspaper reporters mistakenly took to calling any racketeer's girl a *gun moll.*

guvnah A pronunciation of *governor.*

gwan! A pronunciation of *go on!*

hackie A name for the driver of a hack or a taxi cab. More often called a *cabbie* today. A *hoople* used to be a hackie working a 24-hour stretch.

hahbuh A pronunciation of *harbor*, as in "Poil Hahbuh." *See* LEO THE LIP.

hairbag See quote.

> Meeting Muldoon for the first time, one would note his bulbous nose, the broken veins in his cheeks. If close enough one would smell the beer on his breath, would note the stains on his tie, the garish sportscoat buttoned taut over his belly. Some cops called him a hairbag, though not to his face. *Hairbag* is [NYC] slang for men who don't care anymore, who are waiting on retirement. (Robert Daley, *Tainted Evidence*, 1993)

halavah *Halavah* or *halva* is a Yiddish word, deriving ultimately from the Arabic *haluva*, "sweet confection," for every sweet flakey candy of Turkish origin made chiefly of honey and ground sesame seeds.

hall bedroom A hallway turned into a small bedroom by partitioning part of it. Also called a *hall room*.

Hall of Fame *See* NEW YORK UNIVERSITY.

hammer An enforcer for the Mafia, usually the chief enforcer in a Mafia family, who kills or intimidates the family's enemies. "'You will go out and live permanently in Vegas,' he [the Don] said . . . 'However you will remain the Family Hammer.'" (Puzo, *The Last Don*) Sometimes called the *number one hammer*. A *hammer man* is black slang for a very strong authoritative person, but the two terms seem to have arisen independently.

handball Handball became popular in America in about 1882, when it is said to have been introduced by Irish immigrant Phil Casey in Brooklyn, New York. The name of this popular sport can be traced back to 15th-century England, but it originated in Ireland over four centuries earlier and was known as the *game of fives* for the five fingers of the hand, used to hit the ball.

77

Hanukkah A Jewish festival of eight days that usually fall in December commemorating the rededication of the Temple of Jerusalem by the Maccabees after their victory over the Syrian Antiochus IV. The festival is characterized by the lighting of the *menorah* on each of the festival nights, the giving of small cash gifts (*Hanukkah gelt*) and games such as one played with a four-sided top, or *dreidel. Hanukkah* is the Hebrew word for "a dedicating." It is also spelled *Chanukah* and is called *The Feast of Lights* and *The Feast of Dedication. See* MENORAH.

hardie A common name in the New York area for a hard-shell blue claw crab. A soft-shell blue claw is often called a *softie*.

Hard Rock *See* BLACK ROCK.

Harlem A section of New York City in northeast Manhattan that has largely been populated by African Americans since World War I. Harlem was named in Dutch colonial days after the city of Haarlem in the Netherlands. After the war it was the site of the *Harlem Renaissance,* a renewal and flourishing of black culture, especially in literature and music. *See* SUGAR HILL.

Hart Island Named for Peter Hart, a New York City policeman and hero of the Civil War, this East River Island, off City Island in the Bronx, has been the home since 1869 of New York City's Potter's Field, or city cemetery, where the city's unknown

and unwanted poor are buried. The dead are taken to the potter's field from City Island by the "Last Ferry" and buried in mass graves containing hundreds of cheap pine coffins. Few New Yorkers have been to Hart Island, and few would want to go there, before or after death. It is a dreary, barren place where little respect is shown for the dead, and where their bones, called *leather* by the Riker's Island prisoners who do the burying, are frequently washed to the surface of the graves after heavy rains.

Hasidim Members of a movement of popular mysticism founded in Eastern Europe in the 18th century. Their name derives from the Hebrew word *hasidh,* "pious." The Hasidic movement was founded by the mystic Israel ben Eliezer (Baal-Shem-Tov), who taught that simple faith and joyous worship are more important than learning and religious formalities, among many other precepts. There are a number of Hasidic communities in New York, especially in Brooklyn. The word is also spelled *Chasidim*.

have a catch New York youngsters usually *have a catch* when they go out to throw a ball around, not *play catch* as kids do in other parts of the country.

have half a heat on To be half drunk. "In fact, she is nothing but an old haybag . . . and in all these years I seldom see her but what she seems *to have about half a heat on* from drinking gin." (Runyon, "Madame La Gimp")

haybag An old-fashioned term for a slovenly woman; a woman hobo. "She is nothing but an old haybag, and generally ginned up." (Runyon, *Guys and Dolls*)

hazarae Yiddish for junk or trash of any kind, including food, books, movies, cheap goods, etc. "I don't want hazarae like that in my store."

headline Newspaper headlines are an American invention, the first one appearing in the Tory *New York Gazette* on October 20, 1777. Fortunately for the United States, the headline was all wrong:

> Glorious News from the Southward. Washington Knocked up—The Bloodiest Battle in America—6000 of his Men Gone—100 Wagons to Carry the Wounded—General Howe is at Present in Germantown—Washington 30 miles Back in a Shattered Condition—Their Stoutest Frigate Taken and One Deserted—They are Tired—And Talk of Finishing the Campaign.

heavy cruiser A hardbitten, tough-looking prostitute. *Cruiser* has been a New York term for a prostitute since the mid-19th century.

Hebe An offensive name for a Jew first recorded in 1932. A shortening of *Hebrew*.

he eats babies Said of a vicious killer. "The gang . . . was formed in 1890 under the leadership of Raymond the Wolf. He ate babies. Raymond the Wolf passed away in his sleep one night from natural causes;

his heart stopped beating when three men who slipped into his bedroom stuck knives in it." (Jimmy Breslin, *The Gang That Couldn't Shoot Straight,* 1969)

Heinz's 57 varieties John Heinz, the original Mr. (Henry John) Heinz, forebear of the millionaire senator John Heinz, adapted his company's famous slogan from a New York City billboard ad he saw featuring "21 Styles of Shoes." Heinz actually had 60 varieties of assorted products and condiments at the time he coined the slogan in 1896, but he thought an odd number sounded better. The company used its "57" slogan until 1969.

Hell's Hundred Acres A name in the early 19th century for what is now SoHo in Manhattan; of unknown origin. *See* SOHO.

Hell's Kitchen There are several theories about the term's origin, but the following letter from John H. Knubel to the editor of the *New York Herald Tribune* on January 25, 1942, gives an interesting, unusual derivation of the name:

> Years ago on thirty-ninth street between tenth and eleventh avenues there existed a combination "Beer Saloon and Restaurant" conducted by a German and his wife with the name of "Heil" and having a sign on the front reading "Heil's Kitchen" where patrons were served with various dishes, the most popular being pigs knuckles and sauerkraut accompanied by a very large glass of good beer, which was extremely to the liking of those in the neighborhood and from others . . .

When the "rough" boys wished to partake of the above or other food they would call out to one another, "Let's go down to 'Heil's Kitchen,'" not pronouncing the name "Heil" properly, through an innocent error or by deliberate [mis]pronunciation, as it may have been more musical to their ears, and this name consequently had to be borne by the neighborhood to this day.

helluva   A compression of *hell of a,* which itself dates back to the 18th century. *Helluva* seems to have first been recorded in George S. Chappell's novel *The Younger Married Set* (1926), according to William Safire in his *On Language* column (*New York Times Magazine,* September 7, 1996). Also pronounced *helluvuh,* it can express irritation, as in "That's a helluva thing to say," or even admiration, "That's a helluva halavah they make."

Hemlock Forest   A virgin forest in the Bronx, of all places, Bronx Park to be exact, containing some 3,000 trees. New York City, according to several sources, still has more trees than buildings!

here   Often heard as a superfluous interjection, as in "This here book is mine."

hero   New Yorkers, too, have their special names for things. That long sandwich crammed with edibles on Italian or French bread and called a *poor boy* in the South and a *grinder* in New England is a *hero* in most of the metropolitan New York speech area.

Other New York names for the comestible include *Italian sandwich,* much less used, *Italian hero,* and the derogatory *Guinea hero* and *Guinea sandwich.*

hersted   A pronunciation of *hoisted* heard in New York.

her (his) stomach thinks her (his) throat is cut   Said of someone very hungry, starving. "'. . . the best thing to do right now is to throw a feed into her, as the chances are her stomach thinks her throat is cut.'" (Runyon, "Little Miss Marker")

highbinder   A highbinder can be a swindler and cheat, especially a confidence man, or a gangster or rowdy. The word, first used in its latter meaning, derives from a gang of ruffians called the *Highbinders* that plagued New York City about 1800. Later their name was applied (in the lower case) to members of American-Chinese secret societies believed to be employed in blackmail and assassination.

high hat   Jack Conway, a former baseball player and vaudevillian, who became editor of the New York show business newspaper *Variety,* coined the expression *high hat* for a snob in 1924. It suggests an affected rich or nouveau riche man in a high silk hat and tails strolling about town with his nose in the air almost as high as his hat. The term gave birth to the expression to *high hat,* to snub or act patronizingly. *See* PALOOKA.

High Hill   *See* TODT HILL.

him   Very often used in place of *his*, as in "I don't like him being here," instead of "I don't like his being here."

hindu!   A cry of foul in the game of boxball and Chinese handball. *Hindu!* (probably a corruption of *hinder*) was cried out if the ball accidentally hit an object or went out of play because of some other interference. Today *Do over!* is usually heard instead.

hitching   In the 1940s *hitching* meant not only putting your thumb out for a ride from a passing car, but catching onto the bumper of a car or truck while on your sled and getting a ride through city streets that way, a practice definitely not to be recommended. (How did we survive our childhood?)

hit in the kishkas   To hit someone in the stomach. *Kishka* is Russian for "intestines." The word came to describe a sausage-like food of the Jewish cookery and finally suggested the Yiddish expression above.

hitter   An assassin or hit man. "'. . . this much I know, if you guys can double your pressure on every joint operating in the five boroughs, I think it's possible that somebody might give you the hitter.'" (Condon, *Prizzi's Honor*)

hit the hammer   To push the accelerator pedal in a car to the floor to make it go very fast or as fast as it can.

hizzonah   A pronunciation of *his honor* (de Mayah).

hobboh   *See* BONAC.

Hoboken   For no good reason the New Jersey city across the river from New York has been the butt of jokes for over a century, just the mention of its name getting a laugh. Hackensack and Secaucus (once noted for its pig farms) have had much the same trouble.

hoid   A pronunciation of *heard* or *herd*.

Holland Tunnel   The tunnel connecting lower Manhattan and Jersey City has nothing to do with Holland or the Dutch. It is named for the great chief engineer who designed it: Clifford M. Holland. The tunnel opened in 1927.

holler New York   Used in other areas for *vomit*. "He was hollering New York."

holly   A common mispronunciation of *challa* (KHAHL-leh), a braided glazed white bread of Jewish cuisine. *Challa* is the Hebrew word for the bread.

hook   1) *See* DIP. 2) *See* GIVE 'EM THE HOOK.

hoople   *See* HACKIE.

hootoadjuh?   Who told you? A pronunciation recorded in the Federal Writers' Project *Almanac for New Yorkers* (1938).

Horseshoe Bend   See quote. "Jackie Dunne is from the Horseshoe Bend section of Jersey City, which is perhaps the world's leading supplier of Irish gunmen." (Breslin, *The Gang That Couldn't Shoot Straight*)

Hosackia   *See* ELGIN GARDENS.

hot dog   A mainstay of sports cuisine, *hot dogs* were probably first served at a sports event at New York's Polo Grounds. According to concessionaire Harry Stevens, who first served grilled franks on a heated roll there in 1901, the franks were dubbed *hot dogs* by that prolific word inventor and sports cartoonist T. A. Dorgan after he sampled them at a Giants ballgame; but Dorgan may only have popularized the word. Dorgan, or whoever invented *hot dog,* possibly had in mind the fact that many people believed *frankfurters* were made from dog meat at the time, and possibly had heard Stevens's vendors crying out "Get your hot dogs!," leading the indignant Coney Island chamber of commerce to ban the use of the term *hot dog* by concessionaires there (they could be called only *Coney Islands, red hots* and *frankfurters*). *Hot dog!* became an ejaculation of approval by 1906 and is still heard occasionally. *Hot dog* is also a term for a *grandstanding* baseball player or other crowd-pleasing athletes.

Hotel Underwood   A nickname for the Coney Island boardwalk, underneath which was a popular courting place. Also applied to the Rockaway's 5½-mile boardwalk in Queens.

houghmagandy   See quote. "'His lawyer probably advised him to quit the houghmagandy till we reach a [divorce] settlement.' 'What's houghmagandy?' Mollie asked. 'Hanky-panky,' Heather said." (Hunter, *Criminal Conversation*)

House That Ruth Built   A name for Yankee Stadium, which Babe Ruth made famous.

housink   A pronunciation of *housing* in the New York area. "She lived in a New York housink project."

Howard Beach wait   See quote. "When speaking on the phone, people developed what became known as the Howard Beach wait. Every twenty seconds the one on the phone had to say 'Wait a minute' and let the plane go over the house." (Jimmy Breslin, *He Got Hungry and Forgot His Manners,* 1988) The wait is for the jets landing at and taking off from John F. Kennedy International Airport, their flight paths often directly over Howard Beach. The same could be said of all the communities bordering JFK. Some seven miles to the east in Nassau County, the village of Cedarhurst is noted for what is called *Cedarhurst Alley,* a flight path directly over the residential community.

how 'bout that   *See* GOING, GOING . . . GONE.

how come? Bartlett's *Dictionary of Americanisms* (1848) says *how come?* is "Doubtless an English phrase, brought over by the original settlers . . . the meaning . . . [being] How did what you tell me happen? How came it?" Others opt for the Dutch *hockum,* "why," which the "original settlers" heard in New Amsterdam.

howda A pronunciation of *how to. See quote under* TING.

hows about An excrescent "z" sound is frequently added to the expression *how about,* as in "Hows about coming wid me to the party."

how they hangin' A greeting among men, short for "How are your balls hanging?" "'Hey, Cholly!' Pop said. 'How they hangin'?'" (Condon, *Prizzi's Honor*)

howzigohin? A common New York pronunciation of "how's it going?"

Hoyt is hoit! The immortal words of that anonymous Brooklyn Dodger broadcaster who on a linguistically memorable day at Ebbets Field in the 1930s saw that pitcher Waite Hoyt was knocked down by a line drive and exclaimed: "Oh, no—Hoyt is hoit!"

hozzabotutbabe Hows about it, babe. "A prelude to romance," a pronunciation recorded in the Federal Writers' Project *Almanac for New Yorkers* (1938).

Hudson River 1) Named for Henry Hudson, English explorer for hire who in 1609 sailed for the Dutch East India Company on the *Half Moon* trying to find a new route to the Indies and explored the river that now bears his name. His name was not Hendrick Hudson as is widely believed. The confusion probably resulted because Dutch explorer Hendrick Christiaensen was the first to sail the river after him and made numerous voyages to the Hudson from 1610 to 1616, when he was killed by an Indian near Albany. *See also* VERRAZANO BRIDGE. 2) *See* NORTH RIVER.

huh A pronunciation of *her.* "I'm not talkin' to you, I'm talkin' to huh."

Hymie; Hymietown *Hymie* is an insulting name for a Jew, from the often Jewish name *Hyman. Hymietown,* similarly, is a derogatory name for New York City, home to many Jews. The Reverend Jesse Jackson used these words in private conversation during his campaign for the Democratic presidential nomination in 1984, causing great national controversy. He apologized for his language, insisting that he had not believed the words were anti-Semitic.

icebox Still used by some older New Yorkers who owned real iceboxes in earlier times. Today, out of habit, they call refrigerators *iceboxes.*

icky 1) Used to describe anything overly sweet, or sickeningly sentimental, especially music. 2) Something sticky, such as candy stuck on one's hands or face.

ID To identify. "He ID'ed himself as a cop and went inside."

Idaho baked potato Strangely enough, this well-known brand name was made famous by a New York department store "taster." William Titon, better known as Titon the Taster, worked 60 years for Macy's and was the store's final authority on all groceries, wines and liquors. Among other accomplishments, Titon discovered the Idaho potato in 1926 while buying apples for Macy's and promoted it until the spud's name became synonymous with baked potato, for which Idaho's governor wrote a letter of thanks to the store.

idear A pronunciation of *idea;* New Yorkers often add an *r* in such words, another example being *sofa;* pronounced SO-fer.

Idlewild A former name for John F. Kennedy International Airport. *See* KENNEDY.

if Often omitted in dependent clauses, as in "She asked him would he go" instead of "She asked him if he would go." One of many New York shortcuts.

if I can't dance, it's not my revolution The expression originated with the American anarchist Emma Goldman in the early 1900s. She supposedly said this when her lover and fellow anarchist Alexander Berkman berated her one night for dancing wildly in a radical Village hangout. Copublisher of the anarchist paper *Mother Earth* with Berkman, Goldman was deported to Russia in 1919 but left that country two years later after a disagreement with communist authorities.

"If We Must Die" Claude McKay, a Jamaican who immigrated to the

85

United States, worked as a waiter for many years while writing his poems, stories and novels. His poem "If We Must Die" was written in reaction to the 1919 Harlem race riots, but its stirring words of resistance were chosen 20 years later as a World War II rallying cry by both Senator Henry Cabot Lodge Jr., who read the poem into the *Congressional Record,* and Prime Minister Winston Churchill, who read it to the British people.

if you can make it in New York, you can make it anywhere Probably coined by a New Yorker, this phrase dates back at least 30 years, possibly more. It was popularized in the song "New York, New York," written by Fred Ebb and John Kander and recorded by Liza Minelli in 1977 and by Frank Sinatra in 1980.

if you can't do the time, don't do the crime See quote. "Easy time . . . If you can't do the time, don't do the crime. That's what they say on the yard." (Hamill, *Flesh and Blood*)

if you'll pardon the expression Frequently used apologetically to preface any remark the speaker thinks is indelicate or prying, etc.

I have seen the future and it works Muckraking New York writer Lincoln Steffens made a trip to Russia in 1919. Upon meeting financier Bernard Baruch after his return, Steffens made his famous remark about Communist Russia. "I have seen the future and it works." Actually, his exact words were, "I have been over into the future, and it works." Steffens's companion on the trip to Russia, William Bullitt, claimed that Steffens's remark wasn't spontaneous, that he had invented it even before he set foot on Russian soil.

I'll be a turkey's asshole! A recent variation on *I'll be damned.* "'Well I'll be a turkey's asshole!' Jo Ann screamed. 'Thas where I found it.'" (Sapphire, *Push*)

I'm gonna make him (her, etc.) an offer he (she, etc.) can't refuse Used jokingly today, but popularized by the film version of Mario Puzo's *The Godfather* (1972) when the godfather, played by Marlon Brando, uses it as a veiled threat. One of his confederates tells him that a certain Hollywood producer will never give his godson an important part in a movie he is making. "I'm gonna make him an offer he can't refuse," the godfather says, implying the potential of violence to the producer.

in a New York minute Very quickly, in a heartbeat.

Indian burn The pain resulting from the act of grabbing someone's wrist or forearm with both hands and twisting the skin in opposite directions. This mean trick has been inflicted by kids upon each other for many a generation. So far as is known the practice did not originate with any Indian tribe.

I (he, she, etc.) need it like a hole in the head A common expression influenced by Yiddish that is said of something totally disagreeable. "More taxes? I need it like a hole in the head." Much stronger than the similar *Who needs it?* or *This I need yet?*

infamita   Italian used in the Mafia for a terrible thing to do, a violation of the code, a sin. "'The brother is right. It would be an infamita to lay hands on her.'" (Condon, *Prizzi's Money*)

infattago   A pronunciation of the common children's skin disease *impetigo*.

in line   *See* ON LINE.

innarupted   A pronunciation of *interrupted*. "'It looks like we coulda just innarupted a mob hit.'" (Condon, *Prizzi's Money*)

intiment   Often a pronunciation of *intimate*.

intimidatore   An enforcer. "[Violente's] second man was Joey Cloacacino. Violente, who was the chief intimidatore of the Prizzi family, would have frightened Siegfreid, El Cid . . . or Arnold Schwarzenegger. . . ." (Condon, *Prizzi's Money*) (Incidentally, Condon's last name for Joey translates as "little sewer.")

in your hat   Short for "shit in your hat." "'Ah, in your hat, Charley, and right down over your ears.' She hung up heavily." (Condon, *Prizzi's Honor*)

I only regret that I have but one life to give for my country   The last words that American spy Nathan

Hale supposedly said on the New York City gallows before he was hanged by the British. According to the recently discovered diary of British officer Captain Frederick Mackenzie, what he really said was "It is the duty of every good officer to obey any orders given him by his commander-in-chief." Hale was executed on September 22, 1776. British author Joseph Addison's play *Cato* (1713) has the words "What pity it is that we can die but once to serve our country."

I really appreciate it   New Yorkers are not nearly so rude as they are portrayed. Instead of a simple "thank you," New Yorkers will often say, "I really appreciate it."

Irish fight   An all-out, no-holds-barred brawl, a donnybrook.

Irish tea   Tea strongly seasoned with whiskey.

Irishtown   An old term, not heard much since the 1960s or so, for an area, often with a great number of bars or saloons, where there is a large Irish-American population. One that comes to mind is the 10–20 block area around the now demolished Rockaway Playland in Queens, not far from Brooklyn. The bars were noted for a lot of drinking, talking, singing, arguing and fighting. In some other states Irishtowns have been called *Dublins,* but I've never heard that term in New York.

Irish turkey   A humorous term for corned beef and cabbage.

Iron Horse New York Yankee first baseman Lou Gehrig, who played in 2,130 consecutive games and was also called *The Pride of the Yankees. The Iron Horse* died in 1941 of a rare spinal disease named *Lou Gehrig's disease* after him.

I say it's spinach and I say the hell with it E. B. White wrote the caption that became this catchphrase for a 1928 Carl Rose cartoon in the *New Yorker* showing a spoiled little girl who rejects her mother's offer of broccoli with these words. The phrase has come to mean, "When I'm indulging my prejudices, I don't want to be confused with facts." The phrase's abbreviated form, *spinach*, however, means the same as *baloney, malarkey, bull*, etc.

ish kabibble An old term, its origin unknown, that means I should worry, I couldn't care less, etc. In the 1940s trumpet player–comedian Merwyn Bogue in Kay Kyser's band was featured as Ish Kabibble, giving the term wide currency.

I should have such luck A common expression probably influenced by Yiddish.

I should worry A common term, possibly Yiddish in origin, meaning it's not my concern, I don't care. *See* ISH KABIBBLE.

I shuddah stood in bed widda doctor! A classic example of pure early Brooklynese. Rarely, if ever, heard anymore, but there may be a Brook-lyn legion of angels flying around mouthing the economical words, which translate roughly as: "I should have stayed in bed this morning and had the doctor make a house call to treat me instead of being here (at work, etc.)." *See* STOOD; WE WUZ ROBBED!

I swear on my mother's eyes! An old mob oath still used today.

Italian Geography See quote.

> As a reporter, however, he is considered an expert in what is known as Italian Geography . . . Italian Geography is the keeping of huge amounts of information on gangsters: the price they pay for clothes, the restaurants in which they eat, the names of all relatives out to the fifth cousins, their home addresses, and their visible daily movements. (Breslin, *The Gang That Couldn't Shoot Straight*)

Italian ice Used frequently in the New York City area for smooth crushed ices infused with fruit-flavored syrup that are sold by street vendors and in stores. Also called an *ice*.

Italian pepper In New York City this does not mean a round bell pepper but a long (4–6 inches) green or red pepper. It can be sweet or hot.

Italian sandwich Very infrequently used for a hero sandwich made with Italian cold cuts and cheese.

It Does Not Soil the Breakfast Cloth *See* NEW YORK TIMES.

itch A nickname for any old, run-down movie theater. "In fact, most people in the parish called it The Itch, implying that you could get fleas just by sitting on its hard seats." (Hamill, *Snow in August*)

it doesn't go on all fours   Unlike similar Madison Avenue expressions, this saying, meaning "something isn't quite right," goes back to the ancient Latin proverb *Omnis comparatio claudicat,* which literally means "every simile limps," but which British historian Thomas Babington Macaulay translated as "No simile can go on all fours."

it shouldn't happen to a dog   A common saying lamenting a person's extremely bad luck. The expression probably derives from or was influenced by Yiddish.

it's how you played the game   New York sportswriter Grantland Rice who coined the term the *Four Horsemen* to describe Notre Dame's famous backfield in an account of a Notre Dame–Army game ("Outlined against a blue-gray October sky, the Four Horsemen rode again . . .") is also responsible for *it's how you played the game*. The much loved writer, who died in 1954 at the age of 73, first recorded the expression in a poem he published in one of his "The Sportlight" columns:

> When the One Great Scorer comes
> To mark against your name,
> He writes—not that you won or lost—
> But how you played the game.

it's o.k. by me   A New York idiom that probably has its roots in Yiddish and means *it's all right with me, I approve.*

jabronie An old term, origin unknown, for a stupid, clumsy or inept person. Also pronounced *jiboney*.

Jack Robinson Contrary to popular belief, the saying *as quick as you can say Jack Robinson* has no connection with Brooklyn Dodger Jackie Robinson, the first black major league baseball player, although Jackie Robinson was quick enough to beat out many a bunt and to steal many a base. Notable attempts have been made to trace this 18th-century British phrase, all unsuccessful. One popular explanation has the saying's origin in the habit a certain Jack Robinson had of paying extraordinarily quick visits to his friends, the gentleman leaving even before his name could be announced. But *Jack Robinson* was probably used in the phrase simply because it is a very common name in England and is easy to pronounce.

jalettum A pronunciation heard in New York for *did you let him*. "Jalettum go to the movies?"

jeet An amazing condensation of *did you eat* that would make a *Reader's Digest* editor proud. "Jeet jet? Les gedda frank."

jeez! A euphemism for *Jesus* that is frequently used as an interjection by New York speakers, as in "Jeez! I didn't recognize you."

jerk around To take advantage of, con, lie to, etc. "'You dumb fucken shit, this ain't *me* you're jerkin around, this is Frankie Palumbo whose money you bet.'" (Hunter, *Criminal Conversation*)

Jesus H. Christ! Though it is not noted in the *Dictionary of American Regional English*, this oath has long been common in the New York City area.

Jesus, Mary and Joseph! A common exclamation, especially among Irish Catholics. "Dolores's mother blessed herself. 'Jesus, Mary, and Joseph, to think that kind of money.'" (Breslin, *Table Money*)

jever? Did you ever. "Jever see anythin' like that?"

Jewel of Cities   A nickname for New York or Manhattan.

Jewish penicillin   A humorous term for homemade chicken soup common almost since the invention of penicillin.

Jewish pickles   A kosher dill pickle. Also called a *Jewish dill* and a *Kosher dill*.

JFK airport   *See* KENNEDY.

jih-drool   An Italian expression meaning a fool, dope, jerk. "'So who is this jih-drool, you're goin' out on a limb for him?'" (Hunter, *Criminal Conversation*)

Jim-Dandy   No particular Jim Dandy seems to be the eponym behind the century-old term *Jim-Dandy*, which is still heard for someone or something that is especially fine or admirable. *The Dictionary of Americanisms* traces the term back to January 1887, but not in a sports context. Etymologist Gerald Cohen has cited a published sports usage of it some six months later in a New York Giants game, indicating a possible New York baseball origin.

jive-ass   Mainly a black term, with some white usage, for a lying, false, ignorant person, someone almost totally worthless. "Get out of here, you jive-ass motherfucker!"

Joe Echo   A feature of New York speech that seems to be fading now but led to the popular designation of

Joe Echo 100 years ago. People known as *Joe Echoes* (or *Johnny Echoes, Eddie Echoes*, etc.) in late 19th- and early 20th-century New York weren't so called because they echoed *other* people's words. Those bearing this common nickname, usually the offspring of poor, recent immigrants, often echoed *themselves* in sentences such as *I betcha ya can't do it, I betcha*, or *I tell ya it's mine, I tell ya!*

John   Slang for a prostitute's client, said to have originated from the habit of 19th-century New York City prostitutes of calling every prospective customer "Johnny."

John F. Kennedy International Airport   *See* KENNEDY.

Johnny on a pony   The name of a game played by older children.

> There are two teams, usually of five or six boys each. The first team is the Pony, the second is Johnny. The Pony team lines up this way: One member stands upright with his back braced against a tree [or wall, etc.]; then the second player bends down, thrusts his head into the first person's stomach, and grabs him tightly around the waist. The next bends down, placing his head between the legs of player 2 and grabbing him tightly around the thighs. Players 4, 5 and 6 repeat what number 3 did. The whole team then braces. The Johnny team . . . races at them, one at a time, and vaults atop the row of backs as far forward as he can, shouting "Johnny on a pony, one, two, three!" The object is to cave in the backs of the Pony team. If the jumping team can do that, the other must brace themselves again for the

onslaught. If they hold and support all the members of the other team, then that team becomes the Pony and the jumpers have to bend over. (Fred Ferretti, *The Great American Book of Sidewalk Games*, 1975)

Johnston Smith Stephen Crane published at his own expense his first novel, *Maggie: A Girl of the Streets* (1893), borrowing the money from his brother and issuing it under the pseudonym Johnston Smith (the two most frequently listed names in the New York telephone book.) The grim paperbound novel, set in a New York neighborhood called Rum Alley, sold just two copies. However, Crane, who shared a small rundown studio apartment with three young artists, was practical enough to put the unsold copies to some use. One cold winter's night he used a pile of them to start a fire in his room.

Joisy A pronunciation of *Jersey*, as in "New Joisy."

Joltin' Joe A nickname for New York Yankee centerfielder Joe Di-Maggio, one of baseball's greatest players, who hit safely in 56 consecutive games, a record that still stands. The popular song "Joltin' Joe Di-Maggio" was written in his honor. DiMaggio was also called the *Yankee Clipper*, both for the way he "clipped" the ball and for his grace as a fielder, moving as effortlessly as a clipper ship, or possibly the popular Yankee Clipper airline of the 1930s, across the field to make even the hard catches seem easy.

Joosh A pronunciation of *Jewish*. "She had brought in a dinner from the delicatessen: boiled ham, potato salad, Joosh rye, a six-pack . . . and a gang of coleslaw." (Condon, *Prizzi's Money*)

juhhirmee A pronunciation of *do you hear me*. "Juhhirme this noise? So now y'know I godda thousand dollars wortha CD's, when I go way some people insure clothes, on gana sure my music." This was heard on the Eighth Avenue subway line.

jujubes A favorite candy in New York and elsewhere over the past 100 years, especially as a "movie candy" because there were so many of them, enough to last through the entire show (at one time two pictures, a serial or two, cartoons and a newsreel). The candy has been made by Henry Heide, Inc. since 1869; the company was first located on Hudson Street in Manhattan. Heide also makes the popular Gummie Bears.

juice man A collector for the mob.

juke To stab or kill someone with a knife. "'Even a *knife* costs money [the policeman said], what d'you think? A person's gonna throw it away cause he just *juked* someone with it? Don't be ridiculous. There's switchblades cost fifty, a hundred bucks." (McBain, *Romance*)

keeab A pronunciation of *cab*.

keepers A name dating back to at least the 1940s for a game of marbles in which the marbles won in the game are kept. One plays "for keeps."

keeping up with the Joneses According to his own account, New York cartoonist Arthur "Pop" Momand (1887–1987) lived in a community where many people tried to keep up with the Joneses. Momand and his wife resided in Cedarhurst, New York, one of Long Island's *Five Towns,* where the average income is still among America's highest. Living "far beyond our means in our endeavor to keep up with the well-to-do class," the Momands were wise enough to quit the scene and move to Manhattan, where they rented a cheap apartment and "Pop" Momand used his Cedarhurst experience to create his once immensely popular *Keeping Up with the Joneses* comic strip, launched in 1913. Momand first thought of calling the strip "Keeping Up With The Smiths," but "finally decided on Keeping Up With The Joneses as being more euphonious." His creation ran in American newspapers for over 28 years and appeared in book, movie and musical-comedy form, giving the expression wide currency that made it a part of everyday language. Apparently not trying to keep up with the Joneses served Momand well, for he lived to be 100.

keep your nose out of the gutter Don't drink so much that you get drunk.

Kennedy This is most common name for John F. Kennedy International Airport in Queens bordering Jamaica Bay and the Rockaways. The airport was named for President John F. Kennedy after his assassination in 1963. It is also frequently called *JFK,* and many people still occasionally think of it as Idlewild, its original name when it was a small airport bordered by truck farms.

kerchief *See* BABUSHKA.

kielbasa A name in New York and other areas for spicy Polish pork sausage; from the Polish name for the sausage.

Killers Gat Found   *See NEW YORK DAILY NEWS.*

King Kong   Old slang for any strong drink.

King of Storytellers   *See* BAGDAD ON THE HUDSON.

Kings County   Kings County, better known as Brooklyn, takes its official name from King Charles II, who was king of England when it was named. *See* BOROUGH; BRONX; NEW YORK COUNTY; QUEENS COUNTY; RICHMOND.

king's man   A mob member so well positioned that he can go directly to the boss without going through intermediaries.

kishkas   1) A Yiddish word for the stomach or guts. "He hit him in the kishkas." 2) A Polish or Jewish sausage.

kiss the canvas   To be knocked out in a prizefight; by extension, to lose at anything. A phrase probably dating back to the 1920s that is also heard as *kiss the resin.*

klutz   Originally a Yiddish term, deriving from the German *klotz,* "a log or block of wood." *Klutz* describes a clumsy, graceless person; a bungler; a fool. A *klutz,* however, can be an intelligent person, just someone

badly coordinated. The adjective *klutzy* is also widely heard.

Knickerbocker Rules   Baseball's first codified rules; adopted by the New York Knickerbockers baseball team in 1845. *See* FATHER KNICKERBOCKER.

knockdown   Mob talk for a demotion within the ranks, as when a *capo* is demoted to *soldier* when he fouls up the mob's business.

k'nocker   A Yiddish expression pronounced with the *k* a separate sound) meaning a boastful big shot, a showoff. It is said to derive from the German *knocker,* "someone who cracks a whip."

know from nothing   To know nothing at all about something, or to know nothing about the true nature of something, as in "He's read all the books on it, but knows from nothing." Probably Yiddish in origin.

kosher   In *The Joys of Yiddish* (1968) Leo Rosten calls *kosher* "the most resourceful Yiddish word in the English language." It derives from the Hebrew *kasher,* "fit, appropriate," and strictly means fit to eat according to Jewish dietary laws, but by extension in English can mean authentic, trustworthy and legal, among various other shades of meaning. It is often heard in expressions such as "that's not kosher," that's not right or legal.

Koster & Bial's Music Hall   *See* WORLD'S LARGEST STORE.

kreplach A type of Jewish dumpling often served in soup. The word derives from the German *kreppel* meaning roughly the same.

kuduh A pronunciation of *could have,* as in "I kuduh come over."

kugel A dish of noodle pudding famous in Jewish cookeries. In German the word strictly means the pan in which the dish is cooked.

kvetch Very common as both a noun, for a chronic complainer, someone who complains about the smallest things, and a verb meaning to complain incessantly about such things ("Stop your kvetching, will you?"). From the German *quetschen,* "to squeeze, pinch." Pronounced kuh-VETCH.

ladderide   Let it ride. "A warning not to pursue the matter further," a pronunciation recorded in the Federal Writers' Project *Almanac for New Yorkers,* 1938.

Ladies's Mile   A. T. Stewart's Cast-Iron Palace, built in 1862, was the first store encountered when walking north along *Ladies's Mile.* At the top of this stretch of lower Broadway and Sixth Avenue between Ninth and Twenty-third Streets was Stern Brothers. Many early department stores, such as R. H. Macy's, Lord and Taylor and B. Altman, lined the elegant, cobblestoned streets of this shopping district, which played host daily to exquisitely clad ladies in flowing gowns and feathered bonnets who alighted from their horse-drawn carriages and floated toward the grand emporiums. Women promenaded in their best here up until the end of the century, when the shopping district began to move uptown, but many of the old buildings that housed the stores remain. The women who strolled there may have inspired the phrase *window-shopping.*

Lafayette   An old New York name for *Leiostomus xanthurus,* often called the *spot* elsewhere. The pretty little fish was named after the French Marquis de Lafayette, who aided the American cause during the Revolution.

La Guardia Airport   *See* LITTLE FLOWER.

lamb   A name, among confidence men and police, for a victim or dupe of a confidence game. *Mark* and *patsy* are also used.

large   1) Money, big money. "'. . . money buys the dream . . . And the bigger the dream, the more of the large you'll need.'" (Hamill, *Flesh and Blood*) 2) A thousand dollars. "It cost me two large to get rid of him."

Latino   A man born in Latin America or of Latin American descent. *Latina* is the feminine form. The terms are an alternative to *Hispanic,* which applies also to Spaniards and people of Spanish descent and hence acknowledges the Spanish (imperial) presence in Latin America.

latke In Jewish cookery a pancake, usually one made of grated potatoes. Ultimately from a Russian word meaning about the same.

launder *See* BLACK MONEY.

lawyer with his briefcase can steal more than a hundred men with guns A favorite saying of Don Corleone in Mario Puzo's *The Godfather* (1969).

laydown Sally Someone who doesn't fight back, who will take any kind of abuse lying down. "He's a real laydown Sally."

lay on the romance To romance someone. *See quote under* GLADDA.

l'chayim A well-known toast, the Hebrew meaning "to life." Also spelled *le-hayyim.*

lease Least. "At lease, that's what I think."

leather A wallet. ". . . it seems that somewhere on this ride the sailor loses his leather containing a month's salary . . ." (Runyon, "The Brakeman's Daughter") *See also* HART ISLAND.

leave Often used in place of *let,* as in "Leave me alone."

leave flat To desert a friend or friends to go off with someone else or to do something better; often used among kids since the 1930s. "'We

didn't leave you flat, Michael,' Jimmy said." (Hamill, *Snow in August*)

Leaves of Grass Walt Whitman self-published the first edition of his famous book of poems in 1855, setting it in type himself on the printing press of Andrew and James Rome in Brooklyn. The book contained 12 poems on 95 pages, about 1,000 books printed. Whitman also wrote glowing reviews of the poems that he placed anonymously in several periodicals. Other famous books self-published in New York include Washington Irving's *History of New York* (1809) by "Diedrich Knickerbocker," and Stephen Crane's first novel *Maggie: A Girl of the Streets* (1893).

left tit The heart; courage. "'And he taps his heart, you know. He says it depends if you got the heart. The desire. The left tit . . .'" (Pete Hamill, *Blood and Money,* 1977)

lemmeawf Heard in the New York vicinity for *let me off.* "I asked the bus driver to lemmeawf at the next stop."

lemon man An old synonym for a pool shark, especially among confidence men. The origin of the term is unclear.

Leo the Lip A nickname for Leo Durocher in the late 1940s when he managed the Brooklyn Dodgers. One time he threatened Brooklyn's arch rivals, the New York Giants, with the "cherce" Brooklynese: "It's gonna be Poil Hahbuh fuh de Gints." *See also*

NICE GUYS FINISH LAST; PRACTI-CALLY PEERLESS LEADER.

let's slip out of these clothes and into a dry martini A by-now proverbial quip by New York author and wit Robert Benchley. Benchley was known to drink; in fact, he was known to drink more and to be able to hold more than anyone in his circle. "What do you drink so much for?" F. Scott Fitzgerald, of all people, once lectured him. "Don't you know alcohol is slow poison?" "So who's in a hurry?" Benchley replied. *See* MEN SELDOM MAKE PASSES / AT GIRLS WHO WEAR GLASSES.

Lex A verbal shortcut for Lexington Avenue in Manhattan. "Where's his store?" "It's over on Lex."

lezgehgohen A pronunciation of *let's get going.*

Liberty Enlightening the World
See STATUE OF LIBERTY.

life 1) *The life* is term for mob life in the Mafia. 2) The life of prostitution.

life is just one damned thing after another A phrase said to have been invented by *New York Sun* reporter Frank Ward O'Malley, who is also said to have coined the word *brunch. See* MOON HOAX.

like Frequently used excessively, as in "Like, it came in a box, like."

like Grand Central Station Very crowded, packed, hectic. In use since the early 1900s, the phrase refers to New York's Grand Central Terminal, where trains arrive and depart for many destinations, and the busy Grand Central subway stop in the terminal.

like in Macy's window A synonym for the ultimate in public exposure: "We'll be like in Macy's window." Traditional window displays date back to the early 1880s when the use of plate glass on a wide scale made display windows a standard feature of department stores. Macy's display windows in New York were long the most prominent among them, especially those in their flagship store on Thirty-fourth Street, "The World's Largest Store" with over 2.2 million square feet of floor space. In fact, Macy's old Fourteenth Street store in Manhattan was famous for its Christmas displays as far back as the mid-1800s, featuring a collection of toys revolving on a belt. *See also* DOES MACY'S TELL GIMBELS?

likewise Shorthand for "I feel the same way," etc. "'Please to meet you,' the Plumber said. 'Likewise,' said the driver." (Condon, *Prizzi's Honor*)

line *The line* refers to the odds bookmakers give for all the games played on a certain day.

the *li-on* is busy Stuart Berg Flexner tells us in *Listening to America* that this immortal intonation was first used at the Metropolitan Telephone and Telegraph Co.'s old Nassau exchange in New York City, by a Brooklyn-born operator around 1882. Dialing,

Touch-Tone phones and the decline and fall of Brooklynese have made the words rare, possibly obsolete.

lissina   Listen to. "'Eddie, lissina me,' she said." (Condon, *Prizzi's Money*)

Literary Walk   A section of Central Park near Sixty-seventh Street where there are statues of prominent writers such as William Shakespeare and Robert Burns.

Little Church Around the Corner
See BAGDAD ON THE HUDSON.

Little Christmas   Some sources list Little Christmas, another term for Epiphany, January 6, as a New England expression, but it has long been used in the New York City area as well.

Little Flower   A nickname for Fiorello La Guardia (1882–1947), who served as mayor of New York City from 1933 to 1945. Later, after La Guardia headed the American war relief administration in Korea, many Koreans named their newborns Lee Mi Wah, a literal translation of "Little Flower," in his honor. New York's La Guardia Airport is also named after the colorful mayor, who regularly read the Sunday comic strips, or "funnies," to New York kids on the city radio station.

little girls' (boys') room   The bathroom. "'I gotta go the little girl's room.'" (Condon, *Prizzi's Money*)

Little Odessa   Nickname of Brighton Beach, Brooklyn, where a large number of Russian immigrants live.

lobster roll   In Maine, a *lobster roll* is a sandwich made with lobster meat, but in New York City Chinese restaurants, it is essentially an egg roll filled with lobster meat, or at least some lobster meat. It is not as common as it was 40 years or so ago, if it can be found at all.

lockers   *Locker room,* for a changing room containing *lockers* in which to store one's clothes (not to get undressed in), is recorded as far back as 1890, but no dictionary of any kind, so far as I can determine, records the word *lockers* for "bathhouse." The *lockers* has meant bathhouse in the New York City area, especially in resort areas like Coney Island and the Rockaways, since at least the 1930s and probably before this. Someone might ask, for example, "Are you going to the lockers this year?" or "Are you taking a locker?" No one says, "Are you taking a bathhouse?" A *locker* here is a narrow wooden structure about 7–8 feet high attached to others identical to it in rows that are called aisles. There is barely enough room to change in a locker, although there are larger *family lockers.* Lockers are rented by the season or by the day. Keys are provided, but in case you don't have one available a *lockerboy* will open your locker with a pass key.

loin   A New York pronunciation of *learn.* "Will you please loin to speak correctly like me."

Looooo . . . It sounded like a boo, but it wasn't. This was the famous cheer New York Yankee fans used in recent memory to greet their great favorite Lou Piniella when he came to bat.

Lou Gehrig's disease A fatal paralytic disease, amyotrophic lateral sclerosis has been called Lou Gehrig's disease since the Yankee first baseman died of it in 1941. Known as the Iron Man, the Iron Horse and the Crown Prince (to Babe Ruth) of Swat, Gehrig played in 2,130 consecutive games for the Yankees before the disease took its toll.

lox Although *bagels* and *lox* are a staple of the Jewish cuisine, the dish is not a staple of long standing. Jews were generally introduced to lox in late 19th-century New York, and even today lox is not commonly to be found in Europe or Israel. Lox is so valued in New York that there have been cases of *counterfeit lox* made from other fish (notably *saithe* from Germany) treated with chemicals and food dyes and sold as the real thing. Real lox is a highly salted smoked salmon.

Lunk Guylin; Lung Guylin Pronunciations of *Long Island,* the island to the east of Manhattan that comprises the New York City boroughs of Brooklyn and Queens, as well as the separate political (suburban) entities of Nassau County and Suffolk County. Long Island is about 120 miles long and 23 miles wide.

machine politics Volunteer fire-men in the early 19th century learned to work smoothly as a team on the levers of water-pumping machines, and perhaps, as one investigator suggests, their teamwork and well-organized political associations suggested the term *machine politics* for this reason. Aaron Burr, who converted New York's patriotic Tammany Society into the politically powerful Tammany Hall, is often credited with inventing the phrase, but then so are Nathaniel Hawthorne and even the Duke of Wellington. The use of *machine* in a political sense, however, doesn't seem to have been recorded until 1865. *See* TAMMANY; TWEED RING.

made Often takes the place of a more specific verb, as in "She made like a dog," instead of "She barked like a dog."

made man *See* FRIEND OF OURS.

Madonna! A common exclamation. "'He says to me that his wife has him eat macaroni with American cheese on it out of a can. I says to him—*Madonna!*—you ought to put your wife's head in the oven.'" (Jimmy Breslin, *Forsaking All Others,* 1982)

Mad Poet of Broadway As evidenced by his book of verse, *Elixir of Moonshine by the Mad Poet* (1822), MacDonald Clarke (1798–1842) was known as "the Mad Poet of Broadway." The New York poet, among the first of American bohemians, drowned in the East River, possibly a suicide. Author of "The Rum Hole" (1835), in which a groghouse is "the horrible Light-House of Hell . . . built on a ledge of human bones, whose cement is of human blood." Clarke was eulogized by Walt Whitman, among others. The Mad Poet of Broadway had no illusions about achieving fame while he lived, as this epigram of his shows.

'Tis vain for present fame to wish.
Our persons first must be forgotten;
For poets are like stinking fish,
They never shine until they're rotten.

maff A pronunciation of *math* heard mainly among Afro-Americans. "'I don't want to miss no more of maff class,' I tell that stupid ass Mrs. Lichenstein." (Sapphire, *Push*)

105

Mafia See quote. ". . . the word Mafia had originally meant place of refuge. Then it became the name of the secret organization that sprang up to fight against the rulers that had crushed the country [Sicily] and its people for centuries." (Puzo, *The Godfather*) *See* BROTHERHOOD; COSA NOSTRA; OUTFIT.

mahosker Pay, money, paychecks. "'I mean the mahosker isn't here.' 'The what?' 'The checks. The company don't bring them here until after two.'" (Breslin, *Table Money*)

Maiden Lane According to Albert Ulmann, who wrote *Maiden Lane, The Story of a Single Street* (1931):

> There existed in the old days a rippling little stream that pursued its merry course along the curving path that has ever since marked the line of [Maiden Lane] . . . Directly or indirectly it was this very stream that led the old Dutch settlers . . . to bestow on the locality . . . the name of *I Maagde Paatje,* the Maiden's Path. According to one tradition, the housewives and their daughters congregated along the banks of the flowing water to wash the family linen . . . Another and more romantic tale pictured the grassy slope with its murmuring rivulet as a favorite retreat for lovesick maidens and their favorite swains; hence, the popular designation.

main man A term for one's favorite friend. "He's my main man."

make a bulba To make an error or a gaffe. *Bulba* is Polish for "potato," but the expression is Yiddish. "Boy, did he make a bulba!"

make book on it To count on, let on. "He'll be there—I'd make book on it."

make like To imitate. "Gimme a bat and I'll make like Micky Mantle."

make nice 1) To be friendly or show affection. 2) To be accommodating, curry favor.

make one's bones To kill one's first victim, become a *qualified man* in the Mafia. "He had started making his 'bones' at the age of seventeen, and what had made the deed even more impressive was he had done so with the garrote." (Puzo, *The Last Don*) *See also* QUALIFIED MAN.

make out An old term meaning to make love, usually in the sense of kissing and petting, lovemaking short of actual intercourse.

make whoopee *Whoopee!* has been a New Yorkism used to express of joy or approval since about 1860. However, it was apparently newspaper columnist Walter Winchell who coined the expression *making whoopee,* for "wild merrymaking"; the expression was then made very familiar by the popular song "Making Whoopee" (1930).

make with To use or exercise, as in "He's making with the voice again, but he can't sing a note." Possibly from the Yiddish expression *machen mit,* "swing something about."

Man *See* MR. CHARLIE.

man-hands Used to describe a beautiful woman whose brutish, overly masculine hands are her only flaw. "She's gorgeous, except for those man-hands of hers." Coined on the New York–inspired television comedy *Seinfeld*.

Manhattan The Algonquian Manhattan Indians who sold *Manhattan Island* to the Dutch for $24 in trinkets may have gotten the best of the deal. In the 1930s one statistician figured that if the Indians had invested their $24 at the prevailing interest rates, they would have had some $13 billion—$4 billion more than all the real estate in Manhattan was worth at the time. Of course Manhattan real estate is worth many times the $9 billion the statistician estimated in the '30s. The World Trade Center alone is worth about $1 billion.

Manhattan, since 1898, has been the name of New York's central borough and has always been a synonym for the real, though cosmopolitan, New York City itself. A *Manhattanite* is a resident of the borough of Manhattan.

Manhattan clam chowder A clam chowder made with tomatoes, not the milk base used in the traditional New England clam chowder. The term's origin is much disputed, some saying the dish is named *Manhattan clam chowder* because it was invented by one or another New Yorker in Manhattan, and others claiming it is so named because only New Yorkers would be crazy enough to use tomatoes in the soup instead of cream or milk. Doing so, incidentally, remains a heresy to some New Englanders. Some years ago one Maine state legislator introduced a bill making it *illegal* to add tomatoes to chowder within the state of Maine, the penalty being that the offender dig a barrel of clams at high tide.

Manhattan cocktail A mixture of bourbon or blended whiskey, sweet vermouth and bitters that was invented by a bartender at the Manhattan Club to celebrate the election of Governor Samuel Tilden in 1874. There is also a Bronx cocktail, but no Brooklyn, Queens or Staten Island cocktail. *See also* ALEXANDER; BRONX COCKTAIL.

Manhattan eel A *Manhattan eel* is a condom, because so many float in the waters surrounding Manhattan. For the same reason, a condom can be called a *Coney Island whitefish,* which in typical New York humor says much about the dirty waters off the famous resort in Brooklyn. *Coney Island whitefish* is recorded in few slang dictionaries, but I have heard the expression several times. Both terms probably date back to the 1930s.

Manhattanization A relatively new word that seems to have originated in California of all places. In the 1971 fall election, San Francisco residents were urged to vote for an amendment halting the construction of tall buildings to avoid the *Manhattanization* of the West Coast city. The amendment lost, but brings an interesting story to mind that really has no moral to it at all. About 172 years ago there was actually an attempt made to saw Manhattan Island in two because too many tall and heavy buildings were being built near the Battery. To "prevent the tip from breaking off and sinking into the bay," it was proposed that the Island be sawed off near its northern end, rowed into the bay, turned around and attached to firmer ground uptown. Over the two-month period that the project was the talk of the town, hundreds volunteered, huge oars and oarlocks were built, "long-winded" men were recruited to do the underwater sawing, and supplies were finally provided for the workers. But on the appointed day the project's architects, two hoaxers named Lozier and "Uncle John" De Voe, never showed up. They had played one of history's zaniest pranks on the most cosmopolitan of Americans, though they had to wear disguises for a long time after they came out of hiding.

Manhattan Project The name used for the program for the development of the atomic bomb during World War II.

Manhattan schist The thick, tough bed of rock that makes it possible to build the skyscrapers of Manhattan. Exposures of it can be seen in Central Park.

man of respect See quote. "Vito Corleone was now a 'man of respect' in the [Italian-American] neighborhood. He was reputed to be a member of the Mafia of Sicily." (Puzo, *The Godfather*)

Man Who Came to Dinner, The Moss Hart got the idea for *The Man Who Came to Dinner* (1939) after author Alexander Woollcott spent a weekend at his house. After Woollcott left, Hart remarked to George S. Kaufman, "Can you imagine what would have happened if the old monster had fractured his hip and had to stay?" When Woollcott learned of his subsequent caricature as Sheridan Whiteside in the Kaufman-Hart play, he quipped, knowing a good thing when he had one, "The thing's a terrible insult and I've decided to swallow it." Later he toured in the part. *See also* EVERYTHING WORTHWHILE DOING IS EITHER IMMORAL, ILLEGAL OR FATTENING; MEN SELDOM MAKE PASSES / AT GIRLS WHO WEAR GLASSES.

man with a belly A very important, powerful person.

> For one thing, the five New York Dons were in the old Sicilian tradition, they were "men with a belly" meaning, figuratively, power and courage; and literally, physical flesh, as if the two went together, as indeed they seemed to have done in Sicily. The five New York Dons were stout, corpulent men with massive leonine heads, features on a large scale, fleshy imperial noses, thick mouths, heavy folded chests. (Puzo, *The Godfather*)

Mardi Gras Unlike the New Orleans Mardi Gras festival, held on the last days preceding Lent, New York's Mardi Gras has traditionally been held on Labor Day weekend. Until about 30 years ago, it was held at Coney Island and Rockaway Playland, complete with parades, floats and other features of the New Orleans prototype.

maricón A contemptuous Spanish word for a male homosexual; sometimes used by Puerto Ricans but has little general use.

matzo Unleavened bread that is thin and corrugated and shaped like large square crackers. Enjoyed year round but traditionally eaten by Jews on Passover. From the Hebrew word for the same.

matzo ball A dumpling served in matzo ball soup that is made of matzo meal. *See* MATZO.

matzo brei Small matzo pieces mixed with water and beaten eggs and fried. *See* MATZO.

maven A Yiddish term, pronounced MAY-vin, for an expert on something; from the Hebrew for "understanding." One can be everything from a pickle maven to a Beethoven maven. Also spelled *mavin*.

mazel A very common expression for good luck; from the Hebrew for luck.

mazel tov Although the literal meaning of the Hebrew words is "good luck," the widely known Yiddish expression *mazel tov* means "congratulations" or "best wishes" on one's success or good fortune; it is not said to a person when wishing him luck.

mazuma Widely known slang for money or cash; from the Hebrew *mezuman,* "set, prepared, fixed." Often used in a joking sense.

McGurk's Suicide Hall A Bowery saloon of the 1890s. So named because so many people committed suicide in it: six in 1899 alone. Other colorfully named dives of the so-called genteel Gay Nineties included the Rat Pit, the Hell Hole, the Inferno, the Dump, and the Flea Bag. All were staffed with fearsome bouncers like Eat-'Em-Up Jack McManus of McGurk's.

mechanic *See* DIP.

medium lane *See* SPEED LANE.

meennuh A pronunciation of *mean to,* as in "didn't meennuh do it."

meet me between the lions A favorite meeting place for New Yorkers, the lion statues in front of the New York Public Library, one on each side of the library's steps, have become immortalized in the phrase "Meet me between the lions."

melanzana "Eggplant" in Italian, this word is perjorative slang for a black person, in reference to the eggplant's black skin.

menorah 1) A nine-branched candelabrum lit on Hanukkah, the Feast of Lights. 2) A candelabrum with seven branches used in the biblical tabernacle. 3) A candelabrum with any number of branches used in modern synagogues.

men seldom make passes / at girls who wear glasses Author Dorothy Parker's celebrated couplet, proverbial by now, was originally published in her friend Franklin Pierce Adam's "The Conning Tower" column under the title "News Item." One of the great wits of all time, Parker had the sharpest tongue of anyone at New York's celebrated Algonquin Round Table, a luncheon group that met at the Algonquin Hotel in the 1920s and included Adams, Robert Benchley, Heywood Broun, George S. Kaufman, Alexander Woollcott and many others from time to time.

meshuga Crazy, insane; from the Hebrew for the same. Only in New York could you hear, as I did, "He's not a good example of *mens sana in corpore sano;* he's meshuga."

meshugana A crazy person, as in "Get that meshugana out of here!" *See* MESHUGA.

Met The common abbreviated name for the Metropolitan Opera House in New York City; it opened in 1883. It is also used to refer to the world-famous Metropolitan Museum of Art.

Mets theory A stock market theory holding that the market falls when the New York Mets lose a game and goes up when they win. It wasn't meant seriously and shouldn't be taken seriously.

mezuzah A small scroll, inscribed on one side with biblical passages (Deut. 6:4–9 and Deut. 11:13–21) and on the other with the word *Shaddoi,* a name for God, that is inserted in a small tube and attached by some Jews to the door-jamb of the home. An Orthodox Jew touches his lips and then the mezuzah on leaving or entering the house or apartment. From the Hebrew for "doorpost."

Mick Slang for an Irishman since the mid-19th century in New York City, as it has been elsewhere.

mickey A white potato roasted until done in an open fire, often in a vacant lot, skin burned to perfection. This staple of childhood cuisine is also called a *roast mickey.* It is properly eaten charcoal and all.

million-footed Manhattan A phrase used by Walt Whitman in his poem "A Broadway Pageant" (1883). In it he also called the borough "Superb-faced Manhattan." It might more accurately be called *twenty-million footed Manhattan* today, counting visitors.

minyan The number of Jews needed by Jewish law to conduct a communal religious service, traditionally 10 Jewish males over 13 years of age. *Minyan* is also used in slang to mean any quorum.

Miracle of Coogan's Bluff *See* SHOT HEARD ROUND THE WORLD.

mish-mosh Of this word, Groucho Marx wrote to a presidential candidate:

"You'll never get votes in the Bronx if you go on saying *mish-mash* instead of *mish-mosh*." The word means a mixup or a mess and is of uncertain origin.

Miss Astor A pretentious woman, especially one who overdresses. After the Astor family of New York society. *See* MRS. ASTOR'S PET HORSE (PONY, COW).

Miss Lizzie Tish A usually sarcastic term for a girl or woman who acts and dresses as if she were superior to everyone else. "She thinks she's Miss Lizzie Tish with her nose up in the air." No one seems to know the origin of "Lizzie Tish," but the term was common in the 1930s and 1940s and is still occasionally heard in New York today.

moider A pronunciation of *murder,* as in "Moider Incorporated."

moll buzzer Not a purse snatcher but a skilled pickpocket who specializes in opening women's handbags and removing their wallets etc. *See* FINGER.

mom-and-pop store Mom-and-pop stores are an old American institution; there were, for example, thousands of candy stores run by husband-and-wife teams in New York City from the 1920s through the 1950s. But the term *mom-and-pop store* is first recorded in 1951. It is occasionally used today to describe any small business with a few employees.

momzer Frequently heard slang for a bastard, rascal, detestable person; but sometimes used affectionately to describe a bright child. A Yiddish expression from the Hebrew for "bastard." *See* MUMSER.

money talks Now a folk saying rather than slang, *money talks* means that wealth is power or money buys anything. Though it is probably older, no one has been able to trace the phrase back before 1910. J. D. Salinger used it in *The Catcher in the Rye* (1950): "In New York, boy, money really talks— I'm not kidding."

monkey-in-the-middle A children's ball game in which two players try to prevent a third standing between them from intercepting a ball or other object thrown to each other. If the "monkey" intercepts the object, the thrower becomes the monkey.

moom pickcha Moving picture, movie. "'How was the movie?' Bella asked. 'A fine moom pickcha we seen,' replied Mrs. Gross. 'Such moom pickchas my worst enemy should oney see.'" (Kober, "You Mean Common")

moon hoax Quite a few Americans have walked on the moon by now, and none has seen evidence of life there; but in 1835, according to *New York Sun* reporter Richard Adams Locke, the eminent British astronomer Sir John Herschel trained a new, powerful telescope on the moon and observed some 15 species of animals, including what seemed to be a race of winged men. Locke's article, supposedly reprinted from the actually defunct Edinburgh

Journal of Science, raised the circulation of his newspaper from 2,500 to 20,000 and inspired one ladies' club to raise money to send missionaries to the moon. The book that the *Sun* reporter wrote based on the article sold over 60,000 copies and was studied assiduously by a scientific delegation from Yale. Locke finally admitted his hoax the following year, calling it a satire on absurd scientific speculations that had gotten out of hand. His friend Edgar Allan Poe, who never believed a word of the story, nevertheless admitted that it had anticipated most of his own "Hans Pfall," which was the reason he left that story unfinished.

more better I have heard the superfluous *more better* used by a numbre of younger New Yorkers, as in "Burger King is more better than MacDonald's."

mouse gun A small gun with little firepower.

mouser An old term for a mustache. "He is a little guy . . . with a bald head and a small mouser on his upper lip." (Damon Runyon, "Breach of Promise," 1931)

mout' A pronunciation of *mouth*. "'Keep your mout' shut, you unnerstan'?" (Condon, *Prizzi's Money*)

movies *See* PICTURE SHOW.

Mr. Charlie First recorded in 1923, this is a contemptous black term for white men in general and especially those whites regarded as oppressors. Also *Boss Charlie, Charlie, Mr. Chuck, Captain Boss, The Man. See* GOLDBERG.

Mrs. Astor's pet horse (pony, cow) An old expression, not much heard anymore for a woman who behaves or dresses ostentatiously. "She thinks she's Mrs. Astor's pet horse." The Astors are, of course, one of New York City's oldest rich families. Also *Mrs. Astor's plush horse. See* MISS ASTOR.

muddah Mother, as in the song, "Hello, Muddah, Hello, Faddah!" *See* FADDAH.

muffin *Muffin* is an affectionate term for a woman or a man that is not so commonly heard as it was 40 years ago. *Cupcake* was also commonly used in this way, but today it often describes a man who is "soft" and not difficult to deal with. "You won't find many cupcakes pitching in the majors."

mug; mugging; mugger *Mugging* seems first to have been New York City slang for what was called *yoking* in other parts of the country, that is, robbery committed by two holdup men, one clasping the victim around the neck from behind while the other ransacks his pockets. The term either derives from the *mugs* who commit such crimes or from the expression on the victim's face—which can appear as if he is mugging, grimacing or making a funny face—as he is brutally yoked. The term is now well known throughout the country. As often as not, the *mugger* acts alone today, and *mugging* has become a synonym for holding someone up. The spelling *mugg* seems to be yielding to *mug*. The word *mug* for a grimace was introduced to England by the Gypsies and may derive from the Sanskrit word *mukka*, "face." *Mug* was used as slang for face in England as early as 1840. *Mug* for a heavy cup may come from the Swedish *mugg* meaning the same.

multimillionaire   A term that may have first been applied to New York's John Jacob Astor in the mid-19th century.

mumser   A bastard. A variation on *momzer*. "Fifteen minutes later, the assistant walked into his superior's office. 'I cut that mumser from Queens loose.'" (Breslin, *Table Money*) *See* MOMZER.

Murder, Inc.   The enforcement agency of the organized crime syndicate during the 1930s, believed responsible for between 400 and 500 deaths. *Murder, Inc.* was controlled by top crime bosses such as Meyer Lansky, Lucky Luciano and Frank Costello, and led by Lord High Executioner Albert Anastasia, a notoriously violent killer. The group provided the mob with a ready pool of paid assassins to be used around the country. Killings were considered strictly business and carried out to protect the interests of the growing syndicate. Members of the group headquartered at Midnight Rose's, a 24-hour candy store in Brownsville, Brooklyn, where they traded tips on killing techniques and waited for assignments. Most prominent among

the assassins was Pittsburgh Phil Strauss, target of 58 murder investigations, but believed responsible for twice that many deaths. In 1940 law enforcement authorities arrested a number of mob members, including Abe Reles, a Murder, Inc. lieutenant. Reles, fearing others would talk to the police before him, turned informer to save himself, providing details on hundreds of murders and sending many of his colleagues to the electric chair. Before completing his testimony against the highest-ranking mob bosses, Reles fell to his death from the window of a Coney Island hotel where he was under police protection. *See* CANARY THAT COULDN'T FLY.

muscle   Power, physical or financial; influence. "The Prizzis' had the political muscle in the country on every level. . . ." (Condon, *Prizzi's Honor*)

Mustache Pete   A derisive term describing the old-fashioned leaders of the Mafia in America, who often wore mustaches, were out of touch with the times and were out of power by the 1940s. "'The Don was an old 'Moustache Pete,' his day was over but he didn't know it.'" (Puzo, *The Godfather*)

musta   Must have. "You musta gone there already."

mutt   A term used by New York police to describe a criminal, usually a stupid run-of-the-mill criminal, someone without any class at all. The term is also used generally for any stupid person, not necessarily a criminal.

muver A pronunciation of *mother* among some blacks and whites. "One thing I got is clothes, thanks to my muver's charge at Lane Bryant. . . ." (Sapphire, *Push*)

nathin' *See* BONAC.

nebbish Yiddish for a loser; a sorrowfully ineffectual, timid, unlucky person. Probably from the Czech *nebohy,* "poor." "He's such a nebbish." Also *nebech.*

Negro plot A so-called plot of 1741 in which blacks were accused of setting several fires in New York City, a charge never proved. As a result of the accusations 29 blacks were burned at the stake and 100 were transported out of the city.

Nelly Bly New York journalist Elizabeth Cochrane Seaman adopted the pen name Nelly Bly from a song by Stephen Foster. She is said to have taken it when one of her editors insisted that she as a woman use a pseudonym and an office boy happened to walk by whistling the tune. One of the first female reporters, Nelly Bly began her career when only 18. Her forte became exposés, such as her account in *Ten Days in a Madhouse* (1887) of the horrible conditions on New

York's Blackwell's Island, where she was an inmate for 10 days after feigning insanity. In 1889 the *New York World* sponsored her famous trip around the globe, which she completed in the record time of 72 days, 6 hours and 11 minutes, bringing her international fame far exceeding that of any other woman of her day. Flowers, trains and racehorses were named for Nelly Bly, and songs were written in her honor.

nervous pudding *See* BURN ONE WITH A FEATHER.

nerz A pronunciation of *noise.* "The nerz from JFK is terrible."

neveh A pronunciation of *never.*

New Amsterdam The Dutch name for what is now New York City. New Amsterdam, named after the city of Amsterdam in the Netherlands in about 1626, was originally one of the Dutch trading posts in New Netherland. Among other firsts during the New Amsterdam period of the city: the first murder occurred in 1638, the first lottery was held in 1665 and the first "welfare" assistance was given in 1661.

New Jessey   A mostly Puerto Rican pronunciation of *New Jersey*. *See quote under* THAS.

new potatoes   Small red-skinned potatoes that are the first of the year are called *new potatoes* in New York City. Travel less than 100 miles east to Long Island's North Fork, and their name becomes *salad potatoes,* probably because they are used in making potato salad.

news   In times past the word *news* was treated as a plural, Queen Victoria once writing to the king of Belgium: "The news from Austria are very sad and make me very anxious." Horace Greeley demanded, legend says, that his reporters on the *New York Tribune* always treat *news* as a plural noun. "Are there any news?" he cabled a reporter one time. "Not a new," the reporter wired back. Incidentally, Greeley's handwriting was the despair of printers in a typewriterless world. The *New York Tribune* editor wrote so illegibly that an employee he fired used his letter of discharge as a recommendation letter for another job. Another time Greeley gave written instructions for a sign painter to letter ENTRANCE ON SPRUCE STREET over a door. This the sign painter interpreted and painted as EDITOR ON A SPREE.

New School for Social Research   Usually called the *New School,* this institution was founded in 1919 to provide adult education in the social services and other fields. Its graduate faculty of political social science acquired the nickname *University in Exile* because so many of its members were refugees from totalitarian countries.

New York   New York is named for James, duke of York and Albany, who in 1664 was granted the patent to all lands between the Delaware River and Connecticut by his older brother, King Charles II. The duke gave away the Jersey portion but held on to what was up to then the Dutch colony of New Netherlands. York had become the patron of Col. Richard Nicholls, who earlier that same year had set sail for the New World, captured New Amsterdam from the Dutch, and named both the city of New Amsterdam (New York City) and the colony of New Netherlands (New York State) after the duke. New York State's capital, Albany, is also named for the duke of York and Albany.

New York alligators   There are many stories about New Yorkers flushing baby pet alligators down the toilet and the alligators growing to full size in the sewer pipes beneath the city streets. There were, in fact, several stories about New York alligator sightings in the local papers during the 1930s, and Smelly Kelly, a noted city worker who sniffed out gas leaks in the underground tunnels, claimed he had encountered one. True or not, the tales are part of New York City folklore. So are New York "rats as big as cats" in the subway tunnels, but these could simply be raccoons, hundreds of which commute on foot in the tunnels every day along with the 3½ million people who prefer to use the trains.

New York blister Everything has a name, if you dig deep enough. Even the swollen, slightly blackened bubbles on the top of pizza pies. They are called—in the trade, anyway—*New York blisters*. These New York blisters are said to be impossible to make perfectly without traditional Italian coal ovens.

New York City buffalo hunt Fox hunting and horseracing were fairly common in old New York, but the most unusual "sport" held in the city was buffalo hunting. In late 1784 buffalo hunts with hounds were held, the buffalo imported from Kentucky.

New York City Marathon Though it was held in Central Park several years before, the first real New York City Marathon, a 26.2 mile race that winds through all five boroughs, was held in 1976. There were about 3,000 runners, compared with about 30,000 each year presently, and they ran essentially the same course that runners do today, from Fort Wadsworth, Staten Island, to Central Park. Far fewer people crowded the streets to cheer the runners on that first rainy October day than they do now.

New York City's Finest A name for New York City's policemen since the 1890s.

New York County The official name for Manhattan, one of New York City's five boroughs. It is named for James, duke of York, brother of England's king Charles II. *See* BOROUGH; BRONX; KINGS COUNTY; QUEENS COUNTY; RICHMOND COUNTY.

New York Daily News The tabloid newspaper was founded in 1919 by Joseph Medill Paterson, whose motto was "Tell it to Sweeney [the common man]—the Stuyvesants [the rich] will take care of it themselves." The paper became increasingly conservative over the years, after breaking with President Franklin D. Roosevelt over foreign policy in 1940. Notable *News* headlines include KILLER'S GAT FOUND; FORD TO CITY—DROP DEAD! and, after actress Gina Lollobrigida was criticized by an Italian prosecutor, CHARGES GINA / WAS OBSCENA / ON LA SCREENA. Among "New York's Picture Newspaper's" most famous photographs is a front-page shot of murderer Ruth Snyder executed in the electric chair at Sing Sing prison on January 22, 1928. The *News* photographer, Thomas Howard, sitting in the first row, crossed his knee and took the photograph with a camera strapped to his ankle just after the switch was pulled.

New Yorker A name used in other places, but not in New York, for a hair cut with a brush cut on top and long on the sides.

New York Evening Post The original name of today's *New York Post*, founded in 1801 as a conservative Federalist paper. Its most famous editor was poet William Cullen Bryant (1794–1878), who edited the paper for nearly 70 years, until the year of his death. (Bryant wrote lovingly, with his usual nobility and dignity, of the month of June in his poem of the same name. In the poem he concluded that he wanted to die in June, and he did, 10 years later.)

New York game A version of baseball popular in New York in the 1840s. Similar to present-day baseball, it led to the modern game when codified in the *Knickerbocker Rules*. *See* KNICKERBOCKER RULES.

New York Gazette New York City's first newspaper, first published on November 8, 1725. This semiofficial chronicle of current events was edited by its publisher William Bradford, who was the official royal printer at New York and also the first to print an American play. The paper ceased publication in 1744.

New York Giants A New York National League baseball team from 1883 (when they were known as the New York Metropolitans) until they were moved to San Francisco in 1958. Their name was coined by New York sportswriters when their manager, Jim Mutrie, called them "My big fellows! My giants!" in 1885. Fans often called them the *Jints* in true New Yorkese. *See also* COOGAN'S BLUFF.

New Yorkitis A disease that some outlanders think people with a New York accent suffer from.

New York kiss-off A term for a very rude dismissal, a brush-off. "She gave him the New York kiss-off." *Kiss-off* can also mean to die, deriving in this sense from black slang. Often called a *California kiss-off* as well.

New York Knicks *See* FATHER KNICKERBOCKER.

New York Mets *See* AMAZIN' METS.

New York minute A very quick minute, a very short time. "He had it done in a New York minute."

New York Shitty A contemptuous derogatory term for New York City. Its origin is unknown but was probably coined by an outlander.

New York steak Everybody disagrees about just what cut of meat a *New York steak* is. Some opt for a shell steak, others say a porterhouse, still others a sirloin; it also depends on what kind of steak is served at the restaurant. Actually, the name is used more by out-of-towners than by New Yorkers.

New York Stock Exchange The *New York Stock Exchange* (NYSE) was first named the *New York Stock and Exchange Board* (1817), taking its present name in 1863. The *American Stock Exchange* (AMEX), which took its present name in 1953, was formed as the *New York Curb Exchange* in 1842, because it was composed of *curbstone brokers* who were not members of any exchange and conducted business outside on the curb.

New York system   A Rhode Island term for a frankfurther with everything on it.

New York Times   The eminent daily newspaper was founded in 1851 by conservative Henry J. Raymond, whose goal was to oppose the distorted news reporting of the day. In the 1890s it went through a period of decline and then was bought by Adolph Ochs who brought it back to prominence under the slogan "All the News That's Fit to Print" and whose family has maintained the paper's reputation since. The slogan remains on the paper's masthead, unlike another slogan Ochs adopted: "It Does Not Soil the Breakfast Cloth." *See also* YELLOW JOURNALISM.

New York University   Best known as *NYU*. A private, nonsectarian university chartered in 1831. Its *Hall of Fame,* on its former uptown University Heights campus, was established in 1900 to honor 50 Americans with memorial busts and tablets, these including Emerson, Hawthorne, Poe and Whitman. Since then additional persons have been so honored every five years.

nice guys finish last   This cynical proverb has been attributed by Bartlett's *Dictionary of Americanisms* to former Brooklyn Dodger manager Leo Durocher, who wrote a book using it as the title. Back in the 1940s Durocher was sitting on the bench before a game with the New York Giants and saw opposing manager Mel Ott across the field. "Look at Ott," he said to a group of sportswriters. "He's such a nice guy and they'll finish last for him." One of the writers probably coined the phrase *nice guys finish last* from this remark, but the credit for it still goes to Leo the Lip. It is one of several baseball expressions that have become proverbial outside the sport.

nickel a shtickl   See quote. "Atop the meat case [in the deli] stood a teaser, an open display of small knobs of a thickly sliced knublvoorst—garlic wurst—ornamented by a hand-lettered sign, A NICKEL A SHTICKL, or a nickel apiece." (Elliot Willensky, *When Brooklyn Was the World,* 1994)

nickel curve   In baseball a *nickel curve* is a curve that doesn't break much. The term has been taced to William Arthur "Candy" Cummings (1848–1924), a Hall of Famer who is credited with inventing the curveball over 120 years ago. Cummings's curve was inspired by the half clam shells that he skimmed across a Brooklyn beach as a youngster, but he perfected it by experimenting with a baseball that cost a nickel.

Nickel Series   An old synonym for a subway baseball World Series, when the subway cost a nickel a ride. *See* SUBWAY SERIES.

nine   1) *Nine* is obviously a synonym for a baseball team because that's the number of players on a team. The first recorded use of the word *nine* in this sense is in the name of a team called the New York Nine, which played against the New York Knickerbockers Ball Club in 1846. Thus the term nine may derive from the name of a specific team. 2) Short for a 9-millimeter pistol. The following quote gives the full name and its firepower: "They were both armed with Intratec nine-millimeter semi-automatic pistols capable of laying down a barrage of fire at the rate of five or six rounds a second." (McBain, *Mischief*)

Noah's boy with Murphy carrying a wreath   A plate of ham, potatoes and cabbage, as a luncheonette waitress or waiter might order it from the short-order cook.

Noah's brig   *Noah's brig,* a tiny rockbound island in the Hudson River, is named for one Captain Noah, an 18th-century New York City captain of a fleet of rafts, who had the misfortune of encountering the island under adverse conditions one night. Noah sighted "a dark object floating the waters," which looked like a brig under sail. "Brig ahoy!" he cried, but no answer came. "Brig ahoy!" he shouted. "Answer or I'll run you down!" There was still no reply and Captain Noah stubbornly held his course. Then a crash; wood crunched on rock. Noah had mistaken two trees on the island for masts with sails set.

nobody but nobody undersells Gimbels   You can't get it cheaper anywhere else. This slogan of the now defunct Gimbels department store, often used by other stores today, was invented by the irrepressible Bernice Fitz-Gibbon, an English teacher who became Macy's star copywriter before Gimbels shoplifted her from the World's Largest Store. (She had coined Macy's famous *It's Smart to Be Thrifty* slogan, not to mention a legendary ad featuring a voluptuous woman in a strapless evening gown that was captioned "How do you keep it up night after night?") Gimbels's slogan became world famous, Winston Churchill once asking his friend Bernard Baruch if it was "really true that nobody, but nobody, undersells Gimbels?" *See also* DOES MACY'S TELL GIMBELS?; LIKE MACY'S WINDOW.

no-goodnik   A Yiddish term that adds the Slavic suffix *-nik* to *no good,* giving us a word for a low-life of one kind or another.

noive   A pronunciation of *nerve.* "She's got a helluva noive barging in like that."

no more free lunch   *See* FUN CITY.

nookleeuh   A pronunciation of *nuclear.*

no problem   The modest New York way of saying "You're welcome." Who says New Yorkers don't got manners?

North River   The Dutch called the Hudson River the North River. Today *North River* is officially the name of the Hudson from the Battery to about Fourteenth Street.

nosh   To eat, especially between meals, to snack. A true *nosher noshes* whenever there is a *nosh* around. A

Yiddish expression, from the German *nachen,* to eat on the sly.

not to know one's ass from one's elbow To be completely ignorant about something or everything. "He doesn't know his ass from his elbow."

not worth a Continental During the Revolutionary War, counterfeiting in New York City contributed to the coining of the still common phrase *not worth a Continental,* that is, worthless. The financial instability of Continental paper money was increased by the circulation of an immense amount of fake Continentals by the British and Tories after the spring of 1777. These were sent out of New York City literally by the cartloads, and the business was no secret. An ad in a New York paper ran: "Persons going into other colonies may be supplied with any number of counterfeit Congress notes for the price of the paper per ream." Readers were assured that the counterfeits were so neatly and exactly executed "that there was no risk in getting them off."

nudnik; nudge A persistently dull, boring pest can be called a *nudnik,* from the Yiddish *nudyen,* to bore. A *nudge* (*noodge*) is a similar type, though less dull and boring than persistent, one who is always *nudging;* or pestering, someone about one thing or another.

nuffin' A pronunciation of *nothing.* "I still don't say nuffin'. She know so much let her ass do the talking." (Sapphire, *Push*)

numbeh A pronunciation of *number.*

N' Yawk Long a pronunciation of *New York.* "Maybe she'd like t'learna speak N' Yawk!" F. Scott Fitzgerald has a character say in his famous story "The Diamond as Big as the Ritz."

nyesplayshagottere Nice place you got here. "On first looking into a friend's apartment," a pronunciation recorded in the Federal Writers' Project *Almanac for New Yorkers,* 1938.

ocho   *See* DIP.

of   Often used in place of *have*. "'Well,' I said, 'we are in Washington and I could of borrowed from the United States Treasury. I could of pretended I was an Englishman.'" (Ring Lardner, "The Golden Honeymoon," 1922)

ofay   An insulting black term for a white. First recorded in 1925 the word may come from the pig latin for *foe*, as the old story goes, or possibly from a Yoruba word meaning "great enemy." No one knows for sure.

off   To kill. "'But the kidnapping of her own husband and the fact that he was offed—that's very good,' Don Corrado said, nodding approvingly." (Condon, *Prizzi's Money*)

offuh yuh   From you, off of you, as in "I wanna borra ten dollars offuh yuh." The expression has been around for at least 100 years and has a number of variations, including *offa* ya.

O. Henry age   *See* BAGDAD ON THE HUDSON.

oh, forget it   *See* UNDER THE TABLE.

oh yeah?   Still a common feature of New York speech. "In his routine chatter," as the Federal Writer's Project *New York Panorama* (1938) put it, "the New Yorker cannot get along without his *oh yeah?* It is his most valuable buffer, knout, pacifier and bubble-pipe, a necessary protective lubricant in the daily wear and tear."

oim owan da toity-toid flohwah of da Noo Yowak Stadla—can oi hab a cuppa kowaffe an a glazza watta   "I'm on the thirty-third floor of the New York Statler—can I have a cup of coffee and a glass of water." In a "Best New York Accent in Houston" contest held some 10 years ago, contestants had to give the proper New York pronunciation of the room service order. Former Brooklynite John Occhiogrosso won the grand prize expense-paid trip to Brooklyn with the above. When asked about job discrimination he had experienced because of his accent the winner mused (in translation), "If people don't like me for what I am, the hell with them—that's the Brooklyn way."

o.k. by me   In use for at least half a century or so, this expression is a Yiddish one given wider currency by the media. The *by me* in the phrase comes from the Yiddish *bei mir*.

old ackamarackus   *See* ACKAMA-RACKUS.

old lady in Dubuque   Dubuque, Iowa, is named for the area's first settler, a French Canadian lead miner named Julien Dubuque. But what about that famous symbol of prudery, the little *old lady in Dubuque?* The phrase seems to have originated in this sense with Harold Ross, when he promised in a prospectus of the *New Yorker* that his magazine would *not* be edited for "the old lady in Dubuque." According to Brendan Gill, in his fascinating *Here at the New Yorker* (1975), Ross may have been inspired by "Boots" Mulgrew, a former Broadway musical-comedy skit writer forced by drinking and financial problems to retreat from New York to his birthplace. Mulgrew soon after began contributing squibs to a widely read *Chicago Tribune* column called "A Line o' Type or Two." These pieces, describing "the provincial absurdities of Dubuque" were signed with the pseudonym "Old Lady in Dubuque," and Gill suggests that "Ross read them, admired them, and, whether consciously or not, got the old lady in Dubuque fixed in his mind as a natural antagonist."

omerta   The law of silence sworn to by members of the Mafia and observed for over a thousand years in Sicily. ". . . the Mafia cemented its power by originating the law of silence, the *omerta*. In the countryside of Sicily a stranger asking directions to the nearest town will not even receive the courtesy of an answer." (Puzo, *The Godfather*) In *The Last Don* (1996) Puzo adds,

> As a philosophy *omerta* was quite simple. It was a mortal sin to talk to the police about anything that would harm the Mafia. If a rival Mafia clan murdered your father before your eyes, you were forbidden to inform the police . . . The authorities were the Great Satan a true Sicilian could never turn to.

Richard Condon casts more light on the practice today in *Prizzi's Money* (1994):

> It had almost appeared as though he had been about to violate *omerta,* the sacred oath of manhood of the Mafia with which, among other things, he had pledged in blood that he would never violate a woman of the family of a mafiosa. Everyone in the room knew that *omerta* was only a myth, something observed by the people who wrote newspaper stories and movies. But he was expected . . . to pay solemn lip-service to it.

on account   Sometimes used in place of *because*, as in "I did it on account of her."

oncet; twicet   Bona fide Brooklynese that is still heard in New York for *once* and *twice*. The words, however, were first recorded in Philadelphia and

Baltimore by Noah Webster, and they are also heard in the Ozarks.

one foot on a banana peel and the other in the grave Very old or very ill, slipping away fast. *The Dictionary of American Regional English* (Vol. I, 1985) gives 1965 as the earliest date the editors have found this expression used and do not list New York or New York City among the places where it has been heard. However, I recall hearing the phrase many times from the late 1940s to the 1960s and still hear it occasionally among older speakers, always in the form "He's (she's) got one foot on a banana peel and the other in the grave." The words are a humorous extension of the old expression *one foot in the grave*. This, in turn, did not originate with the famous Grecian statue of an old man standing at the bottom of a long flight of stairs with one foot in the grave, as Roman tourist guides frequently claim (or used to). Fifteen centuries before the statue was carved, Roman emperor Julian said, "I will learn this even if I have one foot in the grave," which is probably the origin of this phrase meaning on the brink of death. Julian may have gotten the idea from the ancient Greeks, who had a similar expression *with one foot in Charon's ferryboat*, that is, the legendary ferryboat that transported the dead across the river Styx to the Elysian Fields. Incidentally, *one foot in the graveyard* used to be slang for an order of soup among New York lunchroom workers, soup thought to be food for the old and infirm.

one to go *See* BURN ONE WITH A FEATHER.

one with Commonly heard slang for a frankfurter with sauerkraut. *One off* is a less frequent term, used only by waiters, meaning a frankfurter without sauerkraut. *One with the works* is often used to order a frank with everything: sauerkraut, mustard and even relish.

oney Only. "You're the oney one for me."

on gana I'm going to. *See quote under* JUHHIRMEE.

on line New Yorkers stand *on line*, not *in line* as other Americans do. Those of school age, however, are kept *in line*, or orderly, by their teachers while on line in the schoolyard. And once people are on line in New York, they ideally *stay in line*.

onnafyah On the fire, meaning "a short order is being prepared." A pronunciation recorded in the Federal Writers' Project *Almanac for New Yorkers*, 1938.

onorata società See quote. "The older founders of the American Mafia refer to their group as the *onorata società*, or honored society." (Breslin, *The Gang That Couldn't Shoot Straight*)

on the arm Something free of charge, often used by police. "His meals were always on the arm."

on the job On the police force. "'He was a sergeant. I have two uncles on the job in Long Island.'" (Breslin, *The Gang That Couldn't Shoot Straight*)

op'm *See* BONAC.

Outfit A synonym for the Mafia. "There was a jeweler in New York who The Outfit used to move out hot stones in bulk, and he was switching the good stones for shitty ones. . . ." (Condon, *Prizzi's Honor*)

out in left field Since left field is not any more odd or less active a position than right or center field in baseball, it is hard to understand why it is featured in this common slang expression meaning very unorthodox and wrong, weirdly unconventional, even crazy. In fact, anyone who has ever played sandlot baseball knows that the most inept (and therefore a little odd, to kids) fielders were relegated to *right* field, because there were fewer left-handed hitters to pull the ball to right field. It has been suggested that the phrase refers to the left field seats in Yankee Stadium that are far away from the coveted seats near Babe Ruth's right field position.

out of here; outta here Finished, done with a place or thing. "She stared into the camera . . . until the operator gave her the signal that she was clear . . . and then turned again to her crew and said, "We're out of here." (McBain, *Romance*)

outta sight! Often regarded as college slang of the 1960s, *outta sight* (for something remarkable or wonderful) has been part of the language since the 1840s in the form of the Bowery expression *out of sight*. Stephen Crane used it in his first novel *Maggie: A Girl of the Streets* (1893): "I'm stuck on yer shape. It's outa sight."

oy! "Oy is not a word," Leo Rosten writes in *The Joys of Yiddish* (1968). "It is a vocabulary. It is uttered in as many ways as the utterer's histrionic ability permits. It is a lament, a protest, a cry of dismay, a reflex of delight. But however sighed, cried, howled or moaned, *oy!* is the most expressive and ubiquitous exclamation in Yiddish." *Oy vay,* a shortening of *oy vay iz mir,* is also used as an "all-purpose ejaculation," Rosten notes. He doesn't list *oy gevald,* which Henry Roth used as "a cry of alarm, concern or amazement" in *From Bondage* (1996). But he does list *gevalt* or *gevald* alone as the same kind of cry and cites the folk proverb "Man comes into the world with an *Oy!*—and leaves with a *gevalt.*" I have heard *oy!,* and *oy vay!* for that matter, uttered by New Yorkers of dozens of religions, races and nationalities. *Gevalt* also.

oy vay! *See* OY!

ozone *Ozone* means fresh, pure air in everyday speech, (the reason for the place-name Ozone Park in Queens, New York). But it translates as "stinking air," deriving from the Greek *ozein,* "to stink." German chemist Christian Friedrich Schonbein coined the name of this stable, pale bluish gas in 1840. Schonbein wrote that he named this most reactive form of oxygen "*ozone* because of its strong smell," which he thought was similar to chlorine.

padrino Patron, boss, an Italian title of great respect in the Mafia, meaning literally "godfather" in Italian.

pahrmee A fast-clipped pronunciation of *pardon me*.

paisan Italian for a friend. "He's my good paisan."

palooka Former baseball player and vaudevillian Jack Conway, who became editor of the New York show business newspaper *Variety,* is said to have coined the expression *palooka* in about 1920. Walter Winchell called the prolific Conway "my tutor of slanguage"; *belly laugh, pushover,* to *click* ("succeed"), *baloney* ("bunk"), *S.A.* ("sex appeal") and *payoff* are probably among his other memorable coinages. At first a *palooka* meant only a clumsy boxer lacking in ability (despite the comic strip *Joe Palooka*). Then it came to mean any ineffective athlete, and finally it was applied to any stupid, clumsy person.

pancake See quote. "I can at once see that this Black Mike . . . has little bringing-up, or he will not speak of dolls as tomatoes, although of course different guys have different names for dolls, such as broads, and pancakes, and cookies, and tomatoes, which I claim are not respectful." (Runyon, "Dark Dolores")

papah A pronunciation of *paper.*

pardon my dust New York Algonquin wit Dorothy Parker's famous mock epitaph. She also wrote the epitaph *This is on me* for herself. *See* MEN SELDOM MAKE PASSES / AT GIRLS WHO WEAR GLASSES.

parkies An old term for city park department workers. "The parkies would make great piles of the leaves and set them on fire, and the smell would drift all through the park." (Hamill, *Flesh and Blood*)

Parsons table No old parson or any other clergyman invented the durable easy-to-make *Parsons table*. It was an innovation of Manhattan's Parsons School of Design in the early 1930s.

party Often used in place of *person*. "A certain party I know told me."

passeggiatrice Italian for a "stroller," hence a kind of streetwalker, prostitute. "'You were going to marry the son of your grandfather's old friend but you became a passeggiatrice instead.'" (Condon, *Prizzi's Honor*) Not widely heard in New York.

passel This variation of *parcel* is found in New York City speech as well as in New England and Southern speech. The form dates back to the 15th century, though the use of *passel* as a collective noun indicating an indefinite number dates back to 19th-century America.

pasta fazool There is no such Italian dish—not spelled this way. *Pasta fazool* is the Neapolitan-American pronunciation of *pasta e fagioli,* a soup containing beans (*fagioli*), other vegetables, and little *ditalini* pasta.

patsy According to one theory, *patsy* for someone who is readily deceived or victimized originated in New York in about 1909, deriving from the Italian *pazzo,* a "fool" or "crazy person." Another theory has it deriving from *Pasqualino,* the Italian diminutive for the name Pasquale. *Pasqualino* is Italian slang for a small weak boy, someone very vulnerable. *See also* POTSY.

patza A casual, amateurish chess player, often one who plays chess in New York City parks. The term, which has only been traced back to about 1955, derives ultimately from the German *patzer,* "bungler."

payoff *See* PALOOKA.

pearls before swine There has been some confusion about the origin of this famous New York–born quip. The old story has Clare Boothe Brokaw, who later became Clare Boothe Luce, encountering Dorothy Parker in the lobby of *Vanity Fair* headquarters one morning. "Age before beauty," said the sharp-tongued Clare, holding the door open. "Pearls before swine," said the sharper-tongued Miss Parker, entering first. Luce later denied this story, and a similar quip was used in one of Alexander Woollcott's pieces, but it has nevertheless become part of the Parker legend. It may be true, though. Recalled Mrs. Robert Benchley when she was 80 years old: "I was right there, the time in the Algonquin [hotel], when *some little chorus girl* and Dottie were going into the dining room and the girl stepped back and said, 'Age before beauty,' and Dottie said very quickly, 'Pearls before swine.' I was right there when she said it."

pelter An old horse. "In fact, this Goldberg is a most sagacious old pelter, indeed, and he is called Goldberg by the King in honor of a Jewish friend by the name of Goldberg, who keeps a delicatessen store in Tenth Avenue." (Runyon, "Princess O'Hara")

Penitentiary Row *See* TENEMENTS.

peoples People. *See quote under* CRACKERS.

pernt A pronunciation of *point*.

perp A perpetrator, a criminal who commits an offense. "'. . . the only perp tosses a weapon is the pros. They use a cold piece, they throw it down a sewer afterwards. . . .'" (McBain, *Romance*)

perp walk A term, short for *perpetrator walk*, used for over 50 years by New York City police and newspaper photographers. It describes the moment when a criminal case suspect is walked out of a station house; the exit was designed to allow the police to display their latest catch and to shame the suspect.

personally One of the most common terms heard in New York City is the apologetic *personally*, as in "Personally, I don't believe it," instead of the franker "I don't believe it."

pertater A pronunciation of potato. "'Honest, I was pickin' pertaters. I ain't no rummy. I'm just goddamn hungry.'" (Roth, *From Bondage*)

pessonovante A big shot in mob talk; a .90 caliber. See quote. "'At the end of the month you can go back to Hollywood and the *pezzanovente*, this .90 caliber will give you the job you want. Done?'" (Puzo, *The Godfather*)

Phaff's Cellar Journalist Henry Clapp, writing under the pen name Figaro, reigned as the "King of Bohe-mia" at Phaff's Cellar located on Broadway above Bleecker Street, the intellectual watering hole of the 1850s, where Walt Whitman, Fitz-James O'Brien, Ada Clare (Clapp's mistress) and many others could be seen.

phonus bolonus Something phony, an imitation, inferior; based on *phony baloney.* "Dave sells him good champagne when most guys are trying to hand him the old phonus bolonus." (Runyon, "Madame La Gimp")

phudnik A *nudnik* with a Ph.D. *See* D.PH.; NUDNIK.

pickpocket *See* DIP.

picture show Still used in New York by some older residents instead of the far more common *movies,* or *flicks,* or *film* for a motion picture. Frequently used in its shortened form *show,* as in "Let's go to the show." I've even heard *cinema* used once or twice in this fashion fairly recently, perhaps humorously: "Let's go to the cinema."

pig in a blanket A small-sized frankfurter encased in dough and baked; often served as hors d'ouerves. The plural is sometimes heard as *pigs in a blanket.*

pinstriper Another name for the New York Yankees; after their pinstriped uniforms. The uniform was *not* introduced to make Babe Ruth appear slimmer, as the old story has it.

pinzone A courageous mob member who can handle difficult situations.

pisher A Yiddish expression from the German *pisser,* "to urinate." A *pisher* is thus a bedwetter, and by extension someone young and unexperienced, or a nobody, a young squirt: "He's just a pisher."

pissbum A drunk. "'Oh, yes, Father, that's what happens when you get some guy got his own business and he's nothing but a real, excuse me, ladies, but a real pissbum.'" (Breslin, *Table Money*)

pistol A name for pastrami in New York delis, where a waiter might convey your order to a counterman or short order cook as "A pistol on rye."

pizza parlor *See* SLICE.

play footsie To be intimately involved with. The expression first meant amorous touching between two people and was then extended to mean two people having any close relationship. "Whatsa matter with ya, playin' footsie with the Commies," Thelma Ritter says in the movie *LO* (1946).

play piano New Yorkers often say "I play piano" instead of "I play the piano," leaving out the *the.*

play the duck To avoid someone or something. ". . . many citizens are commencing to consider Marky something of a nuisance and are playing the duck for her. . . ." (Runyon, "Little Miss Marker")

pleece A pronunciation of *police.*

plotz To *plotz,* as in "I could plotz," is to collapse or faint, from surprise, exhaustion, etc. The slang term comes from the Yiddish *platsn,* "to split," "burst." *Plotzed* is slang for drunk or worn out.

pock A pronunciation of *park.*

Poet of the D.T.'s The nickname of New York author John Bartholomew Gough (1817–86), who became a temperance author and lecturer after he was saved from alcoholism by a pledge he took. His moral authority was diminished somewhat when in 1845 he was found drunk in a New York brothel after being missing for a week. No one seemed to believe his story that he had been carried to the brothel after accidentally drinking drugged cherry soda.

poil A pronunciation of *pearl,* not as common as it was in the past, as shown in the rhyming nickname of Knicks basketball player "Earl the Pearl" Monroe, which I've never heard as "Oil The Poil."

Poil Hahbuh *See* LEO THE LIP.

point A percentage point. "'You are going to get five percent for this job. Five points on two million five is a nice score." (Condon, *Prizzi's Honor*)

poiple A pronunciation of *purple.*

Polar Bear Club An organization of winter swimmers based in Coney Island whose New Year's Day dip is traditionally televised every year. But the most famous of New York's cold water swimmers didn't belong to the Coney Island group; it was playwright Eugene O'Neill, who when he lived in Rockaway Beach swam every day through the winter.

Poor Man's Paradise   An old name for Coney Island, which has also been called *America's Playground, The Nickel Empire,* and *City of Fire,* for its bright lights at night (when it opened in 1904 the park was lit by a million lights, more than most cities at the time). *See* CONEY ISLAND.

poosh 'em opp!   "A call to action in the sense of *Get going! Get rolling! Let's see you go in there now!*" according to the Federal Writer's Project's *New York Panorama* (1938). Possibly Italian in origin, the expression is rarely heard anymore and was "definitely limited in usage" even when *New York Panorama* was written.

pop   Mob talk meaning to kill, as in "I'd like to pop him"—stated by Al Pacino in *Donnie Brasco* (1997).

Popeye   The Federal Writers Project's *New York Panorama* (1938) tells us:

The keen-eared movie-goer may have observed that Popeye, gnarled knight of the clenched fist and the corncob pipe, speaks Tenth Avenue's indigenous tongue. Betty Boop, epitome of short-skirted innocence in the 1920s scolds her little dog and sings her ditties in exaggerated New Yorkese. It is not unlikely that her creation was suggested by the personality and appearance of a musical

comedy and screen actress Helen Kane, whose short-lived star rose in the Bronx.

See BUGS BUNNY.

Pornographic   *The Pornographic* was the nickname of the long defunct New York *Daily Graphic,* a tabloid newspaper founded in 1924 that competed with the *New York Daily News* and Hearst's *Daily Mirror.*

porterhouse steak   Martin Morrison's Porterhouse in New York City introduced the *porterhouse steak* in about 1814, according to the *Dictionary of Americanisms.* The tender steak taken from the loin next to the *sirloin* is an even more succulent cut than its neighbor but has a lot of waste. In England, there is generally no distinction between it and sirloin. A *porterhouse* was a tavern serving the dark brown beer or ale called *porter,* once favored by porters and other laborers.

Porto   A name, not always derogatory, for a Puerto Rican.

positively   Often added to statements for emphasis, as in "You positively got no idea of it."

potsy   A New York City name for hopscotch, which may take its name from the *potsy,* the object thrown into the hopscotch boxes. The object *potsy,* in turn, may derive from *patsy* for an innocent victim, because the *potsy* like the *patsy* is kicked around. *See* PATSY

Potter's Field   *See* HART ISLAND.

Poverty Gap   *See* TENEMENTS.

PR   Puerto Rico. "'It is only June and it is as hot as it is in PR,' she said." (Breslin, *Forsaking All Others*)

Practically Peerless Leader   A nickname for Leo "the Lip" Durocher when he managed the Brooklyn Dodgers in the late 1940s. *See* LEO THE LIP; NICE GUYS FINISH LAST.

Prime Minister of the Mob   An unusual, old nickname for Frank Costello, once a prominent Mafia chieftain. *See also* THAT GUY.

probly   A common pronunciation of *probably*.

public be damned   In 1882 a reporter asked William Henry Vanderbilt why the New York Central Railroad had continued to run a high-speed train from New York City to Chicago despite the fact that it was losing money. Commodore Vanderbilt told him that he did it to compete with a similar Pennsylvania Railroad train. Wouldn't you run it just for the benefit of the public, competition aside, the reporter continued, and Vanderbilt roared the classic reply that has unfortunately become associated with big business ever since: "The public be damed! Railroads are not run on sentiment but on business principles."

public relations   It is said that publicity writer Eddie Bernays (1891–1995), a nephew of Sigmund Freud, coined the term *public rela-*tions in May 1920, in the wedding announcements heralding his marriage, as a respectable way to describe his profession. He had previously established the first firm doing such work.

punk rock   See quote. "[Legs] McNeil, 40, [who lives in the East Village] has been sober for years now and is often credited with coining the word 'punk' as it is applied to the bands in the mid-70s that played jagged music, took lots of drugs and believed, roughly, in the release of believing in nothing." (Ian Fisher, "Erin's Looking for Leg-Rub Steve . . .," *New York Times Magazine*, December 8, 1996)

purey   A clear marble that is, along with the *boulder*, one of the most valuable marbles in the children's game of marbles. This term dates back to at least the 1920s, though it is heard less today with the game's decreasing popularity.

pushover   *See* PALOOKA.

puta   A Spanish word meaning a prostitute or whore that is increasingly heard as a contemptuous term among Spanish-speaking and some non-Spanish-speaking people in New York. *Puta* is sometimes also heard as slang for a punchboard.

put muscle on someone   To force someone to do something, strong-arm someone. "Then he said harshly, his voice deliberately all East Side, 'You trying to put muscle on me?'" (Puzo, *The Godfather*)

put someone on   *See* PUT THE FEAR ON.

put the blast on   To criticize severely and loudly. "Miss Missouri Martin puts the blast on her plenty for chasing . . . Dave the Dude out of the joint." (Runyon, *Guys and Dolls*)

put the fear on   To intimidate someone by staring him or her down or by one's formidable presence.

> This had never happened to Charley in his life since he had developed the science of putting fear on people . . . "*Now* I remember," Julia said giggling. "You are putting the fear on me. My father used to tell me how your father made you practice blanking out your eyes and hardening all of the muscles in your face. Did you *really* do that in front of a mirror for hours every day when you were a kid." (Condon, *Prizzi's Money*)

To put someone on or *put on someone*, originally black slang, can mean the same.

put under the top of the water   To murder someone by drowning him or her. "'They put Ezmo under the top of the water,' one of the hoodlums from the car yelled." (Breslin, *The Gang That Couldn't Shoot Straight*)

putz   *Putz* is Yiddish for "penis" and has also come to mean a tool, jerk, an obnoxious person. Wrote Judith Krantz in *Scruples* (1978): "'You,' she said, enunciating clearly, 'are a putz, a schmekel, a schmuck, a schlong, and a shvantz. And a WASP at that.'" All of those "s-words" mean penis as well and can also mean a jerk or obnoxious person. So does *schlontz*.

qualified man A Mafia member who has made his *bones,* who is qualified to do a job. Also called by the Italian *qualificato.*

Queens County Queens County, one of the five boroughs comprising New York City, takes its name from Catherine of Braganza, queen of England's Charles II. See BOROUGH; BRONX; KINGS COUNTY; NEW YORK COUNTY; RICHMOND.

rabbi Meaning "my lord" or "master" in Hebrew, *rabbi* of course refers to a teacher and scholar of Jewish law who usually heads a synagogue or temple. In police jargon one's *rabbi* is a person who can help further one's career, the person so called because he has influence with higher-ups—just as a *rabbi* has influence with the ultimate higher-up.

rag trade A name for the garment industry. The city's garment district lies between Eighth and Madison Avenues in the Thirties, but its main artery is Seventh Avenue, also called Fashion Avenue in that area.

rain on one's parade To spoil in any way something someone else is celebrating. "'He's had his turn at bat. Now he's trying to rain on my parade.'" (Condon, *Prizzi's Money*)

rap *The New Dictionary of American Slang* (1986) suggests that *rap*, for to converse, dates from the 1960s, but it seems clearly from the context of "Madame La Gimp" to have been used in this sense in Damon Runyon's tale written in the 1920s: "I get to the Marberry . . . and who opens the door of Madame La Gimp's apartment for me but Moosh, the door man . . . I wish Moosh a hello, and he never raps to me but only bows, and takes my hat." *Moosh*, incidentally, seems to be a popular name among Broadway characters. If I remember correctly, it was the name of the fight manager in Rod Serling's *Requiem for a Heavyweight*.

rat Mob talk for an informer, squealer. "If you're a rat, I'm the biggest fuggen mutt in the history of the Mafia," said Al Pacino in *Donnie Brasco* (1997). *See* MUTT.

rat mother This common curse is a shortening of "rat motherfucker," meaning a despicable person. "'Now let them rat mothers, they think they all so smart, let them figger out what that was about.'" (Breslin, *The Gang That Couldn't Shoot Straight*)

rat out To inform, squeal on someone. "Did he rat me out?"

real macher *Macher* is Yiddish for an operator, a big wheel. From the German *Macher*, "maker" or "doer"; pronounced MOK-er.

real nothing Someone of no worth at all, as in "He's a real nothing." Probably influenced by Yiddish.

real thing *See* UNDER THE TABLE.

Red Hook A section of Brooklyn named *Roode Hoek* by the Dutch after its rich red soil.

regella Regular. "I din know we had a regalla Greta Gobbo in the awfice." (Kober, "You Mean Common")

regular In New York City a regular coffee is coffee with an average amount of milk in it and sugar served on the side. In other areas, however, *regular* means coffee with cream and sugar added to it. *Regular* can also mean real, bona fide. *See* REGULAR GENIUS.

regular genius A common expression, as in "She's a regular genius," that is sometimes used sarcastically and was probably influenced by Yiddish.

Reuben The grilled sandwich of corned beef, Swiss cheese, sauerkraut and dressing on rye bread was possibly invented in the early 1900s at Manhattan's Reuben's Delicatessen. But no one is sure of this, even though the Reuben has long been associated with the city.

revenge is a dish that tastes best when it is cold A favorite saying of Don Corleone in Mario Puzo's *The Godfather* (1969).

rich as Rockefeller *Rich as Rockefeller* refers to the huge family fortune amassed by John Davison Rockefeller (1839–1937). Variations on the phrase above include *he's a regular Rockefeller,* and *Rockefeller* itself is the American equivalent of *Croesus*. John D. may have given only dimes to beggars, but his philanthropies totaled about a billion dollars. John D. Rockefeller Jr. built New York's Rockefeller Center, with Radio City Music Hall completed in 1940.

Richmond The New York City borough is named for the duke of Richmond, son of King Charles II of England. It is rarely called Richmond except in official business, being widely known as Staten Island. *See* BOROUGH; BRONX; KINGS COUNTY; NEW YORK COUNTY; QUEENS COUNTY.

Rockaway Playland An amusement park much smaller than Coney Island but almost as well known to New Yorkers. It was torn down in the 1980s, and nothing but rubble has taken its place.

roller derby A sport in which two roller-skating teams compete on an oval track in a race to complete as many laps as possible in a given time. The sport and its name were invented in 1937 by famed New York author Damon Runyon.

rooster *See* DIP.

roscoe Old underworld slang for a gun. "Regret finds himself brooding so much over the idea of an ever-loving wife who is so handy with a roscoe that he never really asks." (Damon Runyon, "The Bloodhounds of Broadway," 1929) Also called a *John Roscoe*.

rumcake A drunk, a rummy. "'Some rumcake staggering around their house liable to take a pass at the wife while he's supposed to be fixing the faucets." (Breslin, *Table Money*)

rum, Romanism and rebellion This political slogan is usually attributed to the supporters of Herbert Hoover, who used it to defeat New York's Catholic Democratic candidate Al Smith for the presidency in 1928, calling the Democrats the party of *rum, Romanism and rebellion*. Al Smith, "the Happy Warrior" from the East Side, who entered politics as a Tammany appointee, served four terms as governor of New York and later headed the company that built the Empire State Building. The slogan used to defeat him was actually first used in 1884 by New York Presbyterian minister Samuel D. Burchard, who spoke in presidential candidate James Blaine's presence of the Democrats as "the party whose antecedents are rum, Romanism and rebellion," this offending the large Irish Catholic vote in New York City and causing Blaine to lose the state by a scant 1,000 votes and thus the election to Grover Cleveland. Blaine's political reputation didn't help him either. The Democrat's slogan for that election was "James G. Blaine, James G. Blaine, Continental liar from the state of Maine."

Runyonese The language spoken by New York characters invented by author Damon Runyon (1884–1946); a colorful if exaggerated New Yorkese. The author of *Guys and Dolls,* a journalist and short story writer noted for his tales of the New York underworld and New York City itself, requested that his ashes be scattered over Broadway. On his death his ashes were dropped on the Great White Way from a large transport plane flown by his friend, the famous American aviator Eddie Rickenbacker.

rush hour This term describing peak morning and evening hours for commuting to and from work seems to have been invented in New York in about 1890 and is still commonly used here and elsewhere.

S.A. *See* PALOOKA.

Saddy Saturday. A pronunciation recorded in the Federal Writers' Project *Almanac for New Yorkers* (1938).

St. Patrick's Day Parade The first one was held on March 17, 1779, and was actually led by a *British* band. Never mind, though. The band and the 400 marchers were "Volunteers of Ireland" who had been brought over to fight the Americans in the Revolutionary War but went over to General Washington's side in great numbers (after the parade from lower Broadway to the Bowery and the banquet that followed).

sanctioned stool Someone who pretends to be a stool pigeon informing on the mob but is actually working for them, a double agent.

sandwich men Men who wear hinged signs that hang over their shoulders with advertisements on the front and back so that they are sandwiched between the boards. The practice is over 150 years old, and *sandwich men* are still occasionally seen today.

sanguiccio *See quote under* GIOBBA.

sawlauf It's all off, as in "Sawlauf between us."

scapping; scalloping; scalping All terms used for catching a crab with a net in local waters around New York City. *See* DOUBLE.

scarf To eat or drink, often hastily; a black term that is now widely used. "I grab chicken and roll, turn, run out . . . stuffing chicken in my mouth, 'Scarf Big Mama!' this from crack addict standing in front of abandoned building." (Sapphire, *Push*)

schizerino No slang dictionary seems to record this slang substitute for schizophrenic. Henry Miller used it in *Tropic of Capricorn* (1939): "Once you became a real schizerino flying is the easiest thing in the world. . . ." Whether it was coined after or before *schizo* is unknown.

schlemiehl; schlemihl Nothing ever turns out right for the awkward and unlucky *schlemiehl*. The word, by now common American slang, comes from the Yiddish *shelumiel*, "one who is worthless," which is said to derive from the name of the first Shelumiel mentioned in the Bible. Shelumiel appears four times in the Book of Numbers as the son of Zurishaddai and the leader of the tribe of Simeon. Nothing is said about him except that he is the leader of 59,300 people and makes an appropriate offering for the dedication of the altar at the Lord's command, but it has been suggested that Shelumiel lost in battle all the time while the other tribal leaders were victorious. Be that as it may, the word *schlemiehl* got a boost from the allegorical tale *Peter Schlemihls Wunderbare Geschichte* (*The Wonderful Story of Peter Schlemihl*), written by the German botanist and poet Adelbert von Chamisso in 1814. In the story the impecunious Peter Schlemihl makes a foolish bargain with the devil, selling his shadow for a never-empty purse and finding himself an outcast from human society because he has no shadow. Through this story, which was translated into many languages and virtually became legend, *schlemiehl* came to mean anyone making a foolish bargain, both living a life of its own and reinforcing the meaning of the earlier *schlemiehl*.

schmaltz In Yiddish *schmaltz,* from the German *smaltz,* is "chicken fat," a common, sticky, and greasy substance that gives its name to anything common and stickily sentimental.

schmegeggy A stupid oaf, usually rather harmless. The word, possibly born in New York's East Side, is from the Yiddish *shmegegi* of unknown origin and can mean baloney, nonsense or foolishness as well.

schmo A hapless, naive person, a fool. Possibly a euphemistic rendition of the Yiddish *shmuck* or *shmok*, meaning both penis and a dope or jerk. Al Capp gave the name *Shmoo* to the adorable egg-shaped character in the comic strip *L'il Abner.*

schmuck Judging by its common use by New Yorkers, one wouldn't think *schmuck* was an obscene word. *Schmuck* is Yiddish for penis, deriving somehow from a German word meaning "ornament," and has come to mean a stupid obnoxious person of whom there are apparently so many that *schmuck* is one of the best-known Yiddish expressions.

schmutz Yiddish for dirt, filth, garbage.

schnook A timid ineffectual person, one pitied rather than disliked; in fact, a *schnook* can be quite likeable. A Yiddish expression that comes from the German *schnucke,* a "little sheep."

schnorrer An impudent beggar, moocher or sponger who acts like it's one's duty to give him money; a haggler or habitual bargain hunter; a cheapskate; a chisler. *Schnorrer* can mean all these things and more. The word is a Yiddish one, probably deriving from the German verb for to beg.

scimunito Italian for a jerk or a fool. "He had read that some guy had paid fifteen hundred dollars for a dead rose Garbo had kissed maybe twenty years before and he thought that guy was a scimunito." (Condon, *Prizzi's Honor*)

scompiglio A big fuss or argument. "Vincent Prizzi had made a big scompiglio about how he was the boss of the family so he should be the one to attend the meeting." (Condon, *Prizzi's Honor*)

score *See* DIP.

scrag oneself To *scrag* means to kill or murder (or to have sex with) someone, and to scrag oneself means to commit suicide. "'I am figuring on scragging myself,' Feet says . . . 'Yes, I think I will scrag myself.'" (Runyon, "A Very Honorable Guy") Is it possible that *scrag* has something to do with *frag*, used in Vietnam for to kill someone, usually a detested officer? *Frag* is said to come from the fragmentation grenades used for this purpose, but *scrag,* much older slang, may have influenced the coining.

scratch Money. ". . . so I judge Bookie Bob is as tough with his ever-loving wife about scratch as he is with everybody else." (Damon Runyon, "The Snatching of Bookie Bob," 1931)

screwball "King Carl" Hubbell is probably responsible for this 1930s expression meaning an eccentric person. The New York Giants pitcher used his famous *screwball,* which he introduced in the early 1930s, to win 24 games in a row. Hubbell pitched 46 consecutive scoreless innings and, most amazing of all, struck out in order the greatest concentration of slugging power ever assembled—Babe Ruth, Lou Gehrig and Jimmy Foxx—in the 1934 All-Star game.

seeinya Seeing you, as in "I'll be see-inya."

see yuh A shortening of *see you later* often heard in New York. *See yuh later, alligator* was popular for a time but is rarely heard today.

send up the river To send to prison. The river referred to is the Hudson, up which, at Ossining, New York, is Sing Sing Penitentiary, founded in 1830. *See also* SING SING.

seventh-inning stretch These words have become synonymous with a brief break from any long period of sitting. They come from baseball's traditional *seventh-inning stretch,* which dates back to the late 19th century. The tradition originated at an 1882 game at Manhattan College in New York City. Manhattan College baseball coach Brother Jasper, also the prefect of discipline, instructed restless students in the stands to rise and stretch for a minute in the seventh inning before the game continued. This *seventh-inning stretch* became a ritual at all Manhattan College games and spread to the Major Leagues during the 1880s when the college team played exhibition games against the New York Giants at the Polo Grounds.

Shabbes goy In Yiddish *Shabbes* is "Sabbath," and *goy* means "a gentile." A *Shabbes goy* is a gentile who performs such tasks as turning on the lights on the Sabbath, when such tasks are forbidden for Orthodox Jews.

shaddup A pronunciation of *shut up* frequently heard in New York.

shade *See* DIP.

shalom *Shalom,* from a Hebrew root meaning "peace," is an Israeli greeting for both hello and good-bye. Leo Rosten notes that Israelis say they use it so "because we have so many problems that half the time we don't know whether we're coming or going."

shamus This term for a private detective may come from the Yiddish *shammes,* "sexton of a synogogue" (from the Hebrew *shamash,* "servant"), or from the Irish name *Seamus* (James) a typical name of an Irish policeman. Both may have influenced the coining of the word.

Shea Stadium The New York Mets's home field in Flushing Meadows, Queens. Completed in 1964, it is named for attorney William Shea, who was instrumental in getting the stadium built.

shedshoole An often affected pronunciation of *schedule,* imitating the British pronunciation of the word and once fashionable in the New York theatrical world. Said Dorothy Parker

to a young actor who repeatedly affected the pronunciation, "If you don't mind my saying so, I think you are full of skit."

shekel Money; from the Hebrew word for "coin." *Shekel* can be found in the Bible (Gen. 33:12–16) and is a monetary unit in Israel, but it became slang for money here in the mid-19th century.

shield *See* DIP.

shifty as smoke Describes someone sly and untrustworthy. The expression was used in the 1940s and '50s but isn't often heard today. "Watch out for him; he's shifty as smoke."

shiksa A sometimes disparaging term for a girl or woman who isn't Jewish; a Yiddish expression from the Hebrew *sheques,* "blemish."

shine A derogatory term for a black person still heard, mostly among blue-collar whites. "The owner muttered as he picked up a knife, 'These shines.'" (Breslin, *Table Money*) *Shine* is probably based on the brightness of the skin of some black people; possibly the word was influenced by the fact that a good number of black men were once employed as what were commonly called *shoe-shine boys.* No one knows for sure.

shit Heroin. *See quote under* BOO.

shit happens Coincidence plays a major role in human affairs. "Cops knew that shit happens." (McBain, *Romance*)

shlep A widely used Yiddish expression from the German *schleppen,* "to drag"; it usually means to drag, pull, carry, as in "Do I have to shlep all those packages upstairs?" *Shlep* and *shlepper* also widely means a jerk, a fool, as in "What a shlep he is."

shlock This Yiddish expression, for shoddy, cheaply made, defective articles, derives from the German *Schlog,* a "blow," suggesting that the goods have been knocked around and damaged. Pronounced to rhyme with *stock, shlock* is sometimes spelled *schlock.*

shlump Though it is Yiddish deriving from the German *Schlumpe,* a "slovenly woman," *shlump* describes any slow, droopy, lazy person, a drip or drag of either sex.

shmaltz A popular Yiddish word, from the German for "fat," that means cooking fat, usually the drippings from chicken, and by extension anything excessively sentimental, mawkish and maudlin, what is often called *corn.* It is in the extended sense that the term is widely heard, as in "Turn off that shmaltzy music."

shmeer *Schmeer* is Yiddish for to print or smear, from the German for "grease," but New Yorkers widely use the word to mean a bagel with cream cheese spread on it, as in "One with a shmeer." *Shmeer* is also slang for a bribe, grease for the palm.

shmooze To have a long cozy friendly talk with someone, as in "They walked in the park and shmoozed for an hour."

shnozzola The nose, especially a large nose. From the Yiddish *shnoz,* which derives from the German for "snout." The term was popularized by comedian Jimmy Durante, who was called the *Schnozzola* or the *Schnoz* after his huge proboscis, the most famous nose on the stage since that of Cyrano de Bergerac.

shoot the works To gamble or risk everything; probably from the game of dice or craps.

shot *See* DIP.

shot heard round the world The Ralph Waldo Emerson line describing the opening of the American Revolution has a different meaning in New York. It is remembered by many as a name for the home run New York Giant Bobby Thomson hit in the ninth inning of the last game of the 1951 playoffs against the Dodgers to win the pennant. Only Babe Ruth's "called shot" in 1932 is a more renowned homer. The Giant's victory was called *The Miracle of Coogan's Bluff,* after the hill behind the Giant's Polo Grounds stadium. *See* COOGAN'S BLUFF.

should Often used in place of *to* in an infinitive, as in "He wants you should see it," instead of "He wants you to see it."

should be Frequently takes the place of *is* or *are,* as in "Make sure he should be honest," instead of "Make sure he's honest."

shoulder candy   *Candy* for a sexy young woman is documented as dating back to about 1968, when the word possibly originated in New York City, but I haven't seen *shoulder candy* in any dictionary. The term is defined in a *New York Times Magazine* column (November 24, 1996) by John Tierney:

> "Models are visual bait," says David Jones, a gossip reporter at the *Daily News*... "Even the serious playboys, the rich guys who live to chase models, often aren't that interested in sex. They mainly want their fellow wolves to see them walk in with a model. The term they use is 'shoulder candy.'"

shpos   Hospital slang for an obnoxious person, especially a patient; an acronym for *subhuman piece of shit*.

shtarker   Widely used Yiddish word; see quote. "...she was right back where she started, sitting between two professional ruffians, two men exactly the same as her father, *shtarkers*." (Condon, *Prizzi's Money*)

shtik   *Shtik* (rhymes with *lick*) is a Yiddish word, from the German for "piece," that is usually heard in the disparaging sense of a small, contrived piece of theatrical business, often comedic, designed to draw attention to oneself: "He uses the same *shtik* night after night." It can also mean one's special talent.

shtup   A Yiddish word, from the German for "to push," that has general currency only in its slang meaning of to fuck, as in, "He shtupped her."

shudda   Another contraction unconsciously tailored to meet the needs of the hurried, harried city dweller, this one a telescoping of *should have*: "I shudda ordered the special."

Shuttle   *See* DUHSHUH-UL.

shvartzer   A derogatory Yiddish term for a black man, from the German word for "black."

shyster   *Shyster*, an American slang term for a shady, disreputable lawyer, is first recorded in 1846. Various authorities list a real New York advocate as a possible source, but this theory has been disproved by Professor Gerald L. Cohen of the University of Missouri–Rolla, whose long definitive paper on the etymology explores more likely theories. Shakespeare's money-lender Shylock has also been suggested, as has a racetrack form of the word *shy* (i.e., to be shy money when betting). Some authorities trace *shyster* to the German *Scheisse*, "excrement," possibly through the word *shicir*, "a worthless person," but there is no absolute proof for any theory. In any case, shady lawyers in New York have a long history of being called shysters.

Sicilian   *See* SLICE.

sick as a dog   Common for very ill, as in "I was sick as a dog yesterday."

siddown   A frequent pronunciation of *sit down*. "'Siddown, Charley,' Uncle Vincent said." (Condon, *Prizzi's Honor*)

sidekick   New York pickpockets once called the side pants pockets *side-kicks*. These are the hardest pockets to pick because they are closest to the hands of a victim and are constantly moving with the motions of the legs. Therefore, any man wise to the ways of pickpockets kept his wallet in his trusty side pocket, or *side-kick*. *Side-kicker* thus became a slang synonym for a faithful buddy, a partner who is always at one's side. O. Henry first recorded the term in one of his stories in 1904, and about 10 years later *side-kicker* was shortened to *side-kick*.

Silk-Stocking District   The 15th Congressional District, which includes Manhattan's rich Upper East Side.

Sing Sing   The nickname for the New York State prison, Sing Sing Penitentiary, up the Hudson River at Ossining; a place where many New York City criminals have served time since it opened in 1830. *See also* SEND UP THE RIVER.

sit shivah   *Shivah*, from the Hebrew word for "seven," is the seven days of mourning following the funeral observed by Jews for a deceased parent, sibling, child or spouse. To *sit shivah* is to observe this period and is so named because traditionally members of the family sat on stools or low benches while mourning, an ancient custom still observed by many today.

sitting in the catbird seat   A Southern expression, meaning being in an excellent position, that was popularized and spread nationwide by sportscaster Red Barber when he announced the Brooklyn Dodger baseball games on radio in 1945.

$64 question   On the radio quiz program "Take It or Leave It," which premiered in 1941 and was emceed by Phil Baker, topics were chosen by contestants from the studio audience, and seven questions of increasing difficulty on these topics were answered by each contestant. The easiest question was worth $2, and the questions progressed until the ultimate $64 question was reached. The popularity of the show added to the language the expression *the $64 question* for any question difficult to answer and inspired a slew of similar quiz shows. A decade later came television's *$64,000 Question* with its plateaus instead of levels, its isolation booth and its scandals involving contestants who cheated in cahoots with the producers. Then, after a long hiatus, there was the *$128,000 Question*, but despite these programs with their inflated prize, *$64 question* retains its place in the national vocabulary.

skell   New York police slang for homeless men who live on the city streets. The term, however, dates back to Elizabethan England.

skimmer Slang for a hat. A word coined by New York sports cartoonist, T. A. Dorgan, known as Tad. *See* HOT DOG; TAD.

skipper A synonym for a *capo* or *capo regime* in the Mafia. "You're the one who tries to make peace between the skippers." (Hunter, *Criminal Conversation*) Also called a *captain*.

skweet A contraction of *Let's go eat,* as in "Jeet? Skweet." (Did you eat yet? Let's go eat.) *See* JEET.

Skyqueen *See* WOOLWORTH BUILDING.

skyscraper On hearing the word *skyscraper* most people conjure up a vision of Manhattan, but the world's first *skyscraper* office building was the 10-story Chicago office of the Home Insurance Company completed in 1883 by architect William Le Baron Jenney. The fitting name *skyscraper* was given to this first building of steel skeleton construction, a building much higher than any other of its time. The word was borrowed from the triangular sails that had long been used high on the masts of sailing vessels, "scraping" against the sky.

slave bracelet An old name for a silver identification bracelet attached to a chain and worn around the wrist, often given by sweethearts to one another.

Slave Market A name in the 1890s for the area around today's Union Square; after the hundreds of actors who congregated there every day hoping to be hired by the many theaters in the area.

sleep at the bottom of the ocean To die a violent death by assassination. "When he came back he was holding Luca Brasi's bulletproof vest in his hands. Wrapped in the vest was a huge dead fish . . . 'The fish means that Luca Brasi is sleeping at the bottom of the ocean,' he said. 'It's an old Sicilian message.'" (Puzo, *The Godfather*)

sleeper Slang for a reform school inmate; used as the title of a recent book and movie.

slice Usually used by New Yorkers as shorthand for a *slice-a* (a piece of) *pizza* when ordering New York's favorite fast food in a pizza parlor: "Gimme a slice anna small Coke." Whether it's a square cut of thick Sicilian or pie slice–shaped regular (Neopolitan) pizza, it's always a slice. When a whole pizza is ordered it's "Gimme a pie." *Piece* is rarely heard.

sliding pond A *sliding pond* (possibly from the Dutch *baan,* "track") is a metal slide in a New York playground, the term used nowhere else.

Sloppy Louie's A famous landmark restaurant on South Street specializing in a large variety of seafood (they even sold whale steak 30 years ago). The "Sloppy Louie" here was proprietor Louis Moreno. He didn't like the name, but customers who had frequented the place when it was "Sloppy John's" insisted on calling it "Sloppy

Louie's" after he bought the restaurant in 1930.

slow lane   *See* SPEED LANE.

smatter   A contraction of *what's the matter*: "Smatter with you?"

smatterthya?   As in "What's the matter with you?"

Smelly Kelly   *See* NEW YORK ALLIGATORS.

smush   Face. "Hortense plunges right into Feet's arms and gives him a big kiss on his ugly smush . . ." (Runyon, "A Very Honorable Guy")

snatching   Kidnapping. "So I am not surprised to hear rumors that the snatching of certain parties is going on in spots, because while snatching is by no means a high-class business, and is even considered somewhat illegal, it is something to tide over the hard times." (Runyon, "The Snatching of Bookie Bob")

sneeze   Old slang for steal. "Miss Alicia Deering's papa sniffs out where The Lemon Drop Kid plants his roll and sneezes same." (Runyon, "The Lemon Drop Kid")

sod farm   In New York City and vicinity a place where sod grass is grown is called a *sod farm*. The sod is sold to garden nurseries and bought by homeowners who want "instant grass." Yet not 600 miles away in upstate Batavia, New York, a *sod farm* is called a *turf farm*. In New York City *turf* is heard in horseracing circles and

has long been used by criminal gangs to designate an area controlled by a gang: "Don't come on our turf."

sofer   *See* IDEAR.

softie   *See* HARDIE.

SoHo   An area in Manhattan whose name is a shortening of *So*uth of *Ho*uston, the street by which it is bounded on the north. The area, revitalized in the 1970s and 1980s, is a fashionable neighborhood, among the most diverse and vibrant in the city. *See also* HELL'S HUNDRED ACRES.

soldier   The lowest-ranking member of a Mafia family. *See* FAMILY.

solid   Dating back to the 1930s and probably from the world of jazz, *solid* means something or someone remarkable or wonderful. A *solid sender* is usually an admirable jazz musician, while a *solid citizen,* the term often used by Damon Runyon, is any admirable person. The expressions are heard much less frequently today.

sonomagona   *See quote under* GIOBBA.

sottocapo   An underboss in the Mafia. The *sottocapo* serves under the boss, who, in turn, serves under the head (godfather) of the family. "Charley Partanna was . . . Vincent's *sottocapo,* and the Prizzi's enforcer." (Condon, *Prizzi's Honor*)

Soup Nazi   Phrase used on the New York–inspired television comedy *Seinfeld* to refer to a real-life soup merchant located in midtown Manhattan. The impatient Soup Nazi is known for supposedly badgering disorganized patrons and for not including the customary piece of bread with an order of soup for customers who take too long to decide what they want. People tolerate his attitude because he reportedly serves outstanding soup.

sout A pronunciation of *south*.

sowaddyasaybabe So what do you say, babe. Defined as "A prelude to romance," a pronunciation recorded in the Federal Writers' Project *Almanac for New Yorkers* (1938).

spaghetti A New York fireman's term for fire hose. Running out the hose is called *laying spaghetti.*

spaldeen *Spaldeen* is the New York term for a smooth pink rubber ball used in playing stickball, catch, etc. It is named after Spalding, the company that makes it.

spanging The latest New York slang for begging or panhandling; used by young street punks and said to be the result of a slurred and shortened "spare any change?" "I don't spang much because I don't really like doing it. I eat out of trash cans a lot." (Punk street person quoted by Ian Fisher in "Erin's Looking for Leg Rub Steve . . . ," *New York Times Magazine,* December 8, 1996)

Spanglish A combination of *Span*ish and Eng*lish* spoken by many Hispanic people. The hybrid language features words such as *fafu* for "fast food"; *tensen* for a "10¢ store" like the late Woolworth or K Mart; *choping* for "shopping"; and *chileando* for "chilling out." Its combination of Spanish and English might result in a sentence like "Vamos a lonchar, or what?" ("Are we going to have lunch or not?")

speed The use of *speed* as an alternative term for an amphetamine isn't without precedent, for the word has also been used in reference to liquor. In at least one place, anyway:

> As for Judge Henry G. Blake, he is full of speed, indeed. By this time anybody can see that the judge is commencing to believe that all this is on the level and that he is really entertaining celebrities in his own home. You put a quart of good grape inside the old judge and he will believe anything. He soon dances himself plumb out of wind. . . . (Runyon, "Madame La Gimp")

speed lane In New York the *speed lane* is usually the name for the *left lane* on a road or highway, the lane customarily reserved for cars going at least the speed limit, while the *right lane,* or *slow lane,* is for drivers choosing to go slower. Sometimes the *speed lane* is called the *fast lane,* but *fast lane* is usually the term for the lane in a public swimming pool reserved for fast swimmers. In doing pool laps slow swimmers customarily use a lane labeled the *slow lane,* while swimmers of medium ability use the *medium lane.*

sperl A pronunciation of *spoil.*

Spirit of Brooklyn *See* DEM BUMS.

spitter   *See* DIP.

sprinkles   The chocolate or multi-colored flecks of candy that ice cream cones are dipped into or that are sprinkled on ice cream sundaes are generally called *sprinkles* in New York. "Let me have a vanilla cone with chocolate sprinkles, please." *Sprinkles* are called *jimmies* in other regions.

spritz   A little bit, a touch; from the Yiddish for a "squirt." "Just add a spritz of seltzer." Also *shpritz*.

stall   *See* DIP.

Staten Island   One of the five boroughs of New York City. The name derives from the Dutch name for the island. Staten Island is rarely called by its official name, Richmond County, outside official communications. It is frequently pronounced *Statnylant*. *See* CITY.

Statue of Liberty   The official name of the famous statue is "Liberty Enlightening the World," but no one calls it that. Standing 305 feet and 6 inches high, it is the tallest statue in the world.

stay in line   *See* ON LINE.

steerer   *See* DIP.

Stengel, Casey   *See* STENGELESE.

Stengelese   This minor language has been called a confusion of metaphors or double-talk or jabberwocky, but it is sometimes marvelous and was often a tactic used by the late New York Yankee and New York Mets manager Casy Stengel to confuse people who asked him questions that he didn't want to answer. In *The Dickson Baseball Dictionary* (1989) Paul Dickson quotes Stengel's reply to a U.S. senator who in 1958 asked him whether the Yankees intended to keep on monopolizing the world's championship:

> Well, I will tell you. I got a little concern yesterday in the first three innings when I saw the three players I had gotten rid of, and I said when I lost nine what am I going to do and when I had a couple of my players I thought so great of that did not do so good up to the sixth inning I was more confused but I finally had to go and call on a young man in Baltimore that we don't own and the Yankees don't own him, and he is doing pretty good, and I would actually have to tell you that we are more the Greta Garbo type from success.
>
> We are being hated, I mean, from the ownership and all, we are being hated. Every sport that gets too great or one individual—but if we made 27 cents and it pays to have a winner at home, why would you have a good winner in your own park if you were an owner?
>
> That is the result of baseball. An owner gets most of the money at home and it is up to him and his staff to do better or they ought to be discharged.

Mickey Mantle, also present at the Senate hearing, was then asked his views on the same question. "My views are just about the same as Casey's," he replied.

steptidyrearidybuspleez   Step to the rear of the bus, please. A pronunciation recorded in the Federal Writers' Project *Almanac for New Yorkers* (1938).

stick 1) *See* DIP. 2) A marijuana cigarette. "You want a stick?" *See* BOO.

stickball A kid's form of baseball played on city streets with a sawed-off broomstick or similar bat and a rubber ball such as a spaldeen. Among many great New York players who began their careers as stickball players are Willie Mays, Whitey Ford and Joe Pepitone. *See* EGGBALL.

stiff pain A nuisance, as in "That guy's a stiff pain." Variations are *swift pain* and *real pain.*

stink tree *See* TREE GROWS IN BROOKLYN, A.

stock *See* BONAC.

stone in one's shoe In Mafia speech, something or someone who irritates you; an obstacle. "'As for Skannet, he was a stone in your shoe, another family saying, so why shouldn't you get rid of him.'" (Puzo, *The Last Don*) *See also* TAKE THE STONE OUT OF ONE'S SHOE.

stood Often used as the past tense of *stay.* "I stood at the hotel five days."

stoop; stoopball A *stoop*, from the Dutch word for "step," is the front porch and steps of a New York house where games like stoopball are played. *Stoopball,* dating back to about 1940,

is a game resembling baseball where the "batter," the person up, throws a rubber ball hard against the steps so that it rebounds into the air. The number of bases and runs given depends on the number of bounces the ball takes before an opposing player catches it. A long "hit" over an opposing player's head is a home run.

stooper A man or woman who makes a small business of collecting winning pari-mutuel tickets that have been discarded, usually inadvertently, by horseplayers at racetracks. Sometimes the tickets are ripped up into small pieces by the players and pieced together by the stoopers, who have also been called *ground squirrels.*

storm door I had assumed that this term was an Americanism invented in relatively recent times. But lexicographers trace it back to the Dutch *storm deur,* meaning the same, used here in the 17th century, when New York was called New Amsterdam.

straphanger A term for a subway commuter popular at least since the first New York subways were built early in the 20th century and which may even date back to the days of horse-drawn trolleys.

Street People in the diamond trade call Forty-seventh Street *the Street.* It handles more than half of the finished diamonds in the world. Wall Street is also called *the Street.*

Street of the Midnight Sun A colorful old name for Broadway said to have been coined by Diamond Jim Brady and referring to the street's myriad night lights.

Street O' Ships An old name for South Street in lower Manhattan, which 150 years ago was "even more than Broadway the Main Street of the little Metropolis," according to the Federal Writer's Project *New York Panorama* (1938).

street people A term for homeless people who live on the city streets. *Street people* seems to have been invented in New York in the early 1970s.

Subway Series A New York baseball World Series that featured a local team from the American League and a local team from the National League and to which fans could travel by subway. These were traditionally held between the Yankees and Dodgers, before the Dodgers moved to Los Angeles. The Yankees and the Mets played a three-game series in June 1998.

Sugar Hill A prosperous neighborhood in Harlem on upper Edgecombe and St. Nicholas Avenues. The area, possessing many fine private homes and apartment buildings, has been so called since the 1920s. *See* HARLEM.

suit Mob slang for a businessman. "The suits are crookeder than we are."

sumpin' A common pronunciation of *something*. "You're really sumpin' else!" Also *somethin'*.

sumpmscroowie Something screwy, as in "Sumpmscroowie is goin' on." A pronunciation recorded in the Federal Writers' Project *Almanac for New Yorkers* (1938).

supermarket The world's first supermarket was the A&P, the Great Atlantic and Pacific Tea Co., which was founded by tea merchant George Huntington Hartford in 1859 in New York City and had stores across the country by 1917. But the word *supermarket* didn't come into the language until the early 1920s in California. It was probably first applied to one of the stores in the Piggly-Wiggly self-service chain.

Swartwout Samuel Swartwout (1783–1856), collector of the port of New York in Andrew Jackson's administration, stole more than $1 million of public funds and fled to England. Thus *a Swartwout* came to mean an embezzler and to *Swartwout*, to embezzle or abscond.

swear on one's mother's eyes A fairly common oath. "'Andrew, I didn't know it was stolen, I swear on my mother's eyes!'" (Hunter, *Criminal Conversation*)

sweet Street talk for a sissy, someone weak or unmasculine. "You sweet or sumpin'?"

table money   Money for food, rent and other household expenses, the part of one's pay that is brought home and put on the kitchen table. This blue collar expression is used as the title of Jimmy Breslin's novel *Table Money,* 1986.

Tad   A number of references are found in these pages to T(homas) A(loysius) Dorgan (1877–1929), the great American cartoonist better known as "Tad" to millions of newspaper readers early in this century. Dorgan, born in a San Francisco tenement, taught himself to draw with his left hand when at the age of 13 an accident deprived him of the use of his right hand. He worked for a time on San Francisco newspapers, but his great fame came when William Randolph Hearst hired him away to New York. "Judge Rummy," "Silk Hat Harry" and many of Tad's characters, all dogs in human dress, became household words in America, and Dorgan was recognized as the country's most prolific and original coiner of words and catchphrases. If there is a writer anywhere who invented more lasting words and expressions than Dorgan, I've missed him. Just for the record, here are some of the most memorable ones, a good number of which are described at length in these pages. Many were listed by humorist S. J. Perelman, a student and early admirer of Tad, in a *New York Times Magazine* article: *hotdog; yes-man; dumbhead; applesauce* (for insincere flattery); *drugstore cowboy; lounge lizard; chin music* (pointless talk); *the once-over; the cat's meow; press notice; 23-skiddoo; flat tire; for crying out loud; Officer, call a cop; Yes, we have no bananas; The first hundred years are the hardest* (sometimes credited to Wilson Mizner); *See what the boys in the backroom will have; The only place you'll find sympathy is in the dictionary; Half the world are squirrels and the other half are nuts; as busy as a one-armed paperhanger with the hives* (sometimes attributed to O. Henry, who in a 1908 story wrote: "Busy as a one-armed man with the nettle rash pasting on wall-paper").

tag   The signature of a graffiti writer. "He wanted to be known through all eternity as the writer who'd thrown up the most tags ever." (McBain, *Mischief*)

take a cab Mob slang for to be killed. Comedian Alan King on the Arts & Entertainment channel's "Las Vegas" program (December 1, 1996) said he was told of Bugsy Siegel's killing this way: "Bugsy took a cab."

take a dive To fake a knockout in a boxing match and throw the fight; used since the early 1900s.

take it in the arm Said of someone who widely exaggerates; the reference is to a mainline drug user.

taken *See* CLIP (definition 1).

take off To rip off, rob. "He says he's gonna take off that bodega."

take the stone out of one's shoe An old Italian saying used by the mob; to eliminate someone, remove him from my life so that he won't bother me anymore. "'All right,' Don Corrado said with finality. 'After you take the stone out of my shoe, leave her in a rent-a-car at the airport.'" (Condon, *Prizzi's Honor*) *See also* STONE IN ONE'S SHOE.

talking Talking about, as in "This is fifty grand, we're talkin', not chicken feed," or "I'm talking right away, tomorrow."

Tammany; Tweed Ring Tammany Hall has ceased to exist by now, but for over 150 years the machine held sway over New York City politics under such bosses as William Tweed, Richard Croker and Carmine De-Sapio. *Tammany*'s unsavory associa-tion with machine politics dates back to the late 18th century, but Tammany clubs thrived in this country long before that, mostly as patriotic Revolutionary War organizations that ridiculed Tory groups like the Society of St. George. The clubs were named for Tamanend or Tamenund, a Delaware Indian chief said to have welcomed William Penn and signed with him the Treaty of Shakamaxon calling for friendly relations. Tamanend (sometimes his name is given as Taminy or Tammany) may have negotiated with Penn for the land that became Pennsylvania and may have been George Washington's friend. The colonists jocularly canonized this friendly Indian chieftain as St. Tammany and adopted his name for their patriotic societies. These gradually died out, but not before one William Mooney had formed a Tammany Society in New York in 1789. By the Jacksonian era the club became one of the strongest Democratic political organizations in America. Thomas Nast created the famous symbol of the Tammany tiger in his cartoons attacking the machine in the 1870s, when the corrupt *Tweed Ring* was fleecing the city of over $100 million.

tank artist *See quote under* GO IN THE WATER.

tartar sauce Often pronounced *tawtuh sauce*, especially in some parts of Brooklyn, where you'll get a blank look at best if you order *tartar* (tar-TAR) *sauce*.

taykadeezy, taykadeezy "Take it easy, take it easy"; cool it.

tearing up the pea patch Red Barber popularized this southern United States expression for "going on a rampage" when he broadcast Brooklyn Dodgers baseball games from 1945 to 1955, using it often to describe fights on the field between players. Barber hails from the South, where the expression is an old one, referring to the prized patch of black-eyed peas which stray animals sometimes ruined.

teddy bear Brooklyn candy store owner Morris Michtom fashioned the first teddy bear out of brown plush in 1902 and named it after President Theodore Roosevelt. Michtom's inspiration was a cartoon by Washington Post cartoonist Clifford K. Berryman called "Drawing the Line in Mississippi" that had been reprinted throughout the country. Based on a news story about an expedition Teddy Roosevelt made to hunt bears near the Little Sunflower River in Mississippi, it showed the old Rough Rider with his back turned to a helpless bear cub. Gallant Teddy, it had been reported, refused to kill and even set free the small brown bear that his obliging hosts had stunned and tied to a tree for him to shoot. Apocryphal or not, the story enhanced Roosevelt's reputation as a conservationist and made Michtom rich.

Teflon Don A nickname for New York Mafia boss John Gotti because the authorities couldn't make charges stick to him. They finally did get some

to stick, however, and he is now serving a life sentence. Gotti was also called *Dapper Don,* after the stylish clothes he wore.

telling the tale Touting a horse to a prospective client at the racetrack.

> And of course if a guy whose business is telling the tale cannot find anybody to listen to him, he is greatly handicapped, for the tale such a guy tells is always about how he knows something is doing in a certain race, the idea of the tale being that it may cause the citizen who is listening to it to make a wager on this certain race, and if the race comes out the way the guy who is telling the tale says it will come out, naturally the citizen is bound to be very grateful to the guy, and maybe reward him liberally. (Runyon, "The Lemon Drop Kid")

tell me about it I know exactly what you mean, perhaps better than you. "'I hate cops getting shot.' 'Tell me about it,' Sharyn said, and nodded grimly." (McBain, *Romance*)

tenements City tenements are bad enough today, but toward the end of the 19th century they were horrors, often with names like the Dirty Spoon or Bandit's Roost and located on streets actually named Poverty Gap, Bottle Alley, Penitentiary Row, etc. Often they were boarding houses with signs advertising "Five Cents a Spot," "Hallway Space 3¢" and "Standing Room Only."

terlet A pronunciation of *toilet* sometimes heard in New York, though not as commonly today as in the past.

tess A pronunciation of *test*.

tetch inna cup Tens of thousands of days ago I worked on the mike in Coney Island for a much-loved woman whose favorite expression was *tetch inna cup*, which she applied to anyone who acted a little crazy, this including almost everyone. At least that's how the words sounded. I always assumed the expression was Yiddish and meant "touched in the head," *cup* being the Yiddish word for "head." But though I've heard the words since, I've never found them in print and can only offer them in this raw form.

thas A mostly Puerto Rican pronunciation of *that's*. "If there was one thing she could not stand . . . it was that they [Puerto Ricans] said 'thas' and 'New Jessey.'" (Breslin, *Forsaking All Others*)

that Often substituted for *who*, as in "She's the one that went," instead of "She's the one who went."

That Guy An unusual pseudonym, in this case for New York City mob boss Vincent "Vinnie the Chin" Gigante, whose mob members are not permitted to speak his name; they are required to say "That Guy," while rubbing the chin, when speaking of him. *See also* PRIME MINISTER OF THE MOB.

that's a doozy Said of something splendid, outstanding, as in "That's a doozy [of a striped bass you caught]." The term was common in the 1940s and 1950s in New York City, but is less frequently used today. It is first recorded in 1903 and is probably an alteration of *daisy*, influenced by the last name of the great Italian actress Eleonora Duse (1859–1924), who was indeed a doozy of a performer. It can also mean something outstandingly bad, as in "That's a doozy of a cut you got."

that's not kosher *See* KOSHER.

The Bronx? / No Thonx! Poet Ogden Nash (1902–71) created a scandal in the Bronx when he put down the New York City borough with the couplet: The Bronx? / No thonx! Nash never apologized, as Bronx politicians demanded he do at the time, but 20 years later, in 1964, he did make a kind of apology by writing the following poem in response to a request from Bronx Community College:

> I can't seem to escape the sins of
>   my smart-alec youth.
> Here are my amends.
> I wrote those lines, "The Bronx?
>   No thonx!"
> I shudder to confess them.
> Now I'm an older, wiser man
> I cry, "The Bronx, God bless them!"

Which isn't nearly as good as *The Bronx? / No thonx!*

their The personal pronoun is often used instead of *his* or *her*, as in "That type of person needs their sleep."

there Frequently dropped from the phrase *where there is*, as in "You know where's a towel?" instead of "Do you know where there's a towel?"

things happen A shorter alternative to such synonymous observations as *such are the workings of fate; that's the way it goes; that's the way the cookie crumbles* or *the ball bounces*. The term dates back to about 1955 and is often heard today.

think one shits candy To be exceedingly vain, think one is God's gift to the world. "This is those fucking Prizzis again. They think they shit candy." (Condon, *Prizzi's Money*)

30 Rock *See* BLACK ROCK.

33 other McQuades A phrase remembered from the testimony to the Seabury Commission of Brooklyn Tammany leader James A. McQuade, who explained how he had banked $520,000 over a 6-year period on a total salary of $50,000 for that time. He borrowed it, he said, "to support the 33 other McQuades." "They were," vowed McQuade, "placed on my back, I being the only breadwinner, so to speak, and after that it was necessary to keep life in their body, sustenance, to go out and borrow money."

this I need yet? A common expression of lamentation influenced by Yiddish.

this is on me *See* PARDON MY DUST.

this is true An affirmation in response to another's opinion or statement. Often repeated: "This is true, this is true."

thoid A pronunciation of *third*.

Thomas Muffin This is a common name for an English muffin, even though it is a trademark. It honors Samuel Bath Thomas, founder of the S. B. Thomas Company (called Thomas's today), who opened a bakery in Manhattan in 1880 and sold English muffins made from a recipe his mother brought from England.

threepeat This new word, based on *repeat* and meaning to do something three times in a row, this expression seems to have been coined by New York Knicks coach Pat Riley in 1993, when the Chicago Bulls won the National Basketball Association title for the third straight year. Whether *threepeat* will last and pass into general usage remains to be seen.

Times Square Part of midtown Manhattan surrounding the intersection of Broadway and Seventh Avenue. Originally known as Long Acre Square, it was an important commercial center and home to William H. Vanderbilt's Horse Exchange, as well as to an exclusive neighborhood built by the Astor family between 1830 and 1860. It was renamed Times Square around the turn of the century in honor of the newly built *New York Times* building on Forty-third Street, and the newspaper's publisher, Adolph Ochs, sponsored what has since become Times Square's most famous event—an annual New Year's Eve celebration that is still observed today. Following World War I, the district became a major center for the theater and entertainment industries and a popular tourist destination.

But the Depression and the interruption of theater productions by World War II allowed a seedy element to settle there in the form of erotic theaters, peep shows and prostitution. Regardless, Times Square never lost its appeal to theatergoers and visitors, and recent attempts to clean it up have dramatically changed its image. *See* CROSSROADS OF THE WORLD.

ting   A pronunciation of *thing*. "Near the entrance to the Brooklyn Battery Tunnel, a cabdriver screamed, 'Hey, whyn't you learn howda drive dat ting?' and I knew I was home." (Hamill, *Flesh and Blood*)

Tin Pan Alley   Tin Pan Alley is said to have been so named by songwriter Harry Von Tilzer, who in the early years of the 20th century gave us perennial favorites like "I Want a Girl Just Like the Girl Who Married Dear Old Dad," "Only a Bird in a Gilded Cage," "What You Goin' to Do When the Rent Comes Round?" and "Wait Till the Sun Shines, Nellie." He also wrote a pop hit called "Mariutch Make a da Hootch-a-Ma-Cootch," which became a vehicle for New York's Italian dialect comedians, who were starting to be heard along with Irish, German, Afro-American and Jewish dialect comedians of the day. The original Tin Pan Alley was and is located between Forty-eighth and Fifty-second streets on Seventh Avenue in New York City, an area where many music publishers, recording studios, composers and arrangers have offices. The place was probably named for the tinny sound of the cheap, much-abused pianos in music publisher's offices there, or for the constant noise emanating from the area, which sounded like the banging of tin pans to some. *Tin Pan Alley,* the term first recorded in 1914, today means any place where popular music is published, and it can even stand for popular music itself.

to   The preposition is often omitted, as in "Let's go over Harry's house," or "Let's go down the store."

tochis   Pronounced TUCK-iss (and sometimes TOOK-iss) this is a widely known Yiddish word that means the buttocks or ass. It derives from Hebrew for "under, beneath."

Todt Hill   At 409.239 feet above sea level, this hill on Staten Island is said to be the highest natural elevation in New York City. In fact, *The Encyclopedia of New York City* (1995) credits it with being "the highest point on the Atlantic Coast in the United States south of Maine." High Hill, near Huntington on Long Island, is around the same height.

toilet paper   *Toilet paper,* or lavatory paper, which Nancy Mitford says is the "U" (proper) word for it, isn't recorded until the 1880s. The first commercial toilet paper had been marketed, however, in 1857, when Joseph C. Gayetty of New York City began selling an unbleached, pearl-colored, pure manila hemp product at 300 sheets for 50¢. "Gayetty's Medicated Paper—a perfectly pure article for the toilet and for the prevention of piles" had Gayetty's name watermarked on each sheet. Before this the Ward and Sears mail-order catalogs were indispensable in the outhouses of America.

toin A pronunciation of *turn*.

Toity-toid and Toid A pronunciation of *Thirty-third* Street *and Third* Avenue.

tomato *See* PANCAKE.

tomato can *See quote under* GO IN THE WATER.

Tombs *See* CITY COLLEGE.

Tootsie Roll New York candy maker Leo Hirschfield invented the Tootsie Roll in 1896. He named the chewy chocolate for his daughter Clara, whose nickname was Tootsie. Another similarly named candy is the square hunk of chocolate, cashews, brazil nuts and raisins called the Chunky. Candymaker Philip Silverstein invented the confection and named it after his daughter, nicknamed Chunky.

tops Loaded dice. ". . . it seems they soon discover that [he] is using tops on them, which is very dishonest dice. . ." (Runyon, "Madame La Gimp")

toy See quote. "The Herrara kid seemed to be at the bottom of the pecking order, a simple 'toy' in the hierarchy of graffiti writers." (McBain, *Mischief*)

trambo A tramp, a disreputable woman. "'So you are the trambo who keeps my husband out all night, are you, you trambo?'" (Damon Runyon, *Blood Pressure*, 1929)

traveler A name that a New York street punk might call him or herself.

[They] count themselves as "travelers." Which means that they travel with their Mohawks and pierced foreheads and romantic visions of unity against the larger society, in little bands to the St. Marks Places and Haight Streets around the country. Few steal, hustle and beg to support their habits. The major tension in their lives comes from deciding how long to stay in any one city before moving on. (Fisher, "Ernie's Looking for Leg-Rub Steve. . ." *New York Times Magazine*)

Tree Grows in Brooklyn, A Although never named in Betty Smith's novel *A Tree Grows in Brooklyn* (1943) nor the movies made from it, the tree in the book is *ailanthus altissima*, also called the *tree of heaven*. No other tree withstands smoke and other city conditions so well, and the ailanthus seeds easily everywhere, often growing out of cracks in deserted sidewalks. Only female trees should be planted, however, as the odor of the male flower is noxious to many, which is why the ailanthus, a native of China, is also called the *stink tree* or *stinkweed*. The tree was brought to France by a missionary in 1751 and reached America 39 years later. Also called the *backyard tree*.

tree of heaven *See* TREE GROWS IN BROOKLYN, A.

Tricky Dick This nickname for former president Richard Nixon may have its roots in an Irish-American name for another politician named Richard. My grandmother spoke of a New York ward heeler named Tricky Dick, but she may have meant Slippery Dick Connolly, comptroller for the Tweed Ring. In any case, James Joyce named a politician Tricky Dick Tierney in his short story "Ivy Day in the Committee Room" (1914), and it is not inconceivable that it was a felicitous Irish turn of speech, one of so many that came to New York with Irish immigrants.

trombernick Someone who looks like trouble. "'Look at this trombernick,' Weinstein said. He was watching Teenager. . . 'Trouble,' Weinstein said again. . ." (Breslin, *Forsaking All Others*)

troot A pronunciation of *truth*.

true A pronunciation of *through*.

tuh A common pronunciation of *to*, as in "Are y' goin' tuh come with me?"

tumorra A pronunciation of *tomorrow*. "'I'll call you back at the office tumorra.'" (Condon, *Prizzi's Money*)

Tweed Ring Possibly "the greatest plunderers of a great city the world has ever known," the Tweed Ring was headed by political boss William M. "Boss" Tweed, elegant Mayor A. Oakey Hall and Richard B. "Slippery Dick" Connolly. It is said that the ring looted the city treasury of up to $200 million in the period from 1865 to 1874. One public building they commissioned, for example, included a bill of $41,190.95 for brooms! Thanks to crusading journalism on the part of the *New York Times* and cartoonist Thomas Nast, the ring was exposed, but only Boss Tweed went to jail, where he died in 1878.

Twenty-five Foot Mile The last mile, the distance from the holding cell to the electric chair at Sing Sing prison.

twenty-three skiddoo For well over half a century no one has used this expression seriously, but it is still remembered today—mainly as a phrase representative of the Roaring Twenties, which it is *not*. *Twenty-three skiddoo* is important, too. It goes back to about 1900 and for 10 years enjoyed great popularity as America's first national fad expression, paving the way for thousands of other dispensables such as *Yes, we have no bananas; Shoofly; Hey, Abbott!; Coming, mother!* and *I dood it!* Twenty-three skiddoo practically lost its meaning of "scram" or "beat it" and just became the thing to say, anytime. As for its derivation, it is said to have been invented or popularized by that innovative early comic-strip artist "Tad" Dorgan, encountered frequently in these pages under *hot dog, yes man* and other of his coinings. Regarding its composition, *skiddoo* may be a shortening of the earlier *skedaddle*. *Twenty-three* is a mystery; perhaps it was a code number used by telegraphers. There is even a theory that it "owes its existence to the fact that the most gripping and thrilling word in *A Tale of Two Cities* is twenty-three": in the book the hero, Sydney Carton, is the 23rd man to be executed on the 23rd day of the month. Another theory associates *twenty-three skidoo* with the address of the famous Flatiron Building:

> . . . standing on what was traditionally the windiest corner of the city, [the Flatiron Building] was facetiously considered a good vantage point for the glimpse of a trim ankle, in the long-skirted, prewar era; policemen used to shoo loungers away from the Twenty-third Street corner, and the expression "twenty-three skiddoo" is supposed to have originated from this association. (Federal Writers' Project, *New York City Guide,* 1939)

twicet   *See* ONCET; TWICET.

Twin Towers   *See* WORLD TRADE CENTER.

twist it, choke it and make it cackle Colorful waiter's slang of old for an order of a chocolate malted with an egg in it.

twofers   *Twofers* has meant two theater tickets for the price of one in America since about 1948. In New York City today half-price tickets for Broadway plays can be bought at Duffy Square. *Twofer* had previously referred to *two-for-a-nickel* cigars since as early as 1892.

type   Frequently used in place of *kind of,* as in "She's the type person that lies."

U Mob talk for a thousand dollars. "How much would a boat like that cost?" "A boat like that? Oh, about 300 U's." (The movie *Donny Brasco,* 1997)

uddah A pronunciation of *other.*

uf caws Heard in New York for *of course.* "Uf caws he can come with us to the store."

uhparment Heard in the New York area for *apartment.*

under the table New York character George Washington "Chuck" Connors, the so-called Bowery Philosopher in the 1890s and the early years of the 20th century, is said to have coined the expression *under the table* for dead drunk. He is also thought to be responsible for the catchphrases *oh, forget it* and *the real thing.*

underworld Since about 1608, when the term is first recorded, *underworld* had meant hell, or the nether world of the dead beneath the earth. But in the 18th century the word was applied to the world of criminals, who were considered "beneath" proper society. By the 1920s *underworld* was only being used in this second sense to describe organized crime, which the word generally means today.

unemployment *The unemployment* is frequently used for *unemployment insurance,* as in, "I'm waiting to get on the unemployment." But *unemployment* alone, without the *the,* is also frequently used: "I'm waiting to get on unemployment." The same applies for *welfare.*

ungotz Nothing; originally Italian slang. "'You got everything, we got ungotz.'" (Breslin, *The Gang That Couldn't Shoot Straight*)

University in Exile *See* NEW SCHOOL FOR SOCIAL RESEARCH.

unna Under. "I guess I din know how good-lookin' you was because you was right unna my nose." (Kober, "You Mean Common")

unnerstand A pronunciation of *understand*. Also *unnastan'*. *See quote under* MOUT'.

unshushables *The unshushables* are the incessant talkers in a movie theater or any group who refuses to be quiet. Coined by the character Jerry on the New York–inspired television comedy *Seinfeld*.

up in the paints High up. I've been unable to find the origin of this phrase, but I'd guess it derives from the slang *paints* for playing cards, *up in the paints* being the higher valued cards in a deck. "Madame La Gimp's sister is not such a doll as I wish to have sawed off on me, and is up in the paints as regards age. . ." (Runyon, "Madame La Gimp") (Incidentally, this Runyon story was the basis for the very popular film *Lady for a Day,* which won three Academy Awards.)

uppah Manhattan Right before *da Bronx,* is uppah, or upper, Manhattan, below which is *midtown Manhattan* and further down, *lower,* or *downtown, Manhattan,* all of these areas taking in many other distinct areas, such as lower Manhattan's Financial District (Wall Street), Chinatown, etc.

upped Mob talk for promoted. "He got upped when Gotti took over."

uptick Though it has more complicated technical meanings on Wall Street, *uptick* has come to mean an upsurge or a pickup, especially when referring to the state of the economy. A 1980s term, it of course has its roots in Wall Street's stock ticker or ticker tape machine.

vanclla A pronunciation of *vanilla*.

Vaseline Among those flocking to America's first oil strike near Titusville, Pennsylvania, in 1858, was Robert A. Chesebrough, a Brooklyn chemist, who noticed that workmen with cuts, bruises and burns used as a soothing ointment, a waxy substance from the pump rods bringing up the oil. Gathering some of the oily residue, Chesebrough took it back to Brooklyn and made a jelly-like product from it. This he patented at once, giving it the trademark *Vaseline*, a word he formed from the German *Wasser* (pronounced *vasser*), "water," and the Greek *elaion*, "olive oil."

vending machine The term *vending machine* seems to have been introduced either by the Adams' Gum Company (now part of American Chicle) in the 1880s to describe the machine that the company used to sell tutti-frutti gumballs on New York City elevated train platforms, or at about the same time by the Frank H. Fleer Gum Company, whose founder had agreed to an experiment proposed by a young vending machine salesman. The salesman argued that vending machines were so great a sales gimmick that people would actually drop a penny in them for nothing. Frank Fleer agreed to buy several machines if the young man's pitch proved true, and the experiment was conducted at New York's Flatiron Building. The salesman set up a vending machine there, with printed instructions to "drop a penny in the slot and listen to the wind blow." He got Fleer's order when hundreds of people contributed their pennies and continued to do so until New York's Finest hauled the machine away.

Verrazano Bridge Officially named the Verrazano Narrows Bridge, this suspension bridge connects Brooklyn and Staten Island. Its 4,260-feet center span is the longest in North America. The Verrazano is named for Italian navigator and explorer Giovanni Verrazano (c.1480–1527?) who sailed in New York waters 85 years before Henry Hudson. *See* HUDSON RIVER.

verse A pronunciation of *voice*.

vic Police slang for a victim. "'Who's the vic, anyway,' the other one [policeman] said." (McBain, *Romance*)

vichyssoise The chilled potato and leek soup wasn't invented in France as many people believe. Ritz Carlton Hotel chef Louis Diat invented it in New York City in 1910.

vigorish; vig Many people have paid usurious rates of interest to loan sharks. The margin of profit in such transactions, 20 percent or more a week, late payment penalties and other fees, is called *vigorish*, or *vig*, which also means the percentage set by a bookmaker in his own favor. *Vigorish* is one of the few English words with Russian roots, deriving from the Russian *vyigrysh*, "gambling gains or profit," which first passed into Yiddish early in 20th-century America as *vigorish* and was reinforced by its similarity to *vigor*. "The vigorish, or the percentage, or the house cut, the edge that made any gambling a winning proposition for the mob. Even when they lost, they won. Bet a hundred bucks on a football game, the bookie paid you the hundred if you won, but if you lost he collected a hundred and ten." (Hunter, *Criminal Conversation*)

Village *See* GREENWICH VILLAGE.

virgin bagel *See* BIALY.

voitue A pronunciation of *virtue* still hoid in all boroughs.

waddadajintzoodisaft What did the (New York) Giants do this afternoon? A question commonly asked when there was a New York Giants (Jints) baseball team and daytime baseball games were common in New York. The pronunciation is recorded in the Federal Writers' Project *Almanac for New Yorkers* (1938).

wahgoozidoo What good does it do. "Cynical dejection," a pronunciation recorded in the Federal Writers' Project *Almanac for New Yorkers* (1938).

wait'll next year Wait until next year, the loyal, optimistic motto or battle cry of Brooklyn Dodger fans in years during the 1940s when the Dodgers didn't win the pennant or, winning the pennant, failed to win the World Series.

wake me up when Kirby dies An old New York catchphrase not heard anymore but whose story is worth hearing. The tale is told in Charles Hemstreet's *When Old New York Was Young* (1902).

Something more than sixty years ago [in about 1840] the attention of theatre-goers was directed to a young actor who appeared at intervals in the Chatham Theatre. He was J. Hudson Kirby. His acting had not much merit, but he persisted in a theory that made him famous. It was his idea that an actor should reserve all his strength for scenes of carnage and death. The earlier acts of a play he passed through carelessly, but when he came to death-scenes he threw himself into them with such force and fury that they came to be the talk of the town. Some of the spectators found the earlier acts so dull and tiresome that they went to sleep, taking the precaution, however, to nudge their neighbor, with the request to wake them up for the death-scene. And for long years after Kirby's time, the catch-phrase applied to any supreme effort was "Wake me up when Kirby dies."

Waldorf salad Maitre d'hotel Oscar Tschirky of the Waldorf Hotel invented this salad of apples, celery, mayonaise and chopped walnuts in 1893. The nuts weren't added to the popular salad until a few years later.

walking *See* DOUBLE.

Wall Street   *Wall Street,* which is both a street and a term symbolizing varying views of American capitalism in general, is of course located in lower Manhattan, at the southern end of the island, and takes its name from the wall that extended along the street in Dutch times (a wall that was erected against the Indians and parts of which were used for firewood). The principal financial institutions of the city have been located there since the early 19th century. *Wall Streeter, Wall Street broker, Wall Street plunger* and *Wall Street shark* are among American terms to which the street gave birth, *Wall Street broker* used as early as 1836, and Wall Street being called the *Street* by 1863.

Wall Street Journal   The daily newspaper was founded in 1889 by Dow Jones and Company, a financial news agency at the time. In 1901 it was purchased by newspaperman Clarence Walker Barrow, who started it on its way from a journal of business items to the international influential newspaper it is today.

Walt Whitman house   The birthplace of America's greatest poet in West Hills (Huntington), Long Island. Whitman worked for over 25 years on various Brooklyn newspapers and knew the city and Long Island as well as any of his contemporaries.

wannamayksumpnuvit?   Want to make something of it? Defined as an "Invitation to a brawl," this pronunciation was recorded in the Federal Writers' Project *Almanac for New Yorkers* (1938).

warm piece of the sidewalk   A decent living. "Even a dog gets a warm piece of the sidewalk." (The movie *Donnie Brasco,* 1997)

washastep   A pronunciation of *watch your step,* as in "Washastep gettin' off da bus."

wassitooyuh?   What's it to you? "A delicate rebuff to an excessively curious questioner," this pronunciation appeared in the Federal Writers' Project *Almanac for New Yorkers* (1938).

watthitcha?   What hit you? "To a gentleman with a shiner," a pronunciation recorded in the Federal Writers' Project *Almanac for New Yorkers* (1938).

waves   The portion of a public beach where the water is not calm and waves break on the shore. In the Rockaways, for example, the waters are calm from Beach First Street to Beach Twentieth Street because this area is part of an inlet. From Beach Twentieth Street to the end of the Rockaway peninsula the shore faces the rougher open Atlantic and this area is called *the waves,* as in "Let's go down to the waves." Also called *the breakers.*

wazzitooyuh?   What's it to you?

wear it in good health   One of those expressions everyone hears a hundred times over the years, but whose inventor will never be known. It is thought to be a Yiddish contribution or to have been influenced by Yiddish; it is commonly said to someone who buys or is given clothing of some kind.

We Can Kick Your City's Ass A New York City slogan said to be a favorite of (and first uttered by) Rudolph Giuliani, according to the *New York Times* in an article entitled "Welcome to New York, Capital of Curses."

weekend warrior Originally a nickname for a National Guardsman who serves weekends in the military for a certain time. Now, the term is also used to describe professionals who work 9–5 during the week and then go wild on the weekend, either with partying or by playing dangerous sports.

welcome to the club You're not alone, there are many of us in the same sinking boat; words of commiseration. Heard on the street: "With three kids it's getting so I can't afford hospitilization anymore." "Welcome to the club."

welfare *See* UNEMPLOYMENT.

West Side The west side of Manhattan in New York City, west of Fifth Avenue and bordered by the Hudson River. The term was made famous by the musical *West Side Story,* which opened on Broadway in 1957. *See* EAST SIDE.

wet one's beak To partake of some of the rewards of an enterprise, usually a criminal activity. "'After all,

this is my neighborhood and you should let me wet my beak.' He used the Sicilian phrase of the Mafia, '*Fari vagnavie a pizzu.*' *Pizzu* means the beak of any small bird such as canary. The phrase itself was a demand for part of the loot." (Puzo, *The Godfather*)

we wuz robbed! When Jack Sharkey won a decision over Max Schmeling in 1932 to take the world heavyweight championship, Schmeling's manager, Joe Jacobs, grabbed the mike of the fight's radio announcer and shouted, "We wuz robbed!" to a million Americans. The New Yorker's words are still a comic protest heard from losers in any endeavor. Jacobs's "I should of stood in bed" is even more commonly used in fun. He said it after leaving his sickbed to watch the 1935 World Series in Detroit. According to John Lardner's *Strong Cigars and Lovely Women* (1951), *Bartlett's* is wrong in saying Jacobs made the remark to sportswriters in New York after returning from Detroit, and it had nothing to do with his losing a bet that Detroit would win the series. Jacobs made the remark, Lardner says, in the press box during the opening game of the series, when "an icy wind was curdling his blood" at the coldest ballgame anyone could remember.

whack out Mob talk for to kill. "You whack *him* out or I whack *you* out!".

whadda What do. "'Whadda you want me to do?'" (Condon, *Prizzi's Money*)

whaddaya What are you, as in "Whaddaya gonna do?"

what am I, chopped liver? *See* CHOPPED LIVER.

what do you want I should tell you? What do you want me to say?

whatever Whatever you say. "I'll give you ten percent now, the rest when you deliver." "Whatever."

whatsa What's the. "After all, if we can't be frank—well, I mean, whatsa use?" (Kober, "You Mean Common")

what's the big idea! An interjection commonly heard in New York, as in, "What's the big idea, get on the back of the line!"

wheel Common racetrack slang meaning to combine a horse's number in the first race with the numbers of every horse running in the second race in an attempt to win the daily double (that is, to pick the horse that wins the first race of the day and the horse that wins the second race of the day). Playing such a bet at the ticket window, a horseplayer often says, for example, "Wheel eight" and pays for tickets combining "the eight horse" with every other horse in the second race.

when a dog bites a man . . . Crusty *New York Sun* city editor John B. Bogart (1845–1921) is said by some to have originated, in conversation, the old saw: "When a dog bites a man, that is not news, because it happens so often. But if a man bites a dog, that is news." However, the adage may be based on an old story whose particulars have long been lost.

when you've left New York, you ain't goin' nowhere An old saying, its exact origins unknown, which must have been coined by a New Yorker.

where's it at Where is it. "'Do you want a drink of whiskey?' Navy said. 'Never. Where's it at?'" (Breslin, *Table Money*)

white money *See* BLACK MONEY.

whole shebang The earliest recorded use of *shebang* is by Walt Whitman in *Specimen Days* (1862); Mark Twain used it several times as well. Meaning a poor, temporary dwelling, a shack, this Americanism possibly derives from the Anglo-Irish *shebeen*, "a low illegal drinking establishment," older than *shebang* by a century or so. In the expression *the whole shebang*, first recorded in 1879, *shebang* means not just a shack but anything at all—any present concern, thing, business—as in "You can take the whole shebang," you can take all of it.

whole shmeer The entire package, the whole deal, as in "I'll take the whole shmeer." *See* SHMEER.

who needs it? *See* I (HE, SHE, ETC.) NEED IT LIKE A HOLE IN THE HEAD.

who's buried in Grant's tomb? An old joking question on exams or in contests between kids. It's not so obvious as it seems: Both General Grant and his wife, Julia, are buried there. *See* GRANT'S TOMB.

Wickedest Man in New York There may be many more wicked, but historically the title goes to one John Allen, who ran an infamous dance hall on Water Street that was frequented by many prostitutes and their prospects in the 1860s.

wid A common pronunciation of *with*, as in "I'll go widya."

Williamsboig A common pronunciation of *Williamsburg*, an area in Brooklyn that can be reached by the Williamsboig Bridge.

"Will You Love Me in December As You Did in May" *See* FUN CITY.

Winchell, Walter A sensationalist New York newspaper columnist who coined or popularized many slang terms from the 1920s to 1950s. Damon Runyon used him as the model for Waldo Winchester in "Romance in the Roaring Forties" (1929), his first Broadway story and probably the first story with a newspaper columnist of the Winchell type as the central character. Winchell had many admirers, but many detractors as well. While they were fishing in the Gulf of California, John Steinbeck and his friend Doc Ricketts noticed a little fish that lived in the cloaca of the sea cucumber and kept darting in and out of the creature's anus. They named the hitherto unrecorded fish *Proctophilus winchilli* after the gossip columnist who got all the latest dirt.

wise boy A variation of *wise guy*. "'They're what you call wise boys,' Hogan said. 'Don't you know them, too?'" (Ernest Hemingway, "Fifty Grand," *The Short Stories of Ernest Hemingway*, 1953) *See* WISE GUY.

wise guy Another name for a member of the Mafia; made famous in Nicholas Pileggi and Henry Hill's book *Wiseguys* (1985), which became the movie *Goodfellas* (1990).

witchew A pronunciation of *with you*. "'Don't take The Plumber witchew.'" (Condon, *Prizzi's Money*)

with; on New Yorkers rarely use *on* for *with* anymore, as in "Do you want zucchini or salad on your spaghetti?" *On* in this sense probably means "on your order."

without Sometimes substituted for *unless*, as in "I'm not going without you go, too."

woim A pronunciation of *worm*.

Woolworth Building One of New York's most beautiful buildings, inside and out, this downtown structure was once the world's tallest building. According to *New York Panorama* (1939):

> Cass Gilbert, the architect, liked to tell how Frank Woolworth came to put up the tallest building in the world at a time (1913) when the New York skyline was still dominated by the Metropolitan Tower. The Metropolitan

Insurance Company had refused Woolworth a loan, and in so doing had roused his ire. He happened to see a postcard from Calcutta with a picture of the Metropolitan Tower—its fame as the tallest building had spread all over the world. Woolworth made a survey to determine the Metropolitan's exact height, and then ordered his architect to exceed it.

It should also be noted that the Reverend Dr. S. Parker Cadman christened the Gothic-style building with silvery lacework the *Cathedral of Commerce*. Visiting British statesman Arthur Balfour observed: "What shall I say of a city that builds the most beautiful cathedral in the world and calls it an office building." The 50-story *Skyqueen,* modeled after London's House of Parliament, was then the world's tallest skyscraper, at 792 feet, but was proportioned so gracefully by architect Gilbert that it is still regarded as one of the most majestic buildings in the *City of Towers*. Frank Woolworth's office inside is a replica of the Empire Room of Napoleon Bonaparte's palace in Compiègne. But amid all the superlatives about the building, too myriad to catalog here, perhaps the most amazing is that it was built without a mortgage and without a single dollar's indebtedness. Frank Woolworth just shelled out $13.5 million in cold cash—unique in the history of great buildings in the United States, or anywhere else for that matter. *See* CHRYSLER BUILDING.

World's Largest Garbage Dump New York City's Fresh Kills Reclamation Plant No. 1 on Staten Island holds this title. Covering over 3,000 acres it processes some 4.38 million tons of garbage a year. it opened in 1948.

World's Largest Store This is the slogan of Macy's department store and refers to its Herald Square anchor store, which contains 2.2 million square feet of floor space. A good-size house has 2,000 square feet of living space, so you could put 10,000 houses in Macy's at Herald Square, which has as much selling area as many large shopping centers. The Herald Square store (at Thirty-fourth Street and Broadway) opened in 1902 on a site that was once occupied by, among other enterprises, a few fine brothels and Koster & Bial's Music Hall, where "Thomas A. Edison with the 'Vitascope' first projected a motion picture," as a plaque still outside a Macy's entrance informs.

World Trade Center Also called the *Twin Towers*, this 1,350-foot-tall structure in downtown Manhattan is the world's largest office building, with 12 million square feet of rentable space. It is *not* the world's tallest building, however. Sears Tower in Chicago is the tallest building in the United States, and Petronas Tower in Malaysia is the world record-holder at 1,482 feet 8 inches. Over 50,000 people work in the World Trade Center, more than twice as many as in the Pentagon. *See* EMPIRE STATE BUILDING; WOOLWORTH BUILDING.

woulda A pronunciation of *would have.* "'I woulda scared her and she coulda lied to me.'" (Condon, *Prizzi's Money*)

writer   Slang for a graffiti artist. "New walls attracted these writers the way honey did bears. Put up a new wall or a new fence, wouldn't be ten minutes before they were out spraying it." (McBain, *Mischief*)

Wrong-Way Corrigan   Douglas "Wrong-Way" Corrigan may have gone the wrong way unintentionally. The 31-year-old pilot flew from California to New York in a record time of fewer than 28 hours and took off the next day in his battered plane to return to California. His plane had no radio, beam finder or safety devices, and had failed safety inspections, which would indicate that he had no plans for a publicity stunt. But even though extra gas tanks blocked his view, it is hard to explain how, after he took off in a westerly direction over Jamaica Bay, near the present Kennedy International Airport in New York, he swung his plane in a wide arc and crossed the Rockaway peninsula, heading out over the Atlantic Ocean. Presumably, he flew through a thick fog convinced that he was California-bound until the fog lifted that fine morning of July 18, 1938, and he looked down at the grass roofs and cobblestoned streets of Ireland! Corrigan told officials at Dublin's Baldonnel Airport that he had accidentally flown the wrong way, and he promptly became known as "Wrong-Way" Corrigan. As a result he became a hero, made close to $100,000 and even played himself in *The Flying Irishman*, a movie based on his "mistake." When asked if he had really meant to fly to California, Corrigan replied, "Sure . . . well, at least I've told that story so many times that I believe it myself now."

wuh   A pronunciation of *were*. "We wuh there."

wuhduh   A pronunciation of *would have*, as in "I wuhduh done it for y'."

wuntcha   Wouldn't you; a common contraction among New York speakers: "Wuntcha like to go?"

yada, yada, yada A catchphrase popularized by the television show *Seinfeld* (NBC-TV), starring Jerry Seinfeld. *Yada, yada, yada* is akin to *blah, blah, blah* in meaning and usage. "We exchanged greetings, went to lunch, yada, yada, yada, and signed the deal."

yah The Bay Ridge section of Brooklyn has traditionally been the neighborhood of Scandinavians in New York, and the pronunciation *yah* for *yes* or *yeah* is still heard there. But *yah* never became a pronunciation widely used by other New Yorkers, as it has, for example, in Minnesota, where everyone seems to use it. Jacob Riis, a Danish immigrant, was responsible for popularizing the phrase *the other half* for the poor in his book *How the Other Half Lives,* an important contribution to sociological literature. Riis Park in the Rockaways is named for him.

Yankee The most popular of dozens of theories holds that the *Yankee* in the name of the New York Yankees comes from the Dutch expression *Jan Kee,* "little John," which the English used to mean "John Cheese" and contemptuously applied to Dutch seamen in the New World and then to New England sailors. From a perjorative nickname for New England sailors, the term *Jan Kee,* corrupted to *Yankee,* was next applied to all New Englanders and then to all Americans during the American Revolution; the most notable example of this is found in the derisive song "Yankee Doodle." Nowadays, the British and others use it for American northerners, and northerners use it for New Englanders, who are usually proud of the designation. The *New York Yankees's* name was initially the *Highlanders* (in 1903) and then the *Hilltoppers,* becoming the *Yankees* (in 1913), so the story goes, because it was shorter and better suited to newspaper headlines.

Yankee Clipper *See* JOLTIN' JOE.

Yankee Stadium The home field of the New York Yankees since 1923. The stadium in the Bronx is also called *the House That Ruth Built.*

Yaptown An obsolete name for New York coined by O. Henry. "If

177

there was ever an aviary overstocked with jays it is the Yaptown-on-the-Hudson called New York."

yard One hundred dollars. "I am now able to explain to them that I have to wire most of the three yards I win to Nebraska to save my father's farm . . ." (Damon Runyon, "A Story Goes With It," 1931)

yarmulke *Yarmulke,* the skullcap worn by Jewish men, is said by most dictionaries to be a Yiddish word that derives from a Tartar word, which in turn comes from the Polish word for "skullcap." However, in an article published in the *Hebrew Union College Annual* (Vol. 26, 1955), Dr. W. Gunther Plaut concludes that *yarmulke* derives ultimately "from the Latin *almucia* or *armucella,* the amice (vestment) worn by the priest." The theory that *yarmulke* derives from a Hebrew word meaning "awe of the king" is a nice story but only folklore. The skullcap is worn, of course, as a sign of respect before God; this is a custom not only among Jews but is practiced by many people of the East.

yellow An old term for a yellow cab, or any cab. "Johnny stops a Yellow short, and hustles us into it and tells the driver to keep shoving down Eighth Avenue." (Damon Runyon, "The Hottest Guy in the World," 1929)

yellow journalism William Randolph Hearst (1863–1951) American newspaper publisher, editor and model for *Citizen Kane,* is responsible for the term *yellow journalism.* In 1896 Hearst hired R. F. Outcault away from the *New York World* to draw his comic character the Yellow Kid for Hearst's *New York Journal.* But the *World* continued the Yellow Kid cartoon, the first color comic, using another artist to draw the antics of the sassy little kid in his bright yellow nightdress. From the resulting sensational battle between the two Yellow Kids, plus the use of *yellow* to describe sensational books since at least 1846, came the term *yellow journalism* or *yellow press,* for sensational, unscrupulous reporting, which was coined in 1898 and applied to Hearst's Spanish-American War stories.

Yellow Rose of Texas Just as *Dixie,* the marching song of the Confederacy, was written in New York City, so was the famed yellow rose of Texas first grown here. The yellow rose of Texas, which is part of the state's folklore and even has a famous song written about it, actually originated in the 1830s on a New York City farm near the present-day Penn Station. There a lawyer named George Harrison found it as a seedling growing among other roses on his property and began cultivating it. Settlers soon took the yellow rose west with them, and legend has it that Texas finally claimed it as their own when Mexican General Santa Anna, the villain of the Alamo, "was distracted by a beautiful woman with yellow roses in her hair." We have this nice story on the authority of Stephen Scanniello, rosarian of the Crawford Rose Garden in the New York Botanical Gardens. *See also* DOROTHY PERKINS ROSE.

yenta Yiddish for a gossipy woman who talks too much and can't keep a secret, *yenta* may derive from some unknown blabbermouth named Yenta. The proper name Yenta probably derives from the Italian *gentile*. A talkative character named *Yenta Talabenta* in a play by Sholom Aleichem popularized this term.

yes, we have no bananas A popular catchphrase still heard occasionally; from a song written by Frank Silver and Sam Cohen in the mid-1920s. Silver got the idea for the song when he heard a Greek fruit peddler yell up to a woman at a New York tenement window, "Yes, we have no bananas!"

yez Sometimes still heard for you, singular, or in its plural form of *youse*. *See quote under* COME OFF IT!

Yiddish Yiddish, which has contributed many words and expressions to English and the New York dialect, is an entirely separate language from Hebrew. The word *Yiddish* is an Anglicized form of the German word *judisch*, "Jewish," referring to a Jewish German language. Yiddish therefore is an Indo-European language like German and English. Hebrew belongs to the Semitic language family, as does Arabic.

Yinglish A blending of *Yiddish* and E*nglish* to make a word. *See* FANCY-SHMANCY.

yit *See* BONAC.

yiz A plural of you. "All yiz . . . I'll see that yiz get put away." (Hamill, *Snow in August*)

yo Present, or here, often in answer to a roll call. *Yo* is widely used in New York but actually dates back to 14th-century England. ". . . he loved Seigelman, the high school teacher who had forced him to say 'present' instead of *yo*." (Breslin, *Forsaking All Others*) *Yo* is also used to call someone's attention, as in "Yo, John! (Hey, John!)." Sometimes *yo* has the meaning of "Here I am!" In this case someone might call, "Hey, John!" and John would answer, "Yo!"

yob A pronunciation of *job*. "Valentin Perez, walking proudly in the hot sun . . . held the most important thing of all in the life of a person in the South Bronx, he held a *yob*." (Breslin, *Forsaking All Others*)

Yogiism Any saying of Yogi Berra, beloved New York Yankee catcher and later manager and coach of several teams. Of Yogiisms he once said, "I really didn't say everything I said." *See* GOD SHOULD JUST BE ALLOWED TO WATCH THE GAME.

yom A black person. "The whites stare at us one way, wondering what I'm doing with a yom. The blacks stare at Kirk." (Hamill, *Flesh and Blood*) The word's origin is unknown.

you better believe it! An emphatic term popular for the last 25 years or so meaning roughly "You're damned right" or "You can bet on it," as in "You're going to eat that whole thing." "You better believe it!"

your mother! A common curse, short for *fuck your mother!* and thus to an extent euphemistic. "Kid Sully Palumbo swung around in his chair with his eyes flashing wildly. 'Your mother!'" (Breslin, *The Gang That Couldn't Shoot Straight*)

youse *Youse*—the so-called generous plural—is in a class by itself as a New Yorkism, though the expression is definitely heard in several parts of the country, including other eastern cities and the Midwest. New York editor and author Barbara Burn, a New England transplant with a fine ear for regional speech, theorizes that *youse* is usually employed when a speaker is referring to the second person plural, helping the speaker differentiate between one person in the group he or she is speaking to and the group as a whole. It is the New York counterpart of the Southern *you-all* (a

biblical precedent which can be found in Job 17:10), the "mountain tawk" *you-uns* and the localized *mongst-ye* heard in Norfolk, Virginia, and on Albemarle Sound.

you should live to be a hundred and twenty Said to an admired person, often an older person.

you should live so long It is impossible, it will never happen. "The Yankees win the Series? You should live so long."

youvadanuffbud You've had enough, bud; sometimes a bartender's reply to a customer who says: "Filladuppigin." Both pronunciations were recorded in the Federal Writers' Project *Almanac for New Yorkers* (1938).

yuppie *Yuppie* is a recent coinage of the last 20 or so years that originated in the New York City area but already is nationally used. It means and is constructed from *y*oung *u*rban *p*rofessional.

zhlub *Zhlub* during the past 25 years or so has been slang for an insensitive, boorish person. It derives from the Yiddish *zhlub,* meaning the same, which, in turn, comes from a Slavic word. A variation is *zhlob.*

zip Said to be Mafia slang for mob members brought over from Italy to do low-level work. The pejorative term, however, was originally coined in Vietnam as an acronym for *Z*ero *I*ntelligence *P*otential and applied to the Vietnamese.

Zon-gun Here's a new word from the vineyard country of Long Island's North Fork area, a word that hasn't been recorded in any of the big dictionaries, or any dictionary at all so far as I know. A *Zon-gun* is a big gun timed to go off at intervals in vineyards, its sound scaring birds away from ripening grapes. Since the loud guns are sometimes set to go off every 20 seconds for the entire day, seven days a week, their use is not appreciated by neighboring homeowners, who haven't failed to express their displeasure. Some vineyards have turned to netting their grapes, but *Zon-guns* (also called *birdguns*) are much cheaper, costing only about 12¢ a day to operate each, and many growers still use them.

zotz To kill. "'What is the use of zotzing her after she hands over all that money?'" (Condon, *Prizzi's Money*). *Zotz* means nothing or zero in slang, thus to *zotz* someone is to make a person nothing, kill that person.

Zulu Derogatory slang for an African American.